George W. Clark
1998

NO ORDINARY GENIUS

NO ORDINARY GENIUS

The Illustrated Richard Feynman

Edited by Christopher Sykes

W. W. NORTON & COMPANY
New York · London

The text of this book is composed in Melior, with the display set in Britannic.
Composition by Crane Typesetting Service, Inc.
Manufacturing by the Courier Companies, Inc.
Book design by Charlotte Staub.

Library of Congress Cataloging-in-Publication Data

Feynman, Richard Phillips.
    No ordinary genius : the illustrated Richard Feynman / edited by
Christopher Sykes.
        p.   cm.
    Includes bibliographical references and index.
    1. Feynman, Richard Phillips.   2. Physicists—United States—
Biography.   I. Feynman, Richard Phillips.   II. Title.
QC16.F49A3   1994
530′.092—dc20
[B]   93-32449

ISBN 0-393-03621-9

W. W. Norton & Company, Inc., 500 Fifth Avenue, New York, N.Y. 10110
W. W. Norton & Company Ltd., 10 Coptic Street, London WC1A 1PU

1 2 3 4 5 6 7 8 9 0

For my father and mother,
Bernard and Dorothy

Contents

Preface

I first met Richard Feynman in 1981 at Caltech in Pasadena, where he had been a professor of physics for thirty years. I had read about him in a wonderful book called *Disturbing the Universe* by the English physicist and mathematician Freeman Dyson. They had driven across America shortly after the Second World War, and had spent a night together in a brothel in Vinita, Oklahoma. That night they could not sleep, and Feynman told Dyson about his first wife and great love, Arline, about the building of the atomic bomb, about Hiroshima and his deep conviction that the world was going to end rather soon.

I wanted to make a documentary for BBC TV about Feynman's life and work, but over the phone he told me the idea didn't interest him at all. He did agree to meet for ten minutes or so after his Thursday-morning lecture for graduate students "to see what you got to say." I went to the lecture, and although I could understand nothing at all of the physics, I was fascinated by something Feynman did near the end. He looked at the wall clock—11:50— then at the blackboard, and told his students: "There are two ways of dealing with this problem: one is complicated and messy, and the other is simple and very elegant. We don't have much time left, so I'll just show you the complicated and messy way."

Afterwards, we went to his office. He sat back in his chair and said, "Yes, sir?" in such a way that I was certainly scared of him.

I tried to talk about what I thought I wanted to do. He listened, and then he told me again that my idea was "dumb—it would be a 'Do you like lobster?' movie." I didn't understand what he meant. He said, "Well, you know—the answer is either yes or no, and who cares? It's like people who ask each other where they come from—everyone comes from somewhere, but so what?"

We went to lunch at a café near Caltech, and argued a bit about science and art. By now I was convinced that there would be no film. I felt I had nothing to lose, so I told him that I thought his apparent dismissal of anything outside science was narrow-minded and arrogant. This must have done the trick, because Feynman smiled and said, "Well, I did read a novel once. It was called *Madame Bovary* and it was kind of nifty." He winked, and then he asked me what, exactly, did I want him to do?

I tried to explain that I wanted to make a film for laymen (like me) about the excitement of doing science, and that this was difficult unless it was attached to a person and a life. Somehow he warmed to this: "Oh, you mean a sort of a life story with scientific hairs hanging off of it? Yeah, I'll do that!" So he did, and we made a documentary called *The Pleasure of Finding Things Out*. It was a kind of autobiography which consisted of Feynman sitting in a chair, talking for fifty minutes—there was really no need for much else.

I wanted to show Feynman the rough cut, but he said no. "If the thing's any good, that's to your credit," he said, "and if it's lousy, that's your problem."

Feynman often spoke in a strange, ungrammatical way which was very much part of his charm: "There's no such a thing as you do it by algebra"; "Bigger is electricity!"; or "Nature's there, and she's gonna come out the way she is!" He often used the definite article where most of us do not: "the nature," "the physics," or "the science." All this led a pompous *Daily Telegraph* TV previewer to miss the point badly: "Feynman is a 'legendary teacher,' we're told, in view of which I found it curious that he speaks such dreadfully sloppy English—hardly a complete grammatical sentence in fifty minutes' nonstop talk."

Fortunately, everyone else saw Feynman for what he was—a great communicator of what science is, and why people do it.

Feynman was born in 1918 in Manhattan and died in 1988 in Los Angeles. He brought to bear on the world a curiosity so intense and an intellect so powerful that he won a Nobel Prize for a fundamental physics discovery made in his late twenties. He also looked for adventure outside science, and invariably found it—in art, travel, family, and friendship.

In 1984, Feynman and his friend and drumming partner Ralph Leighton published *Surely You're Joking, Mr. Feynman!*—a remarkable collection of autobiographical stories which became a best-seller. Feynman sent me a copy, and on the flyleaf he wrote: "After your program people think I am wise, so I had to publish this to bring the balance back." But Feynman *was* wise, and when he died people all over the world who had never met him felt the loss.

This book is based on *The Pleasure of Finding Things Out* (1981) and the other films I made with and about Feynman for BBC TV—*The Quest for Tannu Tuva* (1988), *No Ordinary Genius* (1993), and a series of six short programs called *Fun to Imagine* (1983). The text is edited from interviews and conversations recorded during research and filming with Feynman, his family, his friends, and some of his scientific colleagues. The arrangement is neither strictly chronological nor thematic, and the only constant is the unique personality of Feynman himself.

Some of the stories have appeared elsewhere. I once asked his daughter, Michelle, whether she and the rest of the family ever got tired of hearing them. Not at all, she said. "He had such a gift for telling them that it was always new. The other thing is that it gave him so much pleasure to tell them. I remember I came downstairs one night, and he was laughing hysterically—tears were running down his face, he was laughing so hard. When I asked him what he was reading, he sheepishly looked up and showed me the cover of his own book, and he said by way of excuse, "I was such a crazy character!"

Freeman Dyson once wrote to his parents that Feynman was "half genius, half buffoon," but has recently changed this to "all genius, all buffoon." Whatever the correct proportions, Feynman seemed to know better than most how to enjoy the world and everything in it, despite his share of tragedy.

The last time I saw him was in February 1988 at a Mongolian barbecue restaurant in Pasadena—Ralph Leighton had arranged a party there. Feynman loved it, although he was obviously in pain. His wife, Gweneth, took him home early, and he went into the hospital for the last time. (Gweneth also had cancer. She died a year later, after adventures in Antarctica and Egypt. I regret that I never recorded an interview with her.)

I remember Feynman as always smiling, and he made me wish I had been a scientist. I think he should be a household name, and that is why I have compiled this book.

Christopher Sykes

A Note on Contributors

I would like to thank the following for allowing me to record our conversations and edit them for this book. Any mistakes and misunderstandings are my responsibility, not theirs.

Hans A. Bethe, *physicist*
Faustin Bray, *musician*
Richard Davies, *physicist*
Freeman Dyson, *physicist*
Carl Feynman, *computer scientist and Richard's son*
Joan Feynman, *physicist and Richard's sister*
Michelle Feynman, *photographer and Richard's daughter*
Edward Fredkin, *physicist*
David L. Goodstein, *physicist*
Albert R. Hibbs, *physicist*
W. Daniel Hillis, *computer scientist*
Donald J. Kutyna, *formerly U.S. Air Force*
Kathleen McAlpine-Myers, *teacher and artist's model*
Marvin Minsky, *computer scientist*
Richard Sherman, *physicist*
Tom Van Sant, *artist*
John Archibald Wheeler, *physicist*
Jirayr Zorthian, *artist*

NO ORDINARY GENIUS

"I'm an explorer, okay? I like to find out." Feynman in 1981, age sixty-three.

CHAPTER ONE

The Pleasure of Finding Things Out

Poets say science takes away from the beauty of the stars—mere globs of gas atoms. Nothing is "mere." I too can see the stars on a desert night, and feel them. But do I see less or more? The vastness of the heavens stretches my imagination—stuck on this carousel my little eye can catch one-million-year-old light. . . . What is the pattern, or the meaning, or the why? It does not do harm to the mystery to know a little about it. For far more marvelous is the truth than any artists of the past imagined! Why do the poets of the present not speak of it? What men are poets who can speak of Jupiter as if he were like a man, but if he is an immense spinning sphere of methane and ammonia must be silent?

Feynman[1]

CS: *Like great chess players, mathematicians, or violinists, you are something of a phenomenon in the particular ways you are able to think. Do you ever wonder about where this ability came from?*

Feynman: No.

Perhaps you just don't find it interesting, but when a mathematical prodigy like, say, Ramanujan[2] *turns up out of nowhere, surely one does wonder how he could*

[1] This footnote and those that follow throughout the text refer to notes found at the back of the book beginning on page 257.

have got hold of such extraordinary mathematical abilities?

I find in the world very many interesting questions such as this one, but I have no way to know the answer to it, and no way to find out. It's not that I am not interested, I simply don't know anything about it, and I don't like to speculate about things I don't know very much about. I don't see that it's useful. It's much more interesting for me (unless I'm working on it) to leave a mystery a mystery, rather than to make believe I know an answer to it. So I can't tell you where Ramanujan got his mathematical desires—I should call them desires, because that's what you really require first. Not so much the ability, but the desire to play around, and to notice. That's what he had to do—to find out funny things about numbers and to explore some more, play with the numbers until he had played enough to discover things that nobody else knew. He was playing, that's all. He had to have the desire to play, and I don't know where that came from.

I've always played around. It's hard to explain it very well. When I was a kid I had a laboratory. Although I'm now in theoretical work, I originally played experimentally. It's a bad term—I mean that I fooled about. I never did experiments in a scientific sense, to find out something. I would make radios, or try to make a photocell work. I had a spark plug from an old Ford car that I would set up and use to burn holes in paper, or see what would happen when I tried to put a spark through a vacuum tube. But I never kept a notebook of things I did every day, or made careful measurements. I wasn't that kind of a "scientist," so to speak. I was just playing, like a child playing, but with different toys.

Freeman Dyson[3] I find the parallel with Ramanujan is quite a good one. Both men discovered things which appeared to be by magic—they didn't go through the ordinary processes of conventional mathematics, because they were able to guess the answers by some weird process that they themselves didn't understand, and certainly we don't.

Feynman was a very unusual scientist. I think it is best described by a friend of mine, Marc Kac. In his memoirs he said that there are geniuses of two kinds. He said that I, Hans Bethe, am an ordinary genius, but that Feynman was a magician.

An ordinary genius is a fellow that you and I would be just as good as, if we were only many times better. There is no mystery as to how his mind works. Once we understand what they have done, we feel certain that we, too, could have done it. It is different with the magicians. They are, to use mathematical jargon, in the orthogonal complement of where we are and the working of their minds is for all intents and purposes incomprehensible. Even after we understand what they have done, the process by which they have done it is completely dark. They seldom, if ever, have students because they cannot be emulated and it must be terribly frustrating for a brilliant young mind to cope with the mysterious ways in which the magician's mind works. Richard Feynman is a magician of the highest caliber.

—from *Enigmas of Chance*, Marc Kac, 1985

Hans Bethe[4]

It's hard to say how people do things, and I think we like to be romantic. It seems to me that in some weird sense what was great about Feynman is that he was normal, and there was nothing unusual about him at all—except that he didn't have very many bugs. It takes me maybe an hour to understand a page of new mathematics. At the end, if I'm lucky, I obviously say to myself, "Why didn't I understand that right away? What took the hour?" Well, you could say that one of the troubles with trying to understand new things is that we all have preconceptions, we're screwed up in one way or another. When Feynman faced a problem he was unusually good at going back to being like a child, ignoring what everyone else thinks, and saying, "Now, what have we got here?"

He was so "unstuck" and if something didn't work he would look at it in another way. He had so many different good ways. He would do something in ten minutes that might take the average physicist a year, so he was just

Marvin Minsky[5]

wonderfully productive. I attribute what they call "genius" to having a bunch of characteristics:

—Don't respond to peer pressure.
—Keep track of what the problem really is; less wishful thinking.
—Have a lot of ways of representing things. If one way doesn't work, switch quickly to another one.

The important thing is not to persist; I think the reason most people fail is that they are too determined to make something work only because they are attached to it. Talking to Feynman, whatever came up he would say, "Well, here's another way to look at it."

The least stuck person I have ever known.

Age two. Richard was born in a Manhattan hospital on May 11, 1918. The family soon moved to the New York suburb of Far Rockaway, on the Atlantic coast near what is now JFK International Airport. Far Rockaway was also the hometown of the polio vaccine pioneer Jonas Salk.

Feynman

I got many influences—from my father, for example. I was born the way I am, and I don't understand these things. It could have been I was something else. I don't know how it works. It's true that my father, even before I was born, told my mother that if it was a boy he was going to be a scientist, and he made an effort in a way to produce that, so no doubt that had a lot to do with it. I think it does.

When I was just a little kid, very small in a high chair, he had brought home a lot of tiles, little bathroom tiles, seconds of different colors, and we played with them, setting them out like dominoes. Vertically, I mean, on my high chair (they tell me this, anyway!), and when we'd got them all set up I would push one end so that they would all go down. But then, after a while, I'd help to set them up and pretty soon we were setting them up in a more complicated way: two white tiles and a blue tile, two white tiles and blue tile, and so on. My mother said that she complained, "Leave the poor child alone! If he wants to put a blue tile, let him." And my father said, "No, I want to show him what patterns are like, and how interesting they are. It's a kind of elementary mathematics." So he started very early to tell me about the world and how interesting it was.

"My father taught me to notice things" Melville Feynman in 1916, age twenty-four.

Lucille, Richard's mother, in 1916, age twenty-one.

If you were a boy, you were to be a scientist. What if you had been a girl?

I haven't the slightest idea. That's his business, isn't it? But my sister (who is a girl!) is also a scientist—she has a Ph.D. in physics. She was in the same environment, so it did work for her too. I don't know whether it was a rub-off from his explaining things to me that she heard, or me explaining things to her, or what. Or whether that had nothing to do with it. Whether my father's influence was as important as it appears, I'm not sure. There are many fathers who've decided what their sons are going to be, and their sons have come out entirely different. His way was never to tell me to be a scientist, or anything like that, but simply to tell me interesting things about the world all the time. He understood science in a way not many scientists do. He understood what it was all about. I don't know how he came to be interested at all. His father was also a kind of rational type of thinking man who liked mathematical and scientific things, and that may have had some influence on him. One can go back into the depths, but really I have no idea.

Joan Feynman

My mother's father was born in Poland. His mother was pregnant when his father slipped through the ice into a river. How he ever got to England I do not know, but he was brought up in an orphanage in England. He had an older brother and sister who were in the United States somehow, and they saved up enough money for his passage when he was fifteen, and he took his passage over to the United States.

The family was so poor they didn't have a bed for him to sleep on. He had only a trunk with a curved top, which is where he slept for a while, and his first job was carrying needles and thread on his back around Long Island and selling them to people.

My great-grandfather was a Polish Jew. He felt that the Jews were better off under Germany than under the czar, so he was smuggling guns to the Russian part of Poland. I guess it must have been in the 1860s or '70s. The Russians caught him, and they were going to hang him. But then the Germans attacked, and in the battle he got away and hid in the basement of the temple in his town. The people got money and sent him to the United States. Then he asked for his children to come, and his oldest daughter was my grandmother. He had a watchmaking store, and she worked there. One day my grandfather brought in a watch to be fixed, and much to his surprise, this beautiful young woman fixed his watch—apparently women didn't fix watches much then. So that's how they met.

In Jewish tradition in Russia and Poland, women were businesswomen, because the men were supposed to study, and somebody had to make a living. So she went into business making hats. Later, he joined her, and they

Joan Feynman, age nineteen.

did very well. One day his older brother came in and said he had a new way to make a collar on a shirt. "You shouldn't be in the hat business," he said. "Why don't you drop this and come join me in the shirt business?" My grandfather said, "I don't know anything about shirts. I'll finance you, lend you some money to get started. But I'll stay with the hats." Well, that was the way the Van Heusen shirt company started. Yes. My grandfather's great mistake!

When my father and mother married, my grandfather set my father up making velveteen dresses. Then came the First World War. Women stopped wearing hats, and they stopped wearing velveteen, and that's what happened— the family fortune disappeared.

My mother kept a very well-regulated house and everything ran smoothly. There were rules that were sort of American-German type rules, you know? One of them was if you were a little kid, then when you went to bed you stayed there. One night I was in bed and Richard got permission to wake me up. I was four, perhaps, and he was thirteen. He woke me up and said there was something wonderful he wanted to show me. We went out of the house and down the street to a golf course. It was night, and out in the middle of the golf course he said, "Look up." And there was an aurora borealis.

Years later, after I got my Ph.D. in solid-state physics, I got interested in the aurora again. I was having a wonderful time and I really wanted to talk to Richard about it. But it occurred to me, you know, he's terribly smart, and if you're doing a puzzle, a crossword puzzle, say, and you're struggling with it, the worst thing that can happen is you put it down, you walk out of the room, and some real puzzle expert comes in and does it for you. I was terrified that Richard would come along and look at this lovely problem that I found and was having fun with, and do it for me. So I went to him and I said, "Listen, I'll make a deal with you: we'll divide up the universe. I take the aurora, and you take everything else!" He agreed.

There's more to this story. A few years ago, Richard went up to Alaska to give some talks or something, and he went around the auroral observatory there. It's run by a guy named Akasofu who has discovered that for some reason or other all the best aurora people are Japanese, so everybody there is very Japanese. Akasofu was showing Richard around and telling him all this stuff, and Richard, of course, was enormously interested in everything. Then Akasofu said, "Wouldn't you like to work on some of these problems?" Richard said, "Well, I would like to, but I can't. I'd have to get my sister's permission. I'll ask her."

I was at a meeting a couple of months later, and a very polite Japanese man came over and said, "I'm not sure whether it's a joke or not, but your brother told me that he would have to get your permission to work on the aurora."

I said, "That's correct. He asked me for it, and I told him no!"

That was the end of Richard and the aurora.

Feynman

Richard on a "fifty-cent horse"—a rental pony—around 1926.

My father taught me to notice things, and one day I was playing with what we call an express wagon, which is a little wagon which has a railing around it that children pull around. It had a ball in it, and when I pulled the wagon I noticed something about the way the ball moved. I went to my father and I said, "Say, Pop, I noticed something. When I pull the wagon, the ball rolls to the back of the wagon. And when I'm pulling it along and I suddenly stop, the ball rolls to the front of the wagon. Why is that?"

"That," he said, "nobody knows. The general principle is that things that are moving try to keep on moving, and things that are standing still tend to stand still unless you push on them hard. This tendency is called 'inertia,' but nobody knows why it's true." Now, that's a deep understanding: he didn't just give me a name. He knew the difference between knowing the name of something and knowing something.

He went on to say, "If you look close you'll find the ball does not rush to the back of the wagon, but it's the back of the wagon that you're pulling . . . against the ball. The ball stands still, or as a matter of fact from the friction starts to move forward really, and doesn't move back."

So I ran back to the little wagon and set the ball up again and pulled the wagon from under it, and looking sideways I saw that indeed he was right—the ball never moved backwards in the wagon when I pulled the wagon forward. It moved backward relative to the wagon, but relative to the sidewalk it was moved forward a little bit. It's just that the wagon caught up with it. So that's the way I was educated by my father, with those kinds of examples and discussions. No pressure, just lovely interesting discussions.

Joan Feynman

When I was little, we used to walk along the beach by the waterside, and you know the way people imagine things in three dimensions? You picture a doughnut in your mind? Well, Richard was imagining things in four dimensions— he was practicing this, to sort of imagine things and manipulate them in four dimensions.

Did he ever speculate on where he got his ability?

No. He thought it was just from doing a large number of problems over and over. But a couple of days before his death we were talking about this—the fact that when he did physics it turned out right, and when he wrote a book it became a best-seller, how no matter what he did it seemed to just happen like that. I said to him, "You know, there is a possible solution to this which we have never seriously considered." He said, "What's that?" "That you really are smarter than other people." And he looked shocked. Oh, no! *That* he would not consider.

You know, he had a normal IQ. When I was a kid, I sneaked off and got into the files and looked up our IQs. Mine was 124, and his was 123. So I was actually smarter than he was!

1929. Joan was nine years younger than Richard. Another child, Henry, died in infancy when Richard was five.

Feynman

In the summertime we used to go to the Catskill Mountains. We lived in New York, and the Catskill Mountains is the place where people went in the summer. The fathers would all go back to New York to work during the week and only come back for the weekend. On weekends, my father would take me for walks in the woods and he'd tell me about interesting things that were going on in the woods. When the other mothers saw this, they thought it was wonderful and that the other fathers should take their sons for walks. They tried to work on them, but they didn't get anywhere at first. They wanted my father to take all the kids, but he didn't want to because he had a special relationship with me—we had a personal thing together. So it ended up that the other fathers had to take their children for walks the next weekend.

The next Monday, when the fathers were all back at work, all the kids were playing in the field, and one kid says to me, "See that bird? What kind of a bird is that?"

I said, "I haven't the slightest idea what kind of a bird it is."

He says, "It's a brown-throated thrush," or something. "Your father doesn't teach you anything!"

But it was the opposite. He had already taught me. "See that bird?" he says, "It's a brown-throated thrush. But in Italian it's a *chutto lapittida*. In Portuguese it's a *bom da*

Far Rockaway, 1929. Richard age eleven, Joan two.

peida. In Chinese, it's a *chung-long-tah,* and in Japanese, it's a *katano tekeda.* . . . You can know the name of that bird in all the languages of the world, but when you're finished, you'll know absolutely nothing whatever about the bird. You'll only know about humans in different places, and what they call the bird. Now, let's look at the bird and what it's doing." (I found out later, but not from him, that to be able to talk to other people, so that they knew which thing you were talking about, you had to know the name of it!) He would tell me things about the birds; we'd be in the woods and we'd see that as the birds walked around on the floor of the forest, they were pecking in their feathers. My father said to me, "Why do you think they peck in their feathers all the time?" I said I thought it was because they were trying to straighten out ruffled feathers. He said, "That's a good possibility. What would make the feathers ruffle?" I said that when they fly it probably ruffles them. He suggested that if that was the case, then the birds would peck more when they first land, and not so much once they had got the feathers straightened out. He said we should watch to see if that was true. And we noticed that when the bird landed, it pecked all right, but it continued to peck in its feathers the whole time it walked around. I couldn't guess the answer, and then my father told me that in the feathers of the bird there lived fleas, and the bird is going after the fleas. But then on the flea, in its leg joints, there is a kind of greasy stuff, and there is a little mite that lives on it. The mite that eats this grease doesn't digest it completely, so from the rear end there comes a stuff which has a little sugar in it, and on this little sugar there can live another animal, and so forth.

Now whether it was really a flea, or a tick, or whatever, he didn't know exactly. If it wasn't in the joint but somewhere else on the flea that the parasite lived, that didn't matter either. He was telling me that everywhere there's any source of food—any kind of a niche that can be used—some form of life finds a way to make use of it. So what I discovered from him, you see, is several things. First, you can find out by thinking about something, and making observations like looking at the birds, whether this idea or that idea is right; but the most important thing I found out from him is that if you asked any question and pursued it deeply enough, then at the end there was a glorious discovery of a general and beautiful kind about the way life behaves. And that's what I mean by saying he knew science better than others.

As I went along I became more interested in radios and a little bit in algebra and mathematics which I . . . I was going to say I picked it up in school, but that's not true. I had found a book, my aunt's old algebra book, upstairs in an attic when I was very young, and one night (I remember this too) when I was in bed, going to sleep, I said to my father, "I found this book on algebra. What's algebra for?" And he told me: "You can do problems with algebra which you can't do with arithmetic. It's like arithmetic, but it's more advanced." Well, that was a big challenge, and I said, "Give me an example of a problem that you can do with algebra that you can't do with arithmetic." He said, "A house and a garage rent for sixty-two hundred pounds" or whatever, some number, and "The house is this big, and the garage is that big . . . how much would the house rent for without the garage?" I said, "You can't answer that by anything!" It was a joke, of course—he gave me a problem that was insoluble. He went out and closed the door, and I fell asleep.

My cousin at that time, who was three years older, was in high school and was having considerable difficulty with his algebra. He had a tutor come, and I was allowed to sit in a corner while the tutor would try to teach my cousin algebra. I'd hear him talking about x. I said to my cousin, "What are you trying to do?" He said, "Well, two x plus seven is equal to fifteen, and you're trying to find out what x is." I said, "You mean four?" He says: "Yeah, but you did it by arithmetic. You have to do it by algebra." That's why my cousin was never able to do algebra. I learned algebra, fortunately, by not going to school and knowing the whole idea was to find out what x was, and it didn't make any difference how you did it. There's no such a thing as "you do it by arithmetic" or "you do it by algebra." That was a false thing that they had invented in school so that the children who have to study algebra can all pass it. They had invented a set of rules which if you followed them without thinking could produce the answer—"Subtract seven from both sides," or "If you have a multiplier, divide both sides by the multiplier," and so on—a series of steps by which you could get the answer if you didn't understand what you were trying to do. So I was lucky. I always learnt things by myself.

Once we were out walking somewhere and my father picked a leaf from a tree. This leaf had a flaw—a little brown line in the shape of a C, that started in the middle of the leaf and ran in a curl to the edge. "Look at this brown line," he says. "It's narrow at the beginning, and it's wider as it goes to the edge. What this is, is a fly—a blue fly with yellow eyes and green wings which has come and laid an egg on the leaf. Then, when the egg hatches into a maggot (a caterpillar-like thing), it spends its whole life eating this leaf—that's where it gets its food. As it eats along, it leaves this brown trail of eaten leaf. As the maggot grows, the trail grows wider until he's grown to full size at the end of the leaf, where he turns into a fly—a blue fly with yellow eyes and green wings—who flies away and lays an egg on another leaf."

Again, I knew that the details weren't precisely correct—it could even have been a beetle—but the idea that he was trying to explain to me was the amusing part of life: the whole thing is just reproduction. No matter how complicated the business is, the main point is to do it again! And that was the way that he would tell me things—I knew that they weren't quite accurate, and yet they were utterly accurate, if you see what I mean, in the character of the story he was trying to tell me.

I don't want to give the impression that my father only taught me about biological things—he told me about inertia, he told me about mathematical things, and the beautiful relationships. He was delighted by the simple, remarkable fact that if you had a circle and you put the same kind, same size circles around it—like a coin with the same size coins around it—exactly six would fit. There

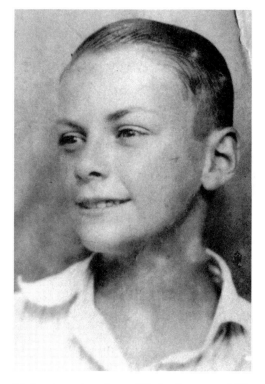

Richard age ten. Joan: "He had a normal IQ. Mine was 124, and his was 123. So I was actually smarter than he was!"

was something profoundly wonderful that six would fit. Things like that. He told me about *pi*, for example—the fact that the circumference of a circle to its diameter was the same for all circles, and that it was a very important and interesting number. I know he told me this, because when I was in school and was learning about decimals, we had to write a decimal for various numbers and the teacher had asked us to write three and a quarter, or three and an eighth . . . let's say I wrote three point five, and that clicked in my mind with something my father had told me, and I wrote, "*Pi* equals"—I thought it was the same number—"*Pi* equals the ratio of the circumference to the diameter of a circle." Fortunately the teacher appreciated it, and she came by and said, "No, *pi* is . . ."—but it showed that I knew about *pi* before I had learned to write very well in school at decimals.

I was always ahead in mathematics and science, naturally, because once my father got me started I read books, and I learned from many, many other places. Later on, when I was about twelve or thirteen, I used to go to the library—I have to explain that we didn't have any sources; nowadays it's very easy to find scientific books which have a lot of detail, any degree that you want, in ordinary libraries. In those days, it wasn't the case.

The library in the town had some scientific books, but mostly they were sort of popularized science, simplified so that you could understand it—not technically detailed, but "explanations-for-people" books that I found particularly good. There were some by Jeans explaining about quantum mechanics or something, and there was a book by Russell on mathematical philosophy that was interesting.

But there was a series of math books, which starts with *Arithmetic for the Practical Man*, and then *Algebra for the Practical Man*, and then *Trigonometry for the Practical Man*, and I learned trigonometry from that—I soon forgot it again because I didn't understand it very well. But the library was going to get *Calculus for the Practical Man*. I knew by this time, by reading the encyclopedia, that calculus was an important subject and it was an interesting one,

FUNCTION	$\int$	$\int$ VALUE	FUNCTION	$\int$	$\int$ VALUE
$x+y+z+\cdots$	$\int(dx+dy+dz\cdots)$	$\int dx+\int dy+\int dz$	$y=\csc\theta$	$\int\csc\theta\,d\theta$	$\log_e(\csc\theta-\cot\theta)$
$y=x+c$	$\int dx$	$x+c$	$y=\sec\theta$	$\int\sec^2\theta\,d\theta$	$\tan\theta$
$y=\pm x$	$\int(\pm dx)$	$\pm\int dy$	$y=\csc\theta$	$\int\csc^2\theta\,d\theta$	$-\cot\theta$
$y=mx$	$\int m\,dx$	$m\int dx$	$y=\sec\theta\tan\theta$	$\int\sec\theta\tan\theta\,d\theta$	$\sec\theta$
$y=x^m$	$\int x^m\,dy$	$\dfrac{x^{m+1}}{m+1}$	$y=\csc\theta\cot\theta$	$\int\csc\theta\cot\theta\,d\theta$	$-\csc\theta$
$y=\sin\theta$	$\int\sin\theta\,d\theta$	$-\cos\theta$	$y=\dfrac{1}{x}$	$\int\dfrac{dx}{x}$	$\log_e x$
$y=\cos\theta$	$\int\cos\theta\,d\theta$	$\sin\theta$	$y=e^x$	$\int e^x\,dy$	e^x
$y=\tan\theta$	$\int\tan\theta\,d\theta$	$-\log_e(\cos\theta)$	$y=e^{ax}$	$\int e^{ax}\,dx$	$\dfrac{e^{ax}}{a}$
$y=\cot\theta$	$\int\cot\theta\,d\theta$	$\log_e(\sin\theta)$	$y=b^x$	$\int b^x\,dx$	$(\log_b e)b^x$
$y=\sec\theta$	$\int\sec\theta\,d\theta$	$\log_e(\sec\theta+\tan\theta)$	$y=\log_e x$	$\int\log_e x\,dy$	$x(\log_e x-1)$
			$y=\log_b x$	$\int\log_b x\,dx$	$x\log_b\left(\dfrac{x}{e}\right)$

(Handwritten notes titled: NOTES ON THE CALCULUS FOR THE PRACTICAL MAN — SUMMARY, a constant C should be added)

"I lied. I said it was for my father. . . ." Notes made from the library book. Richard was thirteen.

and I ought to learn it. (I was older now, I was perhaps thirteen.) Then the calculus book finally came out. I was so excited, and I went to the library to take it out, and she looks at me and she says, "You're just a child! What are you taking this book out for?" It was one of the few times in my life that I was uncomfortable, so I lied. I said it was for my father. I took it home and I learned calculus from it, and I tried to explain it to my father. He'd start to read the beginning of it and he found it confusing. That bothered me a little bit. I didn't know that he was so limited, you know, that he didn't understand it. So that was the first time I knew I had learned more in some sense than he—because I was getting beyond him.

Joan Feynman

We had the *Encyclopaedia Britannica* when I was a kid, and when I married, the *Encyclopaedia Britannica* was Richard's wedding present to me—a house without a *Britannica* just didn't seem right to him.

Feynman

Even when I was a small boy my father used to sit me on his lap and read to me from the *Encyclopaedia Britannica.*

And we would read, say, about dinosaurs and maybe it would be talking about the brontosaurus, or the *Tyrannosaurus rex*, and it would say something like "This thing is twenty-five feet high and the head is six feet across," you see, and so he'd stop always and say: "Let's see what that means. That would mean that if he stood in our yard he would be high enough to put his head through the window, but not quite because the head is a little bit too wide, and it would break the window as it came by."

Everything we'd read would be translated as best we could into some reality, so that I learned to do that: everything that I read I try to figure out what it really means, what it's really saying, by translating. So I used to get read the encyclopedia when I was a boy, but with translation, you see! It was very exciting and interesting to think there were animals of such magnitude (I wasn't frightened that there would be one coming in my window as a consequence of this, I don't think!), but I thought it was very, very interesting, and they all died out, and at that time nobody knew why. From very early times I was interested in the question of what happened to the dinosaurs, and when I hear a new theory like Alvarez's theory about the meteor that came and so forth, it fitted into my past desire to know the answer to this mystery.

Our *Britannica* was the thirteenth edition—the same as the eleventh, but made after the war—which was a famous edition that had good articles by very famous men, and when I got older I read the various articles. They were quite advanced, so there were different degrees of difficulty that I struggled with. There were some articles I never succeeded in understanding—one was on group theory, the other was on gyroscopes.

The articles in the *Britannica* were written by such high-class people that they explained everything; the only problem was that there was so much, but everything was there if you worked at it. I find it very discomforting now that there are many books that claim to explain a subject, in which there's some concept or other which is very poorly explained, and therefore it's not there—no matter how hard you study that book, you'll never come out the other end. You'd have to know the concept wasn't there, and that's hard to do when you're first learning a subject. The problem is not that you are foolish or incapable, but that the writing isn't there. I was lucky in that the sources I had always had everything in them; even if it was in very condensed form, it was all explained very carefully.

I had a trick when a book was hard—like the article on electrostatics in the encyclopedia, which I found difficult. What I'd do is, I'd read the whole article, even though I had stopped understanding it after the first two or three paragraphs. I read the whole article vaguely, and then the next time I'd go through it again and get a little further, and so on, until I went all the way through (with some exceptions, which I'll explain), and then I'd write it in a book and when I did that it was complete. The things I would leave out were things like the calculation of the capacitance of an elliptical condenser, say, but I already knew by reading the whole article that those funny functions and complicated things didn't appear again in the article and were therefore a side issue. I always have had an instinct in reading a complicated book to know what were the essential elements I have to learn, and what were the applications or side issues which, if I didn't understand them, was not an essential lack in understanding the whole thing.

I was always original like that—I did almost everything by myself, getting clues from books as to what was an interesting subject. Not calculus—I didn't work out calculus by myself!

My father was perfectly clear about what he wanted Richard to do and to be. I don't think there was any pressure—I was present at a lot of their conversations, and there was no pressure to do anything. But my father just thought that science was such a wonderful thing. My father had felt that he was trapped in his life, and unable to do these marvelous things, to appreciate them in the way that he would have wanted to. So what he was doing was freeing the children.

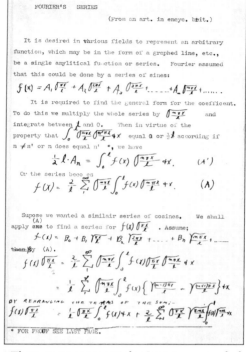

"There were some articles I never succeeded in understanding." Notes on a Britannica article.

Joan Feynman

Nobody really knows where my father got all his knowledge from. Richard and I talked about it, just before he died—where did our father get all this? I mean, he was living in Far Rockaway, Long Island—it wasn't like he lived in the city, and could go to lectures. I guess he went into New York to the museums.

He knew all this stuff very young, and he read every night. It's hard to tell looking back, but yeah, he must have been very smart. I know there was a magician once that came to town and taught him magic. But he must have invented himself.

Between my brother and my father, loving science as they did, it was obvious that this was the thing that was fun to do. I remember even before kindergarten, whenever there was a square, like a door, my brother had me run my finger across it and say, "The sum of the square on the sides is equal to the square on the hypotenuse." I hadn't any idea what a square number was, or what it meant, but because they loved it, there was no escaping loving it.

My father loved nature just as much when I was a kid as when Richard was, although he was ill by then. We'd go down to the beach on Sunday mornings in the spring and the fall when there was nobody else there, and he would take me out on the rocks and show me the barnacles, say. He would tell me about how they start out life free-swimming, and then end up stuck on those posts. He couldn't see anything without wanting to tell you a story about it. Of course, as Richard has pointed out, these stories weren't always enormously accurate about the particular animal, but they gave the general idea about how life works.

He used to tell me about seventeen-year locusts, how they lived all their lives dug in underground, and then every seventeen years they would come up out of the ground and make a lot of noise. Well, years later, long after my father was dead, I was working at Lamont, an old estate above the Hudson River, and one day there was a tremendous noise from a beech tree. The seventeen-year locusts had come up! It was marvelous—just like my father had told me.

When I was about eight or so, I wanted to be an astrono-mer, and my mother informed me that, unfortunately, women's brains were physiologically incapable of doing science. I remember weeping because I wanted to do it—it was taking a little girl and telling her that all her dreams are impossible because she's a girl. There was a time, you know, when biology was destiny—you could only make yourself unhappy by wanting to have a career, or wanting anything besides a family and children. So I think it was to prevent me from being unhappy that my parents dis-couraged me.

The big turning point was when I was thirteen, and Richard was in graduate school. He had been at home, and had left to go back to Princeton. There was a book lying on the table, and I said to my mother, "Richard's forgotten one of his books." I opened it, and inside was my name in Richard's handwriting, and a bookplate with my name on it. It was astronomy! A college textbook on astronomy. He had bought it secondhand in Princeton and left it for me, without saying anything.

Well, I asked him, "How can I read it? It's so hard."

He said, "You start at the beginning and you read as far as you can get, until you are lost. Then you start at the beginning again, and you keep working through until you can understand the whole book."

My great ambition for years was to be an assistant to some man, just to be allowed to look at the stars. Not to do any science, but just to be his assistant—this was my childhood goal. I couldn't imagine anything further than that. My ambition was to be the person that fixed the telescopes so somebody else could look at the stars.

Richard always encouraged me. When I realized that what I really wanted was a telescope, I told Richard, and he said he would buy a piece of glass for me. I could grind the telescope lens at home, and then he would test it at Princeton on the machines there. I was all excited, but my mother and father decided that I couldn't grind it in my room. I don't remember why, but probably because glass dust gets all over everything. But we lived in an apartment block, and downstairs in the basement there were storage-

Joan took her Ph.D. from Syracuse in 1958. It was on "absorption of infrared radiation in crystals of diamond-type lattice struc-ture."

bin rooms for furniture and so on, which were like little rooms. One of the boys who lived in the building had made a wonderful chemistry lab down there in one of these bins, and I used to go see it sometimes. So I figured I could go down there and grind my lens. Wonderful! I told my parents, and the answer was no. No, because they were afraid that I would be raped in the basement. Well, if I had been a boy they would have raised heaven and hell to get me to grind that lens. So I never had a telescope.

In the book there was mention of a woman called Celillia Payne-Gaposhkin. She was at Harvard, she was an astronomer, and she was good enough to be in this book. So there was something wrong with this theory of my parents. I figured, if somebody else could do it, I could do it too. And I did. So—just because things are impossible isn't any reason not to do them!

Feynman I went to a scientific school, MIT. When you first join a fraternity, if you think you're smart, they try to keep you from feeling that you're too smart by giving you what look like simple questions to figure out. It's like a training for imagination, and it's kind of fun.

One of the questions was the problem about the mirror—it's an old problem. You look in a mirror, and let's say you part your hair on the right side. You look in the mirror, and your image has its hair parted on the left side, so the image is left-to-right mixed up. But it's not top-to-bottom mixed up, because the top of the head of the image is there at the top, and the feet are down at the bottom. The question is: how does the mirror know to get the left and right mixed up, but not the up and the down?

You can get a better idea of the problem if you think of lying down on your side and looking in the mirror. All right? Your hair parting is still on the left side. Your left and right was the up and down, whereas the up and the down which look okay were the right and the left before. So did the mirror somehow figure out what you're going to do when you're looking into it?

Well, I worked out the answer to that one.

At MIT, 1937.

See, if you wave one hand, then the hand in the mirror that waves is opposite it—the hand on the "east" is the hand on the "east," and the hand on the "west" is the hand on the "west." The head that's up is up, and the feet that are down are down. So everything's really all right. But what's wrong is that if this is "north," then your nose is to the back of your head, but in the image the nose is to the "south" of the back of your head. What happens is, the image has neither the right nor the left mixed up with the top and the bottom, but the front and the back have been reversed, you see. The nose is on the wrong side of the head, if you like. Now, ordinarily when we think of the image in a mirror, we think of it as another person, and we think of the way that a person would get into that condition over there. It's a psychological thing: we don't think that the person has been squashed and pulled and pushed backwards-forwards with his nose in his head, because that's not what ordinarily happens to people! A person gets to look like he looks in the mirror by walking round the other side and facing you. And when people do that, they don't turn their head into their feet—we leave that part alone. But they do get their right and left hands swung about, you see, when they turn around. So we say left and right are interchanged, but really the symmetrical way is it's along the axis of the mirror that things get interchanged.

Well, that's an easy one. A harder problem, and very entertaining, was: "What keeps a railroad train on the tracks?"

Well, of course, everyone thinks that the answer is the flanges on the wheels. But that's not the answer, because those flanges are just safety devices—if the flanges were up against the tracks, you'd hear a terrible squealing. Sometimes you do. The flanges are there just in case the real mechanism doesn't work.

I'll explain it to you.

People all know this about their automobile: that when you go round a corner, the outside wheels have to travel further than the inside wheels, and so the axle is broken in the middle with a gear system called a differential. Did you ever see the differential on a railroad train? No! You look at those wheels on a freight car, and there are two wheels and a solid steel axle going from one wheel to the other. So now how does it go round a corner, round a curve, when the outside wheel has to go further than the inside wheel? The answer is that the wheels are shaped like cones—they're a little fatter closer to the train, and a little thinner further out, and if you look very closely you'll see that they've got this beveled edge, and it's all very simple. When they go round the curve, they slide out on the track a bit, so that the outside wheel travels on a fatter part—a bigger diameter—and the inside wheel on a smaller diameter. So when they both turn one turn, the outside swings further than the inside. And that's what keeps the train on the track too, in the same way. Suppose the train is running along the track, and the two wheels are exactly balanced, and it's nice and even. Well, then accidentally it hits a bump or something, and swings out to one side. One wheel is now on a bigger circumference than the other, but because they're on a solid shaft, once around carries one wheel forward relative to the other, and steers the train back on the track! Of course, if it

Graduation from MIT, 1939.

goes too far towards the other side, the same mechanism operates the other way round, and it keeps going back or forth.

So, you see? The flanges really are just for safety.

Feynman

You might wonder what my father got out of it all. I went to MIT. I went to Princeton. He was happy with me, I believe. Once, though, when I came back from MIT, where I'd been for a few years, he said to me, "Now that you've become educated about these things there's one question I've always had that I've never understood very well, and I'd like to ask you to explain it to me."

I said, "Okay."

He said, "I understand that when an atom makes a transition from one state to another it emits a particle of light called a photon."

I said, "That's right."

He says, "Well, now. Is the photon in the atom ahead of time, so that it can come out? Or is there no photon in the atom to start with?"

I tried to explain that photon numbers aren't conserved, that they're just created by the motion of the electron. I couldn't explain it very well. I said that the sounds I'm making weren't in me—it's not like my little boy, who said one day that he could no longer say a certain word—the word was "cat"—because his "word bag" had run out of the word. There's no word bag that you have inside that you use up the words as they come out, and in the same sense there's no "photon bag" in an atom. I couldn't do much better. He was not satisfied with me in that respect: that I was never able to explain any of the things that he didn't understand! So he was unsuccessful; he sent me through all these universities in order to find out these things, and he never did find out!

"He was happy with me, I believe. . . ."
Melville Feynman, 1945.

0530 hours, July 16, 1945. Alamogordo, New Mexico. The "Trinity" test of the first atomic bomb.

CHAPTER TWO

Love and the Bomb

Feynman helped build the bombs which destroyed Hiroshima and Nagasaki. In 1992, reviewing James Gleick's biography of Feynman, the British geneticist Steve Jones described Feynman as "a man of profound moral shallowness," and wrote:

"This book contains one of the most shocking admissions in scientific biography: Feynman's confession, while working on the Manhattan Project which led to the atom bomb, that one of the happiest moments of his career was the realization that he need not feel responsible for the horrors which would emerge from his work. . . . Indeed his main comment on the first test in Alamogordo was that everything was perfect except its aim (which should have been at an enemy city)."

Hindsight, of course, makes this kind of judgment easy. The reality of Feynman's predicament in the early 1940s and his response to it was much more complex, as we shall see.

Joan Feynman

Richard was always telling me how terrible girls were. But when he was fifteen and I was six, he went out one night to a party. The next morning I was feeling nasty about myself and I went into his bedroom. I said, "Girls are awful, aren't they, Richard?" He got this faraway look in his eyes and he said, "No! I met the most wonderful girl last night!" That was Arline.

She was thirteen when they started going together. She had hair that came down . . . well, she could almost sit on it. She wore it in braids, and I remember her combing it, and all the boys standing around, fascinated by this gorgeous girl combing her hair.

By the time Richard was in college, when he was seventeen, we knew they were going to get married. Arline was at our house a great deal while Richard was away. She and my father both painted, and she would go paint with him on weekends. She taught me to play the piano, and she used to go to cooking classes with my mother. So she was really part of the family.

One time we all went to a hotel in Atlantic City, and Richard came down for the weekend. We were swimming in the pool—indoor pools were marvelous things in those days—and Arline said she didn't want to swim anymore, she was very tired. She had a swelling on her neck.

It took the doctors a long time to figure it out, but it was tuberculosis. She was going to die, and the problem was whether Richard would catch tuberculosis from her. My

A letter from Arline. "Box 1663, Santa Fe" was the coded postal address for the scientists working on "Project Y" up in the mountains at Los Alamos.

Richard and Arline.

mother was exceedingly upset that he was determined to marry her, but he realized that the only way he could take care of her was if they were married. Otherwise, he was just the fiancé, and he didn't think her family was doing a good job of looking after her. Richard borrowed a station wagon and put Arline's bed in the back. He drove her to a hospital in New Jersey, and they got married on the way. She was never well enough for them to keep house together, and from the time they were married till the time she died, she was in a sanatorium. A twenty-four-, twenty-five-year-old man and his twenty-two-or twenty-three-year-old wife. . . . It was awful. She used to write me letters but I never saw her again. And I loved her.

Arline Feynman died on June 16, 1945, in Albuquerque, New Mexico. This was seven weeks before Hiroshima. Feynman had been recruited into the Manhattan Project at Princeton, where he had gone as a graduate student in

Arline cut her long hair short to make it easier to look after in the sanatorium.

1939, age twenty-one. (This was where, when asked if he would like cream or lemon in his tea, he had said, "Both, please," and his hostess had commented, "Surely you're joking, Mr. Feynman!") His professor and Ph.D. supervisor was John Archibald Wheeler.

John Wheeler[1]

The reason universities have students is so they can teach the professors, and Feynman was one of the best. Through some wonderful freak of fate, I ended up with him assigned to me. He had what so many people with a purely mathematical background lack: he had a feel for the physical world. He had worked in a paint factory, I think, in the summertime before he came to Princeton.

I was very enthusiastic about the idea that in the world there are nothing but particles, with Dirac thinking that the electron is the basic particle, and that if you could understand the interaction between electron and electron, then everything else will follow, everything else would be subsidiary to that simple picture. The idea of an electromagnetic field traveling through space, that's just talk. The real thing is that this electron does something, and later that electron, affected by it, does something. Action at a distance. And we found we could express that in consistent mathematical language, although we didn't get the opportunity to write it up until after the war.

It was so much fun, so beautiful, that the next step seemed to be to translate that classical picture into quantum language, and that seemed to be an attractive thesis topic. So Feynman set to work on that. Someone suggested that he should look at a paper by Dirac, and that furnished a little hint of a way which he later expanded into his "sum-over-histories" way of describing quantum theory, which to me is still so simple, so beautiful. At the time, I went around to tell Einstein about it. Einstein listened to me patiently in his upstairs study, and at the end I said, "Professor Einstein, doesn't this make quantum theory absolutely beautiful, simple, inevitable?" And he said, "I still can't believe God plays dice. But perhaps I've earned the right to make my mistakes." So, he was unshakable!

There were, of course, many important fundamental questions, like "Where does the universe came from?" and so on, that people were working on when I was first learning, and I didn't have a hope—I didn't think to try about that. I had no way to get at them when I was young.

But there were little problems that I would just invent for myself, to find the rule for something—the cubes of the integers, or something like that—and I would solve these things. With that particular example, summing the nth powers of the first n integers, there was one set of numbers which I couldn't find the formula for, and I later discovered that they're called "Bernoulli numbers," and they were invented by Bernoulli, who had the same problem as me in 1748—I was rather delighted that I had gotten

Feynman

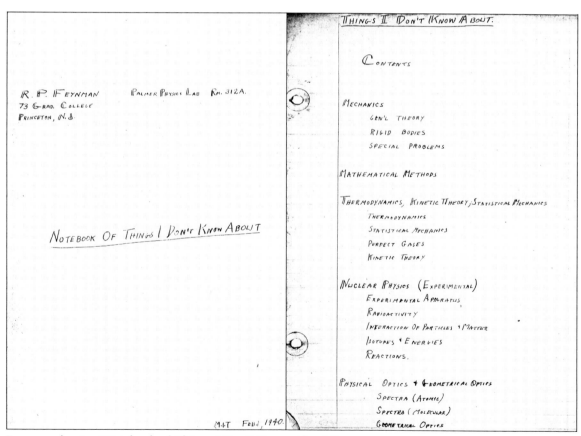

Feynman kept a "Notebook of Things I Don't Know About."

up to 1748! As I went along solving problems independently, I simply got closer and closer to the present, until I was working on problems that were beyond the present.

By that time I had realized that I was mostly interested in physics, in theoretical physics. As a college senior, I had been reading books about the problem of making a quantum theory of electricity and magnetism and electrodynamics. At that time there was a quantum theory[2] proposed, but it gave all kinds of difficulties. I read the books in the same way that I ordinarily did—I didn't understand it, but I went through the whole thing anyway, and I could see where they weren't getting anywhere. So I saw from reading these books that the highest problem of the day in theoretical physics was to get the quantum theory of electrodynamics.

The theory of electricity, magnetism, light, and so on had been worked out according to what's called "classical" principles, and in the meantime the "uncertainty principle" and those other things had been discovered— the quantum mechanical nature of nature, in other words. The problem of how to put the two together to get a quantum mechanical theory of light, magnetism, and electricity was unsolved. It was partly solved, but the equations gave peculiar answers—infinite answers to calculations—so the theory as written seemed unsatisfactory. The people in the high-level books were worrying about this. I couldn't understand the books, but I could understand the worry.

Feynman I was working on my thesis, my research on quantum electrodynamics for a Ph.D. at Princeton, and Bob Wilson came in to say that he has a project. It's being supported by the government—they're going to do something, it's a secret, and he's not allowed to tell me what it is. But since he knows that after he tells me, I'll be sure to work on it, he feels there's no harm in telling me.

So he told me about this business: how they were going to try to make an atomic bomb, and in order to do that they had to separate the uranium isotope that's light from the uranium isotope that's heavy—uranium 235 would explode in a bomblike way, but it had to be separated from the uranium 238. The separation of these two isotopes at that time was a very difficult problem. There were various methods suggested, but none of them was sure to work. "They" had decided that the idea was going to be pursued at Princeton, and Bob Wilson was recruiting people to do it. He wanted someone to do the theoretical work, to figure out which way we should go.

I told him he'd made a big mistake in telling me, because I wasn't going to join the project—I had this thesis work I wanted to do, but never mind, the secret was okay with me. As he left he said, "See you in the meeting at three."

I went back to the desk to work a little bit, but of course I couldn't. I began to think about it and I was worried by the possibility that the Germans would get this thing, this bomb thing, and that to me was a very serious fright. The Germans were already doing such horrible things to the people they had power over.

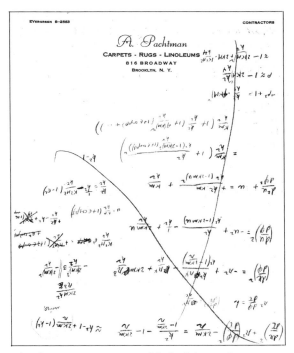

Wheeler: "Feynman would do his work, not on block paper, but on paper lying around."

Part of Feynman's Ph.D. thesis was written on stationery from a college newspaper edited by Arline.

The reason that I didn't want to get involved was that I was working on my thesis. I had gone pretty far with it and I liked this problem in physics. It was a scientific question, and I wanted to be a scientist. This other thing was not a scientific question, it was an engineering problem. It was a completely different kind of a thing. It would mean that I had to stop the research which was my life's desire, to take time off to do this thing which I felt I should do in order to "protect civilization," if you want, okay? So that was what I had to debate with myself. First reaction: I didn't want to get interrupted in my normal work to do this odd job. There was also the moral problem of anything involving war, but it kind of scared me when I realized what the weapon would be. The knowledge of science is universal, an international thing. Everybody cooperates. When we do something we publish it, and when any other country does something they publish it. The discovery of the fission process and so on was made partly in Germany, partly in Italy, partly in the United States, partly in France. There was no monopoly of knowledge or skill at that time as far as I knew, so there was no reason why if we thought it was possible that they [the Germans] wouldn't also think it was possible. They were just humans, with the same information. I don't remember everything I thought—there was a turmoil of a kind between the desire to do my regular physics, and the question as to whether to make such a frightening weapon was something that ought to be done. I decided at the time, I believe, that the morally right thing to do was to protect ourselves; I felt there was a great evil around, and that this evil would only grow if it had more technical power. The only way that I knew how to prevent that was to get there earlier so that we could prevent them from doing it, or defeat them.

We might not have known exactly how big a bomb you could make, or whether in fact it was really possible to make it at all. But it was clear to us that this was a weapon which would release a fantastic amount of energy in a short time, and radioactivity. This would be a very, very powerful weapon which in the hands of Hitler and his crew would let them completely control the rest of the world.

Ph.D., 1942.

So I went to the meeting at three o'clock to decide who was going to do what, and immediately after the meeting I was given an old rolltop desk in a room where the first experiment was being put together. I had to calculate whether this thing [the uranium isotope separation] would work or not, and from that moment on I worked as fast as I could. It was like one of those cartoon movies—each time I looked up the apparatus was getting bigger and bigger, and finally I decided, "Yes, it'll work." (In the end, this particular method wasn't used to separate the uranium.)

Anyway, then we all went to Los Alamos.

Joan Feynman

When I was a child, it was believed that animals became extinct because they were too specialized. My father used to tell us about the saber-tooth tiger's teeth—how they got too big and the tiger couldn't eat because he couldn't take game anymore. And I remember my father saying, with my brother sitting there, "I wonder what it will be with the human beings that will be so overspecialized that they'll kill themselves off?"

My father never found out that my brother was working on the bomb.

Feynman

When I got to Los Alamos, I met all these famous men, scientists I had heard of, and it was a great pleasure for me to meet them.

Los Alamos was very democratic. We had meetings in Oppenheimer's office in which everybody was allowed to say anything to anybody, so it wasn't the kind of hierarchy where you had to know your place. It was a very remarkable organization that Oppenheimer made—the problems of running a bunch of scientists in a new kind of circumstance had never been tried before, and he somehow instinctively knew how to do it so that everybody was happy.

Oppenheimer was extremely human. When he was recruiting all these people to go to Los Alamos—although

Los Alamos. Feynman next to Oppenheimer. In the front row, third from left, Enrico Fermi. In December 1942, in a racquets court at the University of Chicago, Fermi had supervised the world's first nuclear chain reaction.

Los Alamos ID photos: Hans Bethe (who would later win a Nobel Prize for finding out how the sun and stars work), Feynman, and John von Neumann—mathematician, dandy, and computer visionary.

he had all these complicated problems of what the story was going to be, with the secrecy and so on, and he was arranging things with all these big shots—he still worried about all the details. For example, when he asked me to come I told him I had this problem—that my wife had tuberculosis. He himself found a hospital and called me up to say they had found somewhere that would take care of her. I was only one of all the many people he was recruiting, but this was the way he always was, concerned with people's individual problems.

Also he was profounder—well, he could understand everything that everybody was doing. We could discuss everything technically because he understood it all, and he was good at summarizing things and coming to a conclusion. We used to go to his house for dinner. A wonderful man, I thought.

There was a little bit of luck I had at the very beginning—most of the big shots were out of town for one reason or the other, getting their furniture transferred or something. Except for Hans Bethe. It seems that when he was working on an idea he always liked to discuss it with someone. He couldn't find anybody around, so he came down to my office. I was an underling, you see, and he started to explain what he was thinking. When it comes to physics I forget exactly who I'm talking to, so I was saying, "No, no! That's crazy!" and so on. Whenever I objected, I was always wrong, but nevertheless that's what he wanted—someone to look for trouble, and if I had been polite it wouldn't have worked. The result was that when the big shots came back, he still came to my office to discuss things. I got to like him very, very much. That's why, when he went to Cornell after the war, I wanted to go with him.

J. Robert Oppenheimer. "One doesn't always know what he meant with his most profound statements. . . ."

Feynman and Oppenheimer at Los Alamos, 1942.

We met at Los Alamos in the spring of 1943. I knew nothing about him before that. He had only very recently got his Ph.D. from Wheeler, at Princeton. We got to talking, and he obviously was very bright. At the meetings and seminars he always asked questions which seemed partic-

Hans Bethe

Hans Bethe: "We wanted to impress each other . . ."

ularly intelligent and penetrating. We began to collaborate together. First we wanted to impress each other, so we talked about the kind of numerical calculations which were necessary at Los Alamos. For some reason, 46 squared was mentioned, and I said, "That's 2116." He was impressed and astonished, so I told him, "If you are near 50, you go down by 100 for each step, and the fourth step down from 2500 is 2100, and then how much is left over is the square of what's residual—you are four steps, so it's 4 squared . . . 16."

We had to integrate differential equations, and most of them were second-order—that is, with a second derivative. There was a method to do that, but for some reason we also had a third-order differential equation, which had not been very important in physics before. Within a couple of days, Feynman turned up with a method to integrate third-order differential equations, numerically, and it was more accurate than what you do with second-order. Well, this was impressive!

At the very first seminar of our theoretical division, Serber, who was one of the senior members, had given us the formula for calculating the energy yield of a nuclear explosion when the mass is just a little bit above the critical mass. Feynman and I said to ourselves that it would be nice if we could extend that, without elaborate calculation, for any mass—twice, three times, seven times the critical mass. So we sat down after dinner and said, "Let's make a formula for any critical mass." We had no experimental data at that time, of course, but we could look at the quantities which must be important. One quantity, for example, was the rate of neutron multiplication when the reaction first starts. The second thing was: how far can it expand before the nuclear reaction will stop? How long will it hold together? And in a couple of hours, we had concocted a very simple formula for any multiple of the critical mass, and valid for any size of weapon. That formula was extremely successful, and it is used to the present day. Of course, this was long before the weapons were built.

After a while I had to organize the division into groups, and I made Feynman a group leader, the youngest of eight. He had a group of five or six people, and they did very good work. Feynman's enthusiasm was enormous, on any work he did, and it was infectious—everybody else would be enthusiastic as well.

Feynman could do anything, anything at all. At one time, the most important group in our division was concerned with calculating machines, the early computers made by the International Business Machines company—IBM. The two men I had put in charge of these computers just played with them, and they never gave us the answers we wanted. They never gave us any answers, really; they just enjoyed the power of these machines. Well, Feynman enjoyed that too, but since no results were coming out, I asked Feynman to take over. As soon as he got in there, we got answers every week—lots of them, and very accurate. He always knew what was needed, and he always knew what had to be done to get it. That was very well shown later on by his *Challenger* experience, but it was equally true when he was a young man at Los Alamos. He went into everything with full vigor, and because his intellectual powers were very great indeed, "full vigor" really means something.

(I should mention that the computer had arrived in

Feynman opening the combination lock on a Los Alamos filing cabinet.

many parts—about ten boxes for each. Feynman and one of the former group leaders put the machines together from all the small parts. Later we got some professionals from IBM who said, "This has never been done before. I have never seen laymen put together one of these machines, and it's perfect!")

In addition to being a great physicist, Feynman was a clown. Opening the safes at Los Alamos was an example of the clowneries. He liked to fool around and make fun of everything. He liked to play tricks on the military who guarded us. There was a barbed-wire fence around the technical area, and Feynman would quite legitimately go in, with his pass. But there was a hole in the fence somewhere, and he would crawl out of it, and then come back to the front entrance again. Of course, they had no record of his having gone out!

He often affected a Brooklyn accent and attitude, and Pauli, who was a great physicist and who liked Feynman very much, once said to me, "Why does this intelligent young man talk like a bum?" It was true, he did talk like a bum. I think he wanted to cover up his really quite delicate soul, which I think came out in his relation to his first wife.

Feynman had a wife whom he loved dearly. She had

In the sanatorium in Albuquerque, 1944. Visiting Arline on weekends, Feynman sometimes borrowed a car belonging to Klaus Fuchs, the Russian spy.

a very severe case of TB, and she was in a hospital in Albuquerque, about a hundred miles from Los Alamos. Feynman didn't have a car, but every weekend, he would somehow hitch a ride to Albuquerque and visit his wife for those two days. It was quite touching. And during the week, they would write each other letters. Arline didn't have anything to do in that hospital, and so Dick began writing her letters in code. This was, of course, terrible, because we had censorship, and the censor was sure that these letters contained some really deep military secrets. Feynman was asked to provide the code, and it would go with an extra envelope, to the censor. The censor would take off the code, and then his wife would figure out the code in all that very long time that she had.

I greatly admired his performance at Los Alamos while he knew that Arline was dying. It was constantly on his mind, and I believe that this conflict of demands may have had something to do with wanting to appear tough, but I'm not sure. She died within a few weeks of Hiroshima.

At the very end, they were just inventing drugs to help tuberculosis, and Arline did take them for a few months, but it was too late.

Postage stamps Arline had printed while she was in hospital.

Joan Feynman

When Arline died at 9:21 p.m., the clock in her room stopped. Typically, Feynman did not find this mysterious—he knew the clock was faulty, and decided that the nurse must have disturbed it when she checked the time of death.

Feynman I had a short vacation at home, maybe because my wife had just died, and one day I got a telegram that said, "The baby will be born on such-and-such a day." I rushed back to New Mexico and arrived at Los Alamos just as the buses were going off to the Trinity site where they were going to make the test.

I wasn't a very big shot at the time, and there were two different distances—we were observers at twenty miles, and the guys who were actually doing something were much closer, about six miles away. We were supposed to have a radio which would tell us what was happening, and when it would go off, but they were so busy at the other end they forgot to contact us. Then there was this countdown, and this tremendous flash. I was the only one, I think, in the whole world who saw it directly. They had come round and said that we ought to put on goggles, black things, on account of the ultraviolet light. I didn't believe it would be that bright, and I didn't think that light by itself, even though it's very strong, would damage the eye. Ultraviolet, yes, but all I had to do was get in a truck and look through the windshield because the glass would cut the ultraviolet out. So I looked at it directly and I saw all the colors and everything. It was a very white, bright flash, and I could see the clouds. I can't quite remember. They went out, and then they reformed in a wave that spread from this thing. Then it turned gradually yellow, and then orange. Oh, by the way, the first flash of the light was so bright that my natural reaction was to turn my head away and there on the floor of the truck I saw this purple picture of it. I realized that this wasn't the real bomb, so I looked back and then I saw what I told you. So there was a moment when I looked away. Then there formed the black cloud of smoke, smoke with orange light flickering inside it, and gradually this ball that turned into the mushroom shape that you are all familiar with. All this took some time, and finally there was a very sharp noise, like a gun going off nearby. William Laurence, a journalist, said to me, "What was that?" And I said, "That was the bomb." You see, we were so far away that it took a minute and a half for the sound to get to us.

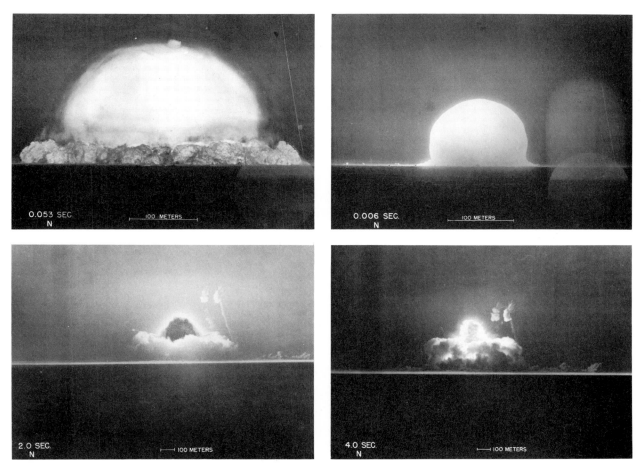

Trinity: the first four seconds. Oppenheimer later told journalists, "If you ask: can we make them more terrible, the answer is yes; if you ask: can we make more of them, the answer is yes; if you ask: can we make them terribly more terrible, the answer is—probably."

Maybe I'm acoustically minded or something, but I was much more impressed by the sound at twenty miles distance—it was so strong. The light lit everywhere, all the mountains, the sky. Even so, the solidity and reality of that sound . . . No one said a word during that minute and a half.

Oppenheimer said later that the words from the Bhagavad-Gita *went through his mind, "I am become Death, the destroyer of worlds," or something like that. What went though your mind?*

My mind was rather dull. What went through my mind was a kind of elation, because during all this time we'd been working very hard to make this thing go, and we weren't sure exactly how it went. I've always had some distrust of theoretical calculations, although that's my business, and I'm never really sure that nature does what you calculate she ought to do. Here she was, doing what we'd calculated.

The only person that I remember who was directly aware of something different was Mr. Wilson, Bob Wilson—the guy who got me into the project. I remember him standing in a hallway and muttering something about this being terrible, and I in my elation couldn't understand it at all.

With regard to moral questions, I do have something I would like to say about it. The original reason to start the project which I had, which was that the Germans were a danger, started me off on a process of action which was to try to develop this system, first at Princeton, and then at Los Alamos, to try to make the bomb work: all kinds of attempts to redesign it (to make it a "worse" bomb, if you like), and we were working all this time to see if we could make it go. It was a project on which we worked very, very hard, all cooperating together, and with any project like that you continue trying to get success, having decided to do it. But what I did immorally, I would say, was not to remember the reason that I said I was doing it, so that when the reason changed—Germany was defeated— not the singlest thought came to my mind about that— that now I have to reconsider why I am continuing to do this. I simply didn't think, okay?

I learned something from this: that one should reconsider perpetually one's reasons for doing something, because it may be that the circumstances have changed. I think the Vietnam War in the case of the United States is another example of the same mistake in morality: whatever the reasons were at the start, good or bad, they should be reconsidered as one goes along. This failure to reconsider the original purpose I would consider a moral weakness on my part during the war.

Love and the Bomb

After Germany was defeated, the question was whether we should use the bomb on Japan. Nobody discussed this at Los Alamos. It was discussed in Chicago. They discussed what advice to give to the President, whether we should use it, or should there be a demonstration explosion, or what? That was discussed there, but not at Los Alamos. The reason may be that in the Chicago laboratory they were finished with their job of making the devices and so on, while at Los Alamos we were still all working very hard, and we weren't thinking about what we were doing anymore. I think so—I don't know human psychology.

Over the public address system came the announcement that our "gadget"—I can't remember the exact words—our gadget has been operated in Hiroshima in Japan, and that it has worked successfully. Something like that. The girl didn't know what she was saying. She was just told to say that, but we knew what it meant.

The only reaction that I remember—perhaps I was blinded by my own reaction—was very considerable elation and excitement, and there was all kind of parties and people got drunk. It would make a terribly interesting contrast of what was going on in Los Alamos at the same time as what was going on in Hiroshima. I was involved with this happy thing—drinking, and drunk, and playing drums sitting on the hood of a jeep, with the excitement running all over Los Alamos at the same time as the people were dying and struggling in Hiroshima.

Oppenheimer said that you physicists had somehow "known sin," and I think that Freeman Dyson says somewhere that what Oppenheimer meant was not that you'd built the bomb, but that you'd enjoyed building it so much. What do you think Oppenheimer meant?

I don't know. What he meant, of course, was that we had made something which had impressive moral consequences, but one doesn't always know what Oppenheimer meant with his most profound statements.

Was it profound?

I don't know. I mean, it's profound in the sense that it's not so clear what it says!

There's been no use of nuclear weapons for a long time. Do you think that will continue forever, or do you think that they will be used sooner or later?

As you can tell from my past experiences, I mispredicted, okay? I thought it would be used long before. So I taught myself that I do not know how to predict the future on matters like this. But in spite of the fact that I learned I was wrong before, I still have this idea that it will be used eventually. I don't see how human beings will avoid it with the present way they behave. But since I don't understand human beings that well, I really don't know what will happen.

Do you feel any sense of personal responsibility for the incredible predicament we are now in: that there is enough explosive equivalent to kill everyone on the planet several times over?

For me the correct question is what one should do, not how one should feel. The feeling may be important to develop in order to convert into some action—"because I feel this way, I ought to do so and so." But I don't torture myself with some sort of remorse. You know that the way to hell is paved with good intentions, and you ask a man who's done a lot of good intentions and found himself in hell how he feels about his moral responsibility. Well, at each stage he thought that he was doing the right thing. It's ignorance and lack of understanding or whatever which leads human beings into their miseries. That's a profound thing, very common in human behavior, that I'm not in a position to understand more deeply or any better than anybody else. The only wrong that I really know is what I've already mentioned—that I didn't think about it again when Germany was defeated. I don't guarantee you as to what conclusion I would have come to if I had thought about it, but nevertheless the fact that I did not think about it was, of course, wrong.

Most of you were very young.

I was twenty-four when I entered the project, and about twenty-eight when I left.

Love and the Bomb

Joan Feynman

After Arline's death he must have been depressed, and he didn't do physics for a while. I'm not a psychiatrist, so I don't know what it was. I can't say how much of it was because Arline died, and how much of it was because of the bomb. His father died then, too. But one thing was clear: after the bomb was dropped, he didn't believe that the world was going to continue for very much longer.

Freeman Dyson

Los Alamos had been a turning point in his life. He had performed splendidly. He ran the numerical computing part of the project, which at that time was all done by humans. So his gifts as a leader of people were vital to the project. He somehow got this team of human computers to work at an inhuman pace, and got things to roll. And that was when his scientific seniors, the big shots of science at that time, first became aware of this fellow. So Los Alamos made him, as far as his relations with people like Bohr and Bethe were concerned. He had this great triumph on the technical level, and then a terrible letdown afterwards—having run this tremendous race and concluding at the end of it that it wasn't worthwhile.

Feynman

I had a very strong reaction after the war of a peculiar nature. It may be from the bomb itself, and it may be for some other psychological reason, like I'd just lost my wife or something. But I remember being in New York with my mother in a restaurant—right after, immediately after—and thinking about New York. I knew how big the bomb in Hiroshima was, how big an area it covered, and so on. And I realized from where we were at, say Fifty-ninth Street, to drop one on Thirty-fourth Street—it would spread all the way out here and all these people would be killed and all the things would be killed. There wasn't only one bomb available, but it was easy to continue to make them, and therefore things were sort of doomed. Already it appeared to me, very early, earlier than to others who were more optimistic, that international relations and the way people were behaving was no different than it

had ever been before, and it was just going to turn out the same way as any other thing, and I was sure that it was going therefore to be used very soon. So I felt very uncomfortable and I thought it was silly—I would see people building a bridge, and I would say, "They don't understand!" I really believed that it was senseless to make anything because it would all be destroyed very soon anyway. So, I had this very strange view of any construction that I would see. I was really in a kind of depressive condition.

I grew out of it somehow. It's a great surprise that things

have lasted so long without it going off. I haven't a very good understanding of international relations and human characteristics, and I thought that no matter what the weapon was, they would soon be at each other's throats with it, so there was no reason to think that it would be any different this time. This was before we knew that the Russians were quickly developing one, but there was no doubt in my mind that they could develop one.

What one fool can do, another can.

In October 1947, two years after Arline died, Feynman wrote her a letter[3] which began

D'Arline, I adore you, sweetheart . . .

and ended

. . . I know you will assure me that I am foolish & that you want me to have full happiness & don't want to be in my way. I'll bet you are surprised that I don't even have a girl friend (except you, sweetheart) after two years. But you can't help it, darling, nor can I—I don't understand it, for I have met many girls & very nice ones and I don't want to remain alone—but in two or three meetings they all seem ashes. You only are left to me. You are real.

My darling wife, I do adore you.

I love my wife. My wife is dead.

Rich.

P.S. Please excuse my not mailing this—but I don't know your new address

October 1965. Red carpet for Feynman at Hughes Aircraft, Malibu, where he gave a regular Wednesday lecture.

CHAPTER THREE

How to Win a Nobel Prize

It was on the news, of course, and they asked me questions about what I had won the prize for and so on. I took a taxi somewhere, and the taxi driver recognized me from the pictures and the TV, and he said, "Boy! You had a hard time. When they asked you to explain in three minutes what you won the prize for? You know what I'd have said? 'If I could explain it in three minutes, it wouldn't be worth the Nobel Prize!' "

quantum electrodynamics (QED) A relativistic quantum theory of electromagnetic interactions. It provides a description of the interactions of electrons, muons and protons, and hence the underlying theory of all electromagnetic phenomena.

In 1965, Feynman shared the Nobel Prize for Physics with another American, Julian Schwinger, and Shin'ichiro Tomonaga of Japan. In the late 1940s all three, independently, had found ways to make quantum electrodynamics "work." At the same time, Feynman developed a completely new way of handling the mathematical complexities of particle physics, a set of tools—"Feynman diagrams"—which are as powerfully useful to the theoretical physicist as, say, circuit diagrams to an electronics designer.

Feynman

65

Feynman's check for his one-third share of the $55,000 Nobel Prize money. He spent it on a beach house in Baja California, Mexico.

For nonspecialists, QED and Feynman's contribution to it are extremely difficult to understand, but in what follows I hope that anyone will be able to get a sense of what Feynman did and why it was worth a Nobel Prize—even if Feynman himself didn't want one.

Feynman (1965)[1]

Usually big words signify very small specialties, but "quantum electrodynamics" is a big word that signifies a very big subject—in fact, it's nearly all of physics.

Let me explain a little about the history of the problem that we three have gotten the Nobel Prize for. The adventure of our science of physics is a perpetual attempt to recognize that the different aspects of nature are really different aspects of the same thing, that all the phenomena that you see, the great variety of different things, can all be explained—perhaps—as different aspects of some underlying business, or some underlying laws, or some underlying simplicity. It's remarkable that as the physics has developed, the fundamental discoveries have shown that things that look completely different are really very closely related.

The history begins mostly with mechanics, and the laws of motion discovered by Newton, who showed, for example, that the motion of pendula and things on the earth and the motions of the planets among the stars are really the same thing, and governed by the same laws.

Later, the phenomena of heat and temperature were discovered, a thing which feels completely different to us than motion—a hot thing doesn't seem like something moving, and yet the phenomena of heat are entirely and ultimately explained as the motions of the parts, so that this is one of those great simplifications of nature.

Again, the phenomena of electricity were studied, and independently those of magnetism, until it was discovered that they were intimately related—they were just different aspects of the same thing.

Maxwell discovered the laws that connected the two of them together, which is called "electrodynamics," and that's part of the word "quantum electrodynamics." As a matter of fact, Maxwell suddenly realized that another set of phenomena—those of light—were nothing but an aspect of electricity and magnetism, so that was another great unification. In fact, he predicted from this the existence of a whole set of phenomena which we now called radio waves. Then as time went on, many other things were discovered, new fields such as X-rays. and most of the time they are found to be some part or some aspect of something already known.

In the meantime, the chemists were working away, and they found that to explain things they had to have "atoms," and then the physicists discovered that atoms are in fact real, and obey certain laws of their own. The problem was to find the mechanical laws of the atoms, and it turns out that the mechanics of atoms is very different than the mechanics of the stars and so on, and new laws were discovered which showed that the behavior of atoms is completely different than ordinary mechanics (involving the uncertainty principle of Heisenberg and so on), a great discovery for which there are many Nobel Prizes, and that's "quantum mechanics."

Well, the next problem was to put together the quantum principles and the uncertainty principle and the laws of electrodynamics. This would make together a unified machinery which could explain all these phenomena, an underlying simplicity behind all this, and that is the subject of "quantum electrodynamics."

The way—the theory—to put together electrodynamics and the principles of quantum mechanics into quantum electrodynamics was developed in 1929. The equations when solved approximately gave nice results, but unfortunately if you tried to get more accuracy out of it, it gave absurd results. That was in 1929.

In about 1947 or '48, an experiment was done on energy levels of hydrogen that were so precise that it required that one used this theory to a degree of accuracy for which is was not possible to use it—that is, for which it gave these absurd results. A Professor Bethe—Hans Bethe—and also Professor Weisskopf discovered a way to get rid of the difficulties for that special problem of the hydrogen atom. What we have done, independently, is to discover the generalization of this, so that the old equations could be used not only for the hydrogen atom problem but for all of the problems that this machinery is supposed to deal with. We found a way of interpreting the equations of quantum electrodynamics in general so that they could be

Feynman at Cornell, late 1940s. "I decided, I'm only going to do things for the fun of it. . . ."

applied to all these phenomena with any degree of accuracy that you would wish.

So—everything is finished, all phenomena are understood, except: in the meantime, we discover nuclear phenomena, and strange particles, and all kinds of things, modern phenomena that are not explained by the laws of quantum electrodynamics.

And then there's one phenomenon which is very old. Way back in the beginning when Newton worked out mechanics, he discovered the laws of gravity. And today we don't understand gravity in terms of anything else like electricity or magnetism. Gravity is independent and different. It sticks out like a kind of sore thumb. So, of course, in solving this problem of quantum electrodynamics, we haven't solved everything, and there are problems left for other Nobel Prize winners to work out in the future!

Feynman (1985)[2]

The theory of quantum electrodynamics has now lasted for more than fifty years, and has been tested more and more accurately over a wider and wider range of conditions. At the present time I can proudly say that there is *no significant difference* between experiment and theory!

Just to give you an idea of how the theory has been put through the wringer, I'll give you some recent numbers: experiments have Dirac's number at 1.00115965221 (with an uncertainty of about 4 in the last digit); the theory puts it at 1.00115965246 (with an uncertainty of about five times as much). To give you a feeling for the accuracy of these numbers, it comes out something like this: if you were to measure the distance from Los Angeles to New York to this accuracy, it would be exact to the thickness of a human hair. That's how delicately quantum electrodynamics has, in the past fifty years, been checked—both theoretically and experimentally. By the way, I have chosen only one number to show you. There are other things in quantum electrodynamics that have been measured with comparable accuracy, which also agree very well. Things have been checked at distance scales that range from one hundred times the size of the earth down to one-hundredth the size of an atomic nucleus. These numbers are meant to intimidate you into believing that the theory is probably not too far off!

We physicists are always checking to see if there is something the matter with the theory. That's the game, because if there *is* something the matter, it's interesting! But so far, we have found nothing wrong with the theory of quantum electrodynamics. It is, therefore, I would say, the jewel of physics—our proudest possession.

Hans Bethe Quantum electrodynamics had been in the forefront of theoretical physics since about 1929—seventeen years or so—before Feynman got to it. The idea is that you have the quantum theory of electrons, which shows you how an atom is built, and shows you how to calculate the energy levels of an atom. Then you have the quantum theory of radiation, which was in fact older than the quantum theory of the electron. The quantum theory of radiation was invented by Max Planck, in 1900. Now, the problem was to put these two things together, and you had to do it paying attention to special relativity.

The trouble was that this quantum electrodynamics worked very well if you calculated everything only in first approximation. If you tried to do it more accurately, it gave the result: infinity. Which was obviously wrong, because neither the mass of the electron, nor its interaction with radiation is infinite. So, a method had to be found to get rid of the infinities.[3]

One thing I can tell you is that I tried, and failed. Many other people, at least two dozen people, tried and didn't get it. In the very early days, Heisenberg and Pauli— perhaps the two brightest theoretical physicists of their generation, of the early 1900s—they tried, and they couldn't make it finite. So it was an extremely difficult problem on which some of the best people worked, and none of them could do it.

My first opportunity after the war had been to be a professor at Cornell. I went there with Hans Bethe, who I had gotten to love while we were at Los Alamos. I had to give two different classes, and I prepared my classes very rapidly because I was used to wartime action at high speed.

I expected to go right back to continue the work that I'd interrupted, but for a long time I didn't seem to be able to do anything. I couldn't sit down at any real problem and work stuff out, like the gamma rays from bromine 82, or something—I started to work on it, but I just couldn't get anywhere. So I got the idea that I was burnt out by the war experience, and I would never really accomplish anything after that. I have no idea why I got into this depressive condition over my own work, but I did. I was saved from that in a way which I'll explain to you if you'd like.

All during this period, there was a kind of inflation of salaries and interest in physicists because the other universities were trying to develop and everybody wanted to get the physicists. I was offered higher and higher salaries by different universities. I wanted to stay at Cornell with Bethe, so I wasn't paying much attention to that, but nevertheless it bothered me psychologically because I knew that I was burnt out, and I certainly wasn't worth the money. People expected me to succeed, and I wasn't going to succeed—or it seemed that way to me. (I now realize, by the way, that preparing and giving two courses was quite a lot of work, but I didn't know that at the time. I thought the teaching was a side issue.) So I got more and more distressed by these offers, but I never accepted any of them. Finally, the Princeton Institute for Advanced Study, where Einstein and all these people were, sent me an invitation to join them. Now I thought this was crazy, that they were absolutely insane. They didn't know that I was burnt out, but even so, it was too high-class a job. It was so ridiculous that it set me thinking and I suddenly realized, while I was shaving, "I can't live up to what other people expect me to do." They expected me to be wonderful to offer me a job like this, and I wasn't wonderful, and therefore I realized a new principle: "I'm not responsible for

Feynman

what other people think I am able to do. I don't have to be good because they think I'm going to be good." And somehow or other I could relax about this. I thought to myself, "I haven't done anything important, and I'm never going to do anything important, but I used to enjoy physics and mathematical things. It was never very important, but I used to do things for the fun of it." So I decided I'm going to do things only for the fun of it.

That afternoon while I was eating lunch some kid threw up a plate in the cafeteria. There was a blue medallion on the plate, the Cornell sign,[4] and as he threw up the plate and it came down, the blue thing went around and it seemed to me that the blue thing went around faster than the wobble, and I wondered what the relation was between the two. I was just playing, no importance at all, but I played around with the equations of motion of rotating things, and I found out that if the wobble is small the blue thing goes around twice as fast as the wobble goes round. Then I tried to figure out if I could see why that was directly from Newton's laws instead of through the complicated equations, and I worked that out for the fun of it.

I went to Hans Bethe and I said, "Hey, I'll show you something amusing," and I explained it to him. He said to me, "Yes. It's very amusing and interesting, but what is the use of it?" I said, "That doesn't make any difference. It hasn't any use. I'm just doing it for the fun of it."

Then Bob Wilson, who was the head of the nuclear lab there, must have had some kind of instinct or something, because that same day he called me in and told me that when they hire a professor at the university it's their responsibility what the professor does; it's their risk, and if he doesn't do anything or accomplish anything, it's not his thing to worry about that. So I should do whatever I want—amuse myself, whatever.

Well, with that double combination I could relax. Somehow I was getting out from some psychological problem, and I started to play with this rotation, and the rotation led me to a similar problem of the rotation of the spin of an electron according to Dirac's equation, and that just led me back into quantum electrodynamics, which was the problem I had been working on. I kept continuing now to play with it in the relaxed fashion I had originally done, and it was just like taking the cork out of a bottle—everything just poured out, and in very short order I worked the things out for which I later won the Nobel Prize.

Freeman Dyson, mathematical prodigy turned physicist, arrived at Cornell in 1947 as a twenty-three-year-old graduate student. "I walked by accident into the delivery room where Feynman's new way of doing particle physics was born," he said later, but this was typically over-modest. In fact, Dyson was the first to grasp what Feynman was trying to do with quantum electrodynamics and he made it accessible to the rest of the physics world.

At Cornell, I was simply puzzled and mystified by Feynman's stuff. I couldn't figure out how he was getting all these amazing answers which turned out to be right. It was just a great mystery. I didn't understand it and, as far as I could tell, nobody else did.

I got to know him gradually. The first time I remember definitely being with him was taking a ride with him to a scientific meeting in Rochester. This meant driving a couple of hours from Ithaca in Feynman's car, and that was a memorable adventure. He was a very good driver, but rather reckless, and he talked all the time while he was driving.

I got to know him much better on another car ride, about a year later. He was driving all the way from Cleveland, Ohio, to Albuquerque, which is about fifteen hundred miles. He invited me to come along for the ride and since I had nothing better to do, I said yes. We spent about four days together.

We were delayed by a major flood in Oklahoma, which was even more fun because it meant that there was a little bit of adventure involved. It was in a little town called Vinita that we were literally surrounded by water. The whole town was completely crammed with stranded motorists. Feynman in his usual fashion, of course, knew

Freeman Dyson

Freeman Dyson at the Institute for Advanced Study, Princeton, in the early 1950s. "I got well rewarded for my part in the business— I got a beautiful job here, set up for life!"

how to find us a room. Namely, we went to the brothel, which was a local hotel of evil repute. This was a miserable night, a real hot, humid, and sticky summer night of the kind you have in Oklahoma. It was raining hard all night long, pouring down—bang, bang, bang on the roof. There was really no prospect of getting much sleep, you know, but we were happy just to have a roof over our heads. So we were stuck in this miserable little stinking room with odd noises, and prostitutes walking up and down the corridor outside. There was no chance of doing any work, or doing anything serious, so we talked the whole night. It was just the one time I had Feynman, essentially to myself, for eight hours, to talk about the problems of the world.

I think that was the time when I got closest to learning what sort of person Feynman was. He was somebody with this completely clear-headed view of things. That was what impressed me most strongly—that he was a sort of *Bhagavad-Gita* ideal of somebody who was engaged in action, but at the same time totally detached.

Quantum electrodynamics was an old theory of matter and radiation, which had been really invented by Heisenberg and Fermi and Dirac in the '30s, or even a little earlier. It was, from a physical point of view, quite a successful theory, and it explained an awful lot of things that were seen. But it got into mathematical difficulties, because one could never calculate very accurately—as soon as you tried to make exact calculations, the thing gave absurd answers. It was an anomalous situation: you had a theory which seemed to be all right, as far as the gross outlines were concerned, but if you wanted to really calculate precisely, it said stupid and nonsensical things. So that was the technical problem.

For Feynman, it was part of a much bigger problem, which was to reconstruct the whole of physics. Feynman, first of all, didn't believe anything that he was told. That was his nature. He was always skeptical about everything that the experts told him. He wanted to understand the basic laws of physics for himself, from a completely new point of view. He had started this already, as a graduate student in Princeton, before the war. He called it a "space-time" approach, where everything in physics was localized in space-time. You thought of microscopic processes—that's processes involving particles—as being "localized," and you could draw little pictures of what was happening. That was the essence of his program, that you had this geometrical view of things, and then you represented this geometrical view with things that he called . . . I forget, but anyway, everybody else calls them "Feynman diagrams" now. These could then be translated into mathematics, but in a very simple fashion, so that once you had the geometrical picture, it was rather simple to go straight to the answer. That made his methods very powerful as compared with the conventional way of doing things, which is much more analytical.

When I came on the scene in 1947, he had this general scheme more or less worked out, and he was trying to apply it, in detail, to the problem of quantum electrodynamics. This meant, for example, understanding the fine details of what a hydrogen atom does when it's in a magnetic field, and these fine details were what was still mysterious—both to him and to everybody else.

There were various people working on this problem of the hydrogen atom. From the orthodox point of view, there were Schwinger and Tomonaga; and from Feynman's point of view there was Feynman alone. So it was a kind of race between the different points of view. The beautiful thing was, of course, that they all arrived more or less at the answer at the same time.

But when I drove to Albuquerque with him, I was still in a state of puzzlement, and trying to figure it all out.

When we had reached Albuquerque, and I had said goodbye to Feynman, I took a bus back to Ann Arbor, Michigan, for the summer school there—at the time it was the main meeting place for physicists during the summer. Schwinger was lecturing there. He was also a young man, about the same age as Feynman, and he had a competing theory of everything. It was much more orthodox—completely in the old style, analytical mathematics, very elaborate and complicated. But it was the kind of stuff I was familiar with, and I was able to understand Schwinger more easily than I could understand Feynman.

I spent six happy weeks in Ann Arbor. I listened to Schwinger in the mornings, and then worked all the afternoons and evenings, going over and over Schwinger's stuff. This was really hard work, because he was a virtuoso performer, and he liked to do everything perfectly. His lectures were so polished that you had to chisel away at them for hours to find out where it all came from. At the end of the six weeks I really understood Schwinger.

I took a vacation, went to California, and simply goofed off for a couple of weeks, in Berkeley mostly. Finally, the summer came to an end, and I took the bus from California all the way back across the country, back to Ithaca. And in that bus, the last bus ride of the summer, the whole thing fell together. That was the big moment. It was a very good situation to be in—too bumpy to read, and too bumpy to write, so there was nothing else to do but just think. I was half asleep, half dreaming in the bus, and suddenly all of Feynman and all of Schwinger fitted together! I realized how Feynman was actually doing the same things, in a totally different language, but it was basically the same mathematics if one did it right.

I think always in terms of equations, and so I had to translate Feynman's stuff into equations to use it myself. That was my major contribution—to translate Feynman back into the language that other people could understand. Ever since, of course, you can think about it both ways—you can do it Feynman's way, or you can do it the conventional way. If you look at the physics literature you'll see pages of equations with "Feynman diagrams" interspersed to summarize what the equations are doing. The diagrams are a convenient language to make a lot of the equations come together in one picture. When Feynman's tools first became available, it was a tremendous liberation—you could do all kinds of things with them you couldn't have done before.

In the autumn of 1948, after coming back from this bus ride, I began writing up a complete version of quantum electrodynamics, explaining to everybody how one could do the Feynman stuff. But there were two snags. Although the theory seemed to work very well for the hydrogen atom, there were two other problems for which it still gave absurd answers, and these had been famous and difficult problems during the 1930s—long and terrible papers were written about it, trying to get sensible answers, and not succeeding. The first problem was scattering of light by an electric field. The other was the problem of scattering of light by light—if you had two light beams, in principle they would scatter against each other, and this was something for which the theory gave infinite answers, which didn't make sense.

I didn't understand, when I was writing this stuff up, how to deal with those two questions. So Cécile De Witt and I went to Ithaca together in the train (which in those days was a very civilized way to get from Princeton to Ithaca). Cécile is a very fine French physicist, and probably the earliest and the most understanding convert to Feynman physics. We spent the weekend talking with Feynman, and we put these two problems to him, and asked him, "Look, how do you deal with those?" Feynman simply said, "Oh, we'll see about that." He proceeded, in front of our eyes, to calculate both these problems and get finite and sensible answers for both of them, showing that the thing really worked, even for the hardest cases. That was just about the most dazzling display of Feynman's powers I've ever seen. These were problems that had taken the greatest physicists months to fail to solve, and he knocked them off in a couple of hours. It was, of course, still calculation, but it was done in this extraordinary economical style, without heavy apparatus—just sort of stitching the answers before even writing down the equations, and deriving things directly from the diagrams. Well, after that there was nothing more to be done, but only to proclaim the triumph of the theory.

Feynman didn't publish what he did; I published it. That's my nature—I enjoy publishing things. He hated writing. There's a famous story about how he actually did finally publish some stuff, and it came about because he went to stay with an old friend called Muleika Corben. She was another of his intellectual friends—I mean, as far as I know, there was no romance between them. But Muleika was an extremely bright young woman, the wife of a physicist in Pittsburgh. She was forceful as well as being bright. She got Feynman into her house, and simply locked him up in a room and refused to let him out until he'd written the paper. I think she even refused to feed him unless he wrote it. So there was nothing for it—he had to sit down and write, and that's how it happened. It did take extreme measures to persuade him to write anything!

So, I had worked out my way of doing Feynman's stuff—my way of doing it was more orthodox than his, but it made it clear how it fitted in with the orthodox theory—and I published this myself. I didn't create the theory, but at least I made it accessible to the rest of the physical community.

And to Oppenheimer?

Right. Oppenheimer was director of the Institute here in Princeton. He was at that time regarded as the spokesman for physics to the outside world. He was the most famous physicist alive, I suppose, at that time, though not necessarily the best, and he took some persuading. Oppenheimer was a man of very strong prejudices, and he was convinced that Feynman's ideas were worthless. He liked Feynman personally, but he couldn't understand what he was trying to do. It took me about two months or so to persuade Oppenheimer to listen. Of course, once Oppenheimer was convinced, he became very generous, and preached the Feynman gospel all over the world.

Hans Bethe Feynman's great secret in solving the problem of quantum electrodynamics was that he developed this way to do it graphically, rather than by writing down formulae. As you know, this led to the famous Feynman diagrams which everybody is using now for any kind of calculation in field theory. The great power of Feynman's diagrams is that they combine many steps of the older calculations in one.

QUANTUM ELECTRODYNAMICS 787

These integrals on y were performed as follows. Since $p_2 = p_1 + q$ where q is the momentum carried by the potential, it follows from $p_2^2 = p_1^2 = m^2$ that $2p_1 \cdot q = -q^2$ so that since $p_u = p_1 + q(1-y)$, $p_u^2 = m^2 - q^2 y(1-y)$. The substitution $2y - 1 = \tan\theta/\tan\theta$ where θ is defined by $4m^2 \sin^2\theta = q^2$ is useful for it means $p_u^2 = m^2 \sec^2\alpha/\sec^2\theta$ and $p_u^{-2} dy = (m^2 \sin 2\theta)^{-1} d\alpha$ where α goes from $-\theta$ to $+\theta$.

These results are substituted into the original scattering formula (2n), giving (22). It has been simplified by frequent use of the fact that p_1 operating on the initial state is m, and likewise p_2 when it appears at the left is replaceable by m. (Thus, to simplify:

$$\gamma_\mu p_2 \alpha p_1 \gamma_\mu \text{ by (4a),} = -2p_1 \alpha p_2$$
$$= -2(p_2 - p_1) \alpha (m + q).$$

A term like $qaq = -q^2 a + 2(a \cdot q)q$ is equivalent to just $-q^2 a$ since $q = p_2 - p_1 = m - m$ has zero matrix element.) The renormalization term requires the corresponding integrals for the special case $q = 0$.

C. Vacuum Polarization

The expressions (32) and (32') for $J_{\mu\nu}$ in the vacuum polarization problem require the calculation of the integral

$$J_{\mu\nu}(m^2) = -\frac{e^2}{\pi i} \int Sp[\gamma_\mu(p - \tfrac{1}{2}q + m)\gamma_\nu(p + \tfrac{1}{2}q + m)]d^4p$$
$$\times((p - \tfrac{1}{2}q)^2 - m^2)^{-1}((p + \tfrac{1}{2}q)^2 - m^2)^{-1},$$

where we have replaced p by $p - \tfrac{1}{2}q$ to simplify the calculation somewhat. We shall indicate the method of calculation by studying the integral,

$$I(m^2) = \int p_\sigma p_\tau d^4p((p - \tfrac{1}{2}q)^2 - m^2)^{-1}((p + \tfrac{1}{2}q)^2 - m^2)^{-1}.$$

The factors in the denominator, $p^2 - p \cdot q - m^2 + \tfrac{1}{4}q^2$ and $p^2 + p \cdot q - m^2 + \tfrac{1}{4}q^2$ are combined as usual by (8a) but for symmetry we substitute $x = \tfrac{1}{2}(1+\eta)$, $(1-x) = \tfrac{1}{2}(1-\eta)$ and integrate η from -1 to $+1$:

$$I(m^2) = \int_{-1}^{+1} p_\sigma p_\tau d^4p(p^2 - \eta p \cdot q - m^2 + \tfrac{1}{4}q^2)^{-2}d\eta/2. \quad (30a)$$

But the integral on p will not be found in our list for it is badly divergent. However, as discussed in Section 7, Eq. (32') we do not wish $I(m^2)$ but rather $I(m^2) - I(m^2 + \lambda^2)$. We can calculate the difference $I(m^2) - I(m^2 + \lambda^2)$ by first calculating the derivative $I'(m^2 + L)$ of I with respect to m^2 at $m^2 + L$ and later integrating L from zero to λ^2. By differentiating (30a), with respect to m^2 find,

$$I'(m^2 + L) = \int_{-1}^{+1} p_\sigma p_\tau d^4p(p^2 - \eta p \cdot q - m^2 - L + \tfrac{1}{4}q^2)^{-3}d\eta.$$

This still diverges, but we can differentiate again to get

$$I''(m^2 + L) = 3 \int_{-1}^{+1} p_\sigma p_\tau d^4p(p^2 - \eta p \cdot q - m^2 - L + \tfrac{1}{4}q^2)^{-4}d\eta \quad (31a)$$
$$= -(8i)^{-1} \int_{-1}^{+1} (\tfrac{1}{4}\eta^2 q_\sigma q_\tau D^{-2} - \tfrac{1}{2}\delta_{\sigma\tau}D^{-1})d\eta$$

(where $D = \tfrac{1}{4}(\eta^2 - 1)q^2 + m^2 + L$), which now converges and has been evaluated by (13a) with $p = \tfrac{1}{2}\eta q$ and $\Delta = m^2 + L - \tfrac{1}{4}q^2$. Now to get I' we may integrate I'' with respect to L as an indefinite integral and we may choose any convenient arbitrary constant. This is because a constant C in I' will mean a term $-C\lambda^2$ in $I(m^2) - I(m^2 + \lambda^2)$ which vanishes since we will integrate the results times $G(\lambda)d\lambda$ and $\int_0^\infty \lambda^2 G(\lambda)d\lambda = 0$. This means that the logarithm appearing on integrating L in (31a) presents no problem. We may take

$$I'(m^2 + L) = (8i)^{-1} \int_{-1}^{+1} [\tfrac{1}{4}\eta^2 q_\sigma q_\tau D^{-1} + \tfrac{1}{2}\delta_{\sigma\tau} \ln D]d\eta + C\delta_{\sigma\tau},$$

a subsequent integral on L and finally on η presents no new problems. There results

$$-(8i) \int p_\sigma p_\tau d^4p((p - \tfrac{1}{2}q)^2 - m^2)^{-1}((p + \tfrac{1}{2}q)^2 - m^2)^{-1}$$
$$= (q_\sigma q_\tau - \delta_{\sigma\tau} q^2)\left[\frac{1}{9} - \frac{4m^2 - q^2}{3q^2}\left(1 - \frac{\theta}{\tan\theta}\right) + \tfrac{1}{3} \ln\frac{\lambda^2}{m^2}\right]$$
$$+ \delta_{\sigma\tau}[(\lambda^2 + m^2)\ln(\lambda^2 m^{-2} + 1) - C''\lambda^2], \quad (32a)$$

where we assume $\lambda^2 \gg m^2$ and have put some terms into the arbitrary constant C'' which is independent of λ^2 (but in principle could depend on q^2) and which drops out in the integral on $G(\lambda)d\lambda$. We have set $q^2 = 4m^2 \sin^2\theta$.

In a very similar way the integral with m^2 in the numerator can be worked out. There results

$$-(8i) \int m^2 d^4p((p - \tfrac{1}{2}q)^2 - m^2)^{-1}((p + \tfrac{1}{2}q)^2 - m^2)^{-1}$$
$$= 4m^2(1 - \theta \cot\theta) - q^2/3 + 2(\lambda^2 + m^2)\ln(\lambda^2 m^{-2} + 1) - C''\lambda^2), \quad (33a)$$

with another unimportant constant C''. The complete problem requires the further integral,

$$-(8i) \int (1; p_\sigma)d^4p((p - \tfrac{1}{2}q)^2 - m^2)^{-1}((p + \tfrac{1}{2}q)^2 - m^2)^{-1}$$
$$= (1, 0)(4(1 - \theta \cot\theta) + 2 \ln(\lambda^2 m^{-2})). \quad (34a)$$

The value of the integral (34a) times m^2 differs from (33a), of course, because the results on the right are not actually the integrals on the left, but rather equal their actual value minus their value for $m^2 = m^2 + \lambda^2$.

Combining these quantities, as required by (32), dropping the constants C'', C'' and evaluating the spur gives (33). The spurs are evaluated in the usual way, noting that the spur of any odd number of γ matrices vanishes and $Sp(AB) = Sp(BA)$ for arbitrary A, B. The $Sp(1) = 4$ and we also have

$$\tfrac{1}{4}Sp[(p_1 + m_1)(p_2 - m_2)] = p_1 \cdot p_2 - m_1 m_2, \quad (35a)$$
$$\tfrac{1}{4}Sp[(p_1 + m_1)(p_2 - m_2)(p_3 + m_3)(p_4 - m_4)]$$
$$= (p_1 \cdot p_2 - m_1 m_2)(p_3 \cdot p_4 - m_3 m_4)$$
$$- (p_1 \cdot p_3 - m_1 m_3)(p_2 \cdot p_4 - m_2 m_4)$$
$$+ (p_1 \cdot p_4 - m_1 m_4)(p_2 \cdot p_3 - m_2 m_3), \quad (36a)$$

where p_i, m_i are arbitrary four-vectors and constants.

It is interesting that the terms of order $\lambda^2 \ln\lambda^2$ go out, so that the charge renormalization depends only logarithmically on λ^2. This is not true for some of the meson theories. Electrodynamics is suspiciously unique in the mildness of its divergence.

D. More Complex Problems

Matrix elements for complex problems can be set up in a manner analogous to that used for the simpler cases. We give three illustrations; higher order corrections to the Møller scatter-

Fig. 8. The interaction between two electrons to order $(e^2/\hbar c)^2$. One adds the contribution of every figure involving two virtual quanta, Appendix D.

"Feynman diagrams" in his 1949 paper "Space-Time Approach to Quantum Electrodynamics."

In the time before Feynman, we would do it all longhand on paper, in algebra, and we would have to consider electrons and positrons separately. This was a very lengthy affair. Feynman was able to combine this, so that only one diagram needed to be calculated.

Why didn't everyone do that?

That's the genius! To get that idea. It never occurred to any of us to put the calculations so graphically, and to combine the electrons and the positrons in this ingenious way. That's just why he was a genius!

Dyson played a very important role, much more than what he told you. He was closest to Feynman, and he listened very closely. He also understood Schwinger. And then he, Dyson, showed that the two are equivalent. Dyson should have much more recognition.

Freeman Dyson Feynman made the big discoveries, and I was just really a publicizer. I got well rewarded for my part in the business—I got a beautiful job here at the Institute, set up for life, so I've nothing to complain about! No, I think that it was entirely right and proper. Feynman's was one of the best-earned Nobel Prizes there ever was, I would say.

Feynman always insisted that he never wanted it, didn't he?

That was quite genuine, I think. He regarded the Nobel Prize as being damaging to the people who won it, and I think that's true. It very often is. He didn't want to have anything to do with it, but his wife persuaded him that the publicity would be even greater if he turned it down. So he reluctantly accepted.

Freeman Dyson, 1954.

Feynman and Gweneth en route for Stockholm.

Richard didn't want to accept the prize, you know. He really didn't. He just didn't think he could face the ceremony and all the big starched speechmaking. So he was in a terrible state, before we went and when we got there. I had to tread on eggs all the time. He had to give a ten-minute acceptance speech, and a scientific lecture. The lecture didn't bother him, because he knew what he was talking about. But the acceptance speech—he agonized over that day after day.

I think we were there for eight or nine days and I enjoyed it. It's not true that Richard didn't enjoy any of it. He sort of liked it after it was over—and he loved the thing where they blow the trumpets, these long, long golden trumpets. That was kind of fun. And then the students entertain you. They have a ball, and that he enjoyed very much, because it was very loose and we were dancing all over the place. Afterwards they took us into a beer cellar somewhere, and the group sat there and drank beer until six the next morning. Our next appointment was something like eight-thirty a.m.

We had to be dressed up almost every day, so Richard had bought a new tuxedo, which was very elegant. I think he's worn it once since. We do get invitations to things I'd very much like to go to, but since Richard won't wear a tuxedo, we just don't go.

Gweneth Feynman[5]

Feynman with Tomonaga and Schwinger to his right at the Nobel Prize ceremony.

Feynman I don't like honors. I appreciate it for the work that I did, and I know that there's a lot of physicists who use my work. I don't need anything else. I don't think there's any sense to anything else, I don't see that it makes any point that someone in the Swedish Academy decides that this work is "noble enough" to receive a prize. I've already got the prize: the prize is the pleasure of finding the thing out, the kick in the discovery, the observation that other people use it. Those are the real things. The honors are unreal to me. I don't believe in honors. It bothers me. Honors is epaulettes, honors is uniforms. My papa brought me up this way. I can't stand it, it hurts me.

When I was in high school, one of the first honors I got was to be made a member of the "Arista," which was a group of kids who got good grades, hmm? Everybody wanted to be a member of the Arista, and when I got into this Arista I discovered that what they did in their meetings was to sit around to discuss who else was "worthy" to join "this wonderful group that we are," okay?

Honors! I had trouble when I became a member of the National Academy of Sciences, and I had ultimately to resign because here was another organization which spent most of its time choosing who was "illustrious enough" to join. This included such questions as "we physicists must stick together because they've got a very good chemist that they're trying to get in, and we haven't enough room" or whatever. . . . What's the matter with chemists? The whole thing was rotten, because its purpose was mostly to decide who could have this honor. Okay? I don't like honors. I'm psychologically distorted. It's my father's doing. I blame him for everything! Almost. I also get a lot from my mother, but I don't blame her for any of my faults!

I didn't see that the publicity would be so terrible. I knew right away I didn't want it. I tried to figure out how not to get it, but like many other people who have gotten it—they realize after a few moments that if they refuse it, it would make more publicity than if you got it. A big shot, he thinks he is! He refuses the Nobel Prize! You don't want that either, and what I think is the solution is that they should at least have the courtesy—I mean the Swedish Academy—when they choose somebody, to call him up quietly and to offer him the prize, and if he doesn't want it he can then say no and there'll be no publicity because nobody has been told yet. That would seem to me to be a rather simple solution.

I have since discovered that I'm not the only nut in the world who felt that he didn't want the prize. It turns out that Professor Dirac felt the same way, and others. They are all caught by this thing. It's not going to be many people that refuse, and it won't make much difference, but what about the poor individuals who want to? Why not? Why do they have to push on it like that? Its only a matter of a telephone call.

I was skeptical about his attitude to the Nobel Prize. He did have an ingrained dislike of pomp and ceremony, but at the same time I think he was torn between that and the

Al Hibbs[6]

Feynman and Paul Dirac in Warsaw, July 1962. It was Dirac who first drew Feynman into quantum electrodynamics when he ended his 1935 book with the words: "It seems that some essentially new physical ideas are here needed."

fact that he did enjoy that his work had been recognized—that people realized that he had made an important contribution to physics. Between the two, he was sort of caught.

He obviously enjoyed getting it, he enjoyed his trip to Sweden. He had many stories to tell about it, and he enjoyed the party that the students at the university gave him. Whenever you saw him with the fellow winners of the prize that year, he was always the one who was smiling the broadest. So I believe he overplayed his dislike of it.

I do know that he didn't want to be a member of the National Academy of Sciences, and that his resignation was kept secret because it was considered such an embarrassment to the Academy.

I suspect that he would have felt worse if he hadn't gotten the Nobel Prize!

Dinner with Scandinavian royalty. Gweneth: "At the Nobel Prize dinner, I sat between the king and Prince Bertil. The king was marvelous. . . . Richard enjoyed sitting next to Christina, the present king's daughter-in-law. But he did have a little trouble with the *old* king's daughter-in-law, Sibylla, who was the epitome of a queen or princess. White hair, not a smile, extremely dignified, ramrod-straight. She really wasn't his kind of girl."

He was very conscious of being famous, and he liked people to know who he was.

He had this van, that was painted all round with large Feynman diagrams. The license plate was PHOTON. Most people would look at these diagrams and they would see some squiggly lines which meant nothing. But every so often, of course, someone would see them and say, "Why do you have Feynman diagrams all over your van?" And he would say, "Because I'm Richard Feynman!"

Ed Fredkin[7]

In a sense, Richard genuinely didn't care about the Nobel Prize; he didn't go around bragging about it. But in another sense, I think it was very important because it gave him the credentials to be "kooky"—to be crazy. The fact that Richard got the Nobel Prize early in life caused everyone to take him a little more seriously, and to write off all the crazy things he did to brilliance. That outside endorse-

Danny Hillis[8]

Feynman's van. Not PHOTON but QANTUM, misspelled because California permits a maximum of six letters on a personalized license plate.

ment freed him up from having to prove himself—he could get away with anything, because everybody knew he was a great and famous physicist.

Of the many things Feynman "got away with," the most famous was probably his passion for drumming, but it irritated him that people should find this amusing and interesting in a Nobel physics laureate. In 1966 a Swedish encyclopedia publisher wrote asking for a photograph of Feynman "beating the drum" to give "a human approach to a presentation of the difficult matter that theoretical physics represents." This was his reply:

Dear Sir,

The fact that I beat a drum has nothing to do with the fact that I do theoretical physics. Theoretical physics is a human endeavor, one of the higher developments of human beings, and the perpetual desire to prove that people who do it are human by showing that they do other things that a few other humans do (like playing bongo drums) is insulting to me.

I am human enough to tell you to go to hell.

Yours,

RPF

Malibu, 1950.

CHAPTER FOUR

Topless Bars and Other Ways to Have Fun

Feynman

I think I've got the right idea, to do crazy things—what other people would consider crazy things. There's so much fun to be had. I must say frankly that I don't understand myself, and I don't know why certain things amuse me. I am not going to try to figure it out. If I enjoy it, I enjoy it, and I don't have to explain it to anybody. I just feel like doing it, and never mind. . . . I don't care! I just do it for the fun of it, and I can't define the fun, because fun is a different thing for different people.

Murray Gell-Mann[1]

What I always liked about Richard's style was the lack of pomposity in his presentation. I was tired of theorists who dressed up their work in fancy mathematical language or invented pretentious frameworks for their sometimes rather modest contributions. Richard's ideas, often powerful, ingenious, and original, were presented in a straightforward manner that I found refreshing.

I was less impressed with another well-known aspect of Richard's style. He surrounded himself with a cloud of myth, and he spent a great deal of time and energy generating anecdotes about himself.

1974.

David Goodstein[2] There certainly is a Feynman legend, to which Feynman contributed with some enthusiasm. Most of us physicists are incapable of doing the sort of things that Feynman did. I'm sure all of those stories he told about himself were true, or at least had some element of truth in them—he was that kind of person. He could excite you and inspire you in ways that ordinary people cannot do. So there ought to be a Feynman mythology, because he was a mythical character.

Feynman and Gell-Mann at Caltech in the 1960s.

Joan Feynman

I talked to him once about the girlie stories in his books, and the story about the prostitute. He was surprised and shocked at the idea that people might have thought he went off with the prostitute, and that he had her—he did not. Nobody's going to believe that. Everybody assumes he did; even I assumed that. But no.

He was out looking for adventure, and I can't say anything about that. I've gone to more distant places, and crazier places than he, looking for adventure—I was in Borneo watching orangutans, in Nepal taking data on rhesus monkeys, chasing a rhinoceros in Africa. Why should anybody take one thing from life, and not the rest?

Al Hibbs

I don't know how he got the time to do all the things he did. Phenomenal. I couldn't do it. I think he never just did nothing. I'd tell him something was happening in the world, and he'd say, "Really?"—very surprised. He didn't listen to the radio, he didn't listen to music, and he didn't read newspapers or novels.

91

Having fun in Las Vegas, mid-1950s.

Feynman once told me he'd like to write a book called *Physics Is Fun*, in which both words would be spelled either with a *Ph* or an *F*. I loved him, and we did some outrageous things together.

While he was away in Las Vegas once, NASA put up *Explorer II*, one of the first U.S. satellites. I got him to come back to help figure out whether it was launched right or not. He bet he could beat the computer, given all the same data, to see whether it was safely in orbit. We had all the data spread out, getting the information by teletype from Florida. The first computer answer said the whole thing came down in Tampa, Florida. Well, the people who lived in Tampa knew that it had not. The next computer run was totally indecisive. Meanwhile, Feynman came to the conclusion that the third stage had failed, and that the thing was in the Atlantic Ocean. It's amazing how people even today—especially today—use a computer to do something you can do with a pencil and paper in less time. Simple equations you can solve in your—well, he could in his head, and certainly with pencil and paper. A computer will grind through for ten minutes, and often you can do it in two. Certainly simple Newtonian trajectory equations. Anyway, he did beat the computer, and then he went back to Las Vegas.

Feynman loved the notion of being a conman. He had read a book called *The Big Con*, a paperback which came out many years ago. It was about the America of the '20s and '30s. I don't know if you ever saw a Redford movie called *The Sting*? Well, that was based on this book. Feynman thought it would be a fascinating intellectual challenge to meet a real con man, so he went to Las Vegas to meet one. He hung around the bars drinking grapefruit juice, but no luck. He was getting very frustrated. Finally he decided, "Well, since I can't meet one, I'll be one!" The only people who ever approached him were the call girls who came round, B-girls. The next time one of them came up, he said, "You don't have to put on anything with me, you know. We're in the same business." She said, "What?" He said, "Well, I'm a conman on vacation." She said, "Oh really?" She was fascinated, and pretty soon he began to meet all kinds of interesting people, including George Hearst, grandson of the famous William Randolph, and had a great time with him. Via George Hearst, he got acquainted with the woman who ran the chorus line in one of the big hotels, and he got acquainted with all the girls who were dancing there. Marvelous!

My wife, Marka, and I held a number of costume parties over the years, with different themes for each one, and Feynman would come to these. One year it was mythological beings, and another year it was something astronomical—a heavenly body. One April Fools' Day, the theme of the party was to come dressed as a king, a queen, a knave, or a joker. Feynman came as Queen Elizabeth II, in a very plain green dress with a perfectly awful white hat, a wig, and a purse and gloves on. He sat very primly on a chair, looking regally at anyone who passed by, and nodding graciously when they spoke to him. At the end of the evening he did a striptease!

He was a showman, there's no question of that, and this is what made his lectures so excellent. But being a showman was just part of his nature, he loved it—he loved

The Ladakhi monk costume made by Gweneth for the "regions of the earth" party.

Dressing up for the "myths and legends" party. As Medusa, Gweneth brought a large round stone as her date.

to show off. Some of the costume parties required a rather complicated costume, and his wife, Gweneth, would always make them. The first party we had, the theme was simply a region of the earth, and you had to come dressed in a traditional costume from somewhere. Gweneth made him the most beautiful costume from Lhasa, with the felt hat and robe. The one she made for him for the myths and legends party was rather simpler—a white robe, and a beard. Somebody asked him, "Are you Moses?"

And of course Feynman said, "No. I'm God!"

Richard Sherman[3] **R**ichard Feynman was the most competitive person I have ever met. Whenever he wanted to do something new, whatever that thing may have been, he wanted to be the best in the world at it. He didn't always succeed, but he tried. It was just second nature.

He had this innate curiosity about everything around

him, not only about nature manifested in physics, but about all kinds of mechanical and electrical devices, how everything functioned, how everything fitted together, and he liked to try everything at least once.

One Saturday Feynman called me up about nine o'clock in the morning and asked if I had a quarter-inch-drive socket set. I said, "Yeah, what do you need it for?" He said, "Are you doing anything today?" Of course, as you do when Feynman calls up, I said no.

He said, "Well, why don't you come on up and bring that socket set with you?"

Sitting out there in his garage was the washing machine, and he says, "It broke this morning. I called the repair man up, and he came over, looked at it, and said it was gonna be three hundred dollars to fix. Which was outrageous, so I decided—why don't we do it ourselves?"

I said, "Fine." So we pulled out all the tools, and he started to pull out the loader and the transmission from the thing, and took it all apart. There was a seized bearing inside the transmission. We pulled the bearing out, went down to the local washing machine store that sold spare parts. We went in and said, "Do you have one of these?" The guy says, "No, but we can get it in a few days." A few days later, Feynman went to pick up the new bearing. The guy in the shop says to Feynman:

"Hey, you look like someone who knows what he's doing. How about a job with me, repairing washing machines?"

I was a yoga teacher in a workshop the first time I met Feynman. Esalen is a Mecca for unusual concepts and, yes, the fruits, nuts, and flakes, no doubt. But there is a lot of good work going on there, and, of course, it's heaven! There are beautiful hot springs at Esalen that come out of the mountain—sulfur springs and baths—and people come here from all over. The baths are very dark, so that people who aren't keen on being seen in the buff can go down there at night.

I was sitting next to him in the dark in the hot tub and

Faustin Bray[4]

Feynman at the Esalen Institute, 1984. In the front row, second from left, is Faustin Bray. Ralph Leighton, Feynman's great friend and drumming partner, is fourth from the left in the second row.

I said, "I heard Richard Feynman is here." And he said, "Hmm?" I said, "I think you're Richard Feynman—Feynman of the Feynman diagrams." He said, "No, I'm not Richard Feynman," and that was the end of that. But I met him again later, out running.

Feynman reminded me of a New York cab driver, and being from New York, I know how to hang out with the cab drivers. I think he was always looking for new territory to explore. He was interested in unusual things to do with his mind, and so he used the flotation tank at John Lilly's house, and tried different meditative techniques. He was willing to look into all sorts of relaxation situations. He took a massage workshop here, and learned how to do it.

He didn't like the word "creative," but he was attracted to creativity and eccentricity He had heard a lot about the "New Age," which has a lot of interesting theories, but picks off a bit of the physics to substantiate them, like Bell's theorem, Einstein's theory of relativity, Heisenberg's uncertainty principle—the whole interpretation (or misinterpretation) of what quantum mechanics is. Richard didn't like the way physics was used, or misused, all over, but especially in California in workshops and lectures. I think he felt it was somewhat his duty to set some of these things straight, and try to have people feel respect for the material as it really is, rather than embellishing it with sort of fairy tales. He called it "hokey-pokey," and he wanted to debunk that sort of thing.

He didn't like people posturing, and one of the things he was trying to do at Esalen was to get people to get their whole "guru thing" under control. One time we awarded him a shirt emblazoned with a serpent with wings and rainbow colors and whatnot going up it. He joked about it: "Oh, yes! This is my guru shirt!"

I don't think he cared at all about what other people thought, and his behavior did look slightly peculiar to the kind of people who are always worried about what other people are thinking. There were younger people around him who were in awe of him, and they behaved in ways that might have been a little obsequious. I think that was something he wanted to disavow himself from, to dilute. So having people see how human he was was something he was keen on. It was very nice that such a magnificent creature turned out to be so normal!

Basically he wanted everybody to just get out of their skin, get on with having a good time, and be infected with the wonder of existence the way he was. He would take something very basic, like the reflections on mud puddles with oil slicks on them, and then he would talk about the relevant physical theories. He was very good, and very entertaining, and participants who would not normally be that rationally organized signed up for those workshops of his.

Workshop member: You are an original thinker. I would like to ask you, how would you go about designing a miniature antigravity machine?[5]

Feynman: I can't. I don't know how to make any antigravity machine.

The Esalen guru shirt.

You would lick the world's problems.

It doesn't make any difference, I still don't know how to do it. The game I play is a very interesting one. It's imagination, in a tight straitjacket, which is this: that it has to agree with the known laws of physics. I'm not going to assume that maybe the laws of physics have changed, so that I can design something or other. I operate as if everything that we know is true. If we're wrong, of course, we can redesign something with the new laws later. But the game is to try to figure things out, with what we know is possible. It requires imagination to think of what's possible, and then it requires an analysis back, checking to see whether it fits, whether it's allowed, according to what is known, okay?

In the case of an antigravity machine, I immediately give up, because my understanding of the laws of gravity are such that it doesn't make sense for antigravity. The only antigravity machines, things which oppose gravity, that is, and which are very effective, are like you're using now—a pillow, or a floor under your behind. Those are antigravity machines and they will support you in a space, above the earth, a few feet in this case, for a relatively unlimited time. Next?

Tom Van Sant[6] Feynman and I met by accident. I was down south of the border, in Baja California, Mexico, in a little town called La Misíon, overlooking the Pacific Ocean. It was winter. There's an isolated beach there, and I used to make and fly large kites with a series of diaphragm-like disks attached together in a big three-line system; I could make a kite a hundred and fifty feet long, with feathers and stuff on it. I was flying a big kite on this deserted beach with little houses up on the cliff, a lot of them owned by Americans. It's a place where they normally see nothing but seagulls or pelicans. This kite was soaring up there in front of the houses, and a man came out on to the porch and looked down at me. I thought, "Oh-oh, I've frightened somebody!" He went back in the house, and came back out with his sweater on, and came down a long set of steps to the beach. He wanted to help me fly the kite.

He flew it, and we just started talking. Then he began coming to my drawing classes in the house I had up in the Hollywood Hills. He'd drive over from Pasadena every Monday night, and that's how we became friends. I don't teach drawing. I don't teach anything. What we would talk about, in a drawing class, is the way you experience a drawing—you let the drawings take care of themselves. What kind of an experience are you having? What's the level of involvement. We'd talk about courage in exploring ways of experiencing things. And we'd talk about things like love.

I had a hot tub, and in the summertime we'd have a hot tub after the drawing class. There'd be several people, or maybe just he and I. We'd sit around in the tub and talk about stuff, but he wasn't much interested in talking physics. We talked about sex, politics, religion—same old things anybody else talks about. We'd talk about worldviews, overviews, on all sorts of different subjects. And philosophy. We just enjoyed talking about the things that one guy knew and the other guy didn't.

Dick acted as a consultant for a company in Switzerland, which took him there every summer. About 1982 or so, I had business in Europe, and I met Dick in Geneva. We decided to kick around for several days. We did the shops and the countryside on the first day, and on the second day, he asked what I'd like to do. I said, "Well, if it isn't too much like a postman's holiday, I'd like to go over to CERN," which is the European particle accelerator, where so much particle physics is done, and where Dick used to work a number of years before. He said, "Sure." So we went over there, and Dick couldn't find his way around because the buildings had changed. We finally found our way in, and looked into a room where there were some physicists doing work on the blackboard. One of them spotted Feynman, and pretty soon there a crowd gathered, and the director came in. He decided they'd take us on a tour. We went into an 007, James Bond cave underneath the ground, with all this wonderful high-technology equipment. There was a giant machine that was going to be rolled into the line of the particle accelerator. The machine was maybe the size of a two-story building, on tracks, with lights and bulbs and dials and scaffolds all around, with men climbing all over it.

Feynman said, "What experiment is this?"

The director said, "Why, this is an experiment to test the charge-change something-or-other under such-and-such circumstances." But he stopped suddenly, and he said, "I forgot! This is your theory of charge-change, Dr. Feynman! This is an experiment to demonstrate, if we can, your theory of fifteen years ago, called so-and-so." He was a little embarrassed at having forgotten it.

Feynman looked at this big machine, and he said, "How much does this cost?" The man said, "Thirty-seven million dollars," or whatever it was.

And Feynman said, "You don't trust me?"

When he wrote his book *Surely You're Joking, Mr. Feynman!* with Ralph Leighton, it got on the best-seller list. A German publisher decided he would like to publish it, but he wrote a letter to Feynman to the effect that he wanted to edit the book to some degree—he wanted to take out passages which he characterized as being not so important to his more serious readership. Dick's response was clever. He wrote back to the German publisher and said, "Thank you for your kind letter about editing the less serious passages of the book so that it could be better appreciated by your more critical readers. I respectfully decline to give you permission to do so because I don't think there are any passages suitable for your more critical readership."

Richard Sherman

Richard and I used to work very hard doing physics, but there was never any protocol dictating that the session had to be thus-and-such length of time. Sometimes Richard would suddenly say, "Let's knock off and go somewhere and fool around!" The usual place we went was a topless bar in Altadena, called Gianone's. There was always something happening at Gianone's in the afternoon, every day of the week. We'd walk in, grab a table. Feynman knew everybody there—all the ladies, Gianone the owner, and anybody who was a regular. He would go behind the bar and pick up an orange juice, because he never drank anything alcoholic. He would also grab a half-inch stack of those paper doilies, or place mats that they put down on tables in restaurants, and come back to the table. We might continue doing physics, or we might watch the ladies dancing on the stage. Frequently people would come by and chat, and this was the sort of entertainment that he liked. But it was kind of deceptive because, believe it or not, although this particular environment might not seem conducive to doing something like theoretical physics, over the years Feynman actually did an enormous number of calculations in that place. I know this because I often used to take care of his house for the summer while he and his family went on vacation. One particular summer I went downstairs in his studio and looked around, and found a stack of these doilies several feet thick. Every one of them was covered from one edge to the other with mathematical computations and theoretical physics!

Dick and I met at a party a long time ago. Originally, we had a lot in common as bachelors. I was going through a divorce, and he had just lost his wife. At this party we were both fighting for the favors of a lady called Alessandra Pondelcini, who was a student from Florence, and somehow after the evening I took her home. Dick liked me because we were competing with each other.

Then there was another time when he was playing the drums, the bongo drums, and at one point I went into the bathroom, took my shirt off, and put shaving cream all over my chest. I wore a wig, and I did a dance which he liked. It was just a personality attraction in the beginning, but I think we loved each other because of this great and interesting contrast between science and art. On his wall, over his mantelpiece, he had a reproduction of Botticelli's *Primavera*. One day he said, "You know, Jiry, this woman drives me crazy. Every time I look at her I get a different

Jirayr Zorthian[7]

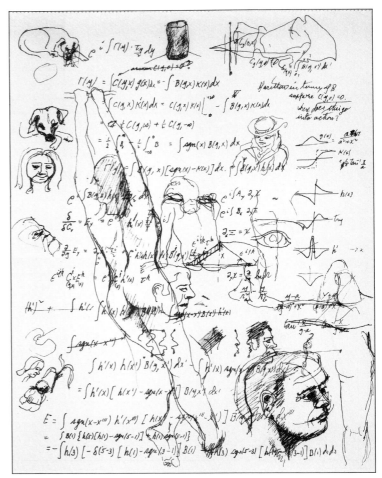

A page from one of Feynman's notebooks.

emotion, different feelings. Sometimes she's the most beautiful person I've ever seen, sometimes I think she's crude, and other times holy. Tell me how an artist achieves all of these contrasting feelings about this painting, how it works?"

I said, "Oh, come on, Dick! I don't know. In fact, I think sometimes the artist himself doesn't know. He just paints. I think we don't know where it comes from; rather than from us, it may come through us."

"Don't give me that stuff!" he said. "Science will someday find out how this kind of thing is done."

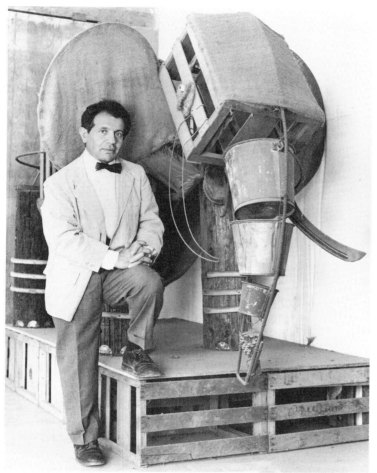

"I have a friend who's an artist. . . ." Jirayr Zorthian with his junk
elephant, 1959.

I said, "Well, good luck!"

We got to know each other very well. He had that same
attitude that a lot of people have: "What is this contempo-
rary art? I don't understand it . . . my child can do better,"
and so on. So one time I said I'd give him some paper and
some crayons, and see what he could do. He looked at this
empty paper, and he became very frustrated.

One day he said to me, "Jirayr, you don't know a thing
about physics, and I don't know a thing about art, and yet
we both admire Leonardo da Vinci. I'm a rather versatile
person, I play the bongo drums and so on, and you do

structures, and sculpture, and architecture. What do you say we become two Leonardo da Vincis? One Sunday I'll give you a day of physics, and the following Sunday you give me a day of art."

Well, I agreed, of course, and we did this for eight years. Most delightful. When he started, it was all absolutely amateur stick figures and that type of thing. I wish I had some of his first drawings to show you. They were just very crude. In the end, he became an accomplished draftsman.

It was just another challenge, frankly. He was interested in so many other things besides physics. He became terribly engrossed in biology at one time. And anthropology. And, of course, the bongo drums. Did you know he was tone-deaf? His musical sense was not strong, but because he was such a great mathematician, he learned to do the bongo drums. He was a concert bongo drummer—very good. So I think art was another thing he wanted to conquer. He told me, "I'm learning all your tricks, and someday I'm going be able to draw as well as you!" He also said, "But there's something I'll never be able to do, and I don't know how you do it. Whenever you have a girl in your studio, within five minutes she's taken her clothes off, and is posing nude!" So I said, "Dick, have you ever asked a woman to pose nude for you?" He said, "What? Is that what you're supposed to do? You mean if I ask them, they might pose for me, too?"

He was genuinely interested in drawing, but the fringe benefits were the girls, of course!

Many of our arguments were about the way an artist looks at nature and the way a scientist looks at nature. I would say, "You scientists don't appreciate nature as much as we do. You look at it too technically. You look at the way a flower grows, how the water goes through the stem and into the petals, and so on. We're not interested in that. We look at it merely as an inspiration for color, red against green, and so on, and it's a very spontaneous, exciting thing."

"Oh no!," he would say. "The more you know about nature, the more you like it, and the more wonderful it becomes."

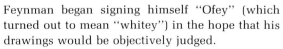

Feynman began signing himself "Ofey" (which turned out to mean "whitey") in the hope that his drawings would be objectively judged.

Kathy: "It was a total, blown-out love affair!"

All this was about twenty-five years ago. Once he came (it was his turn—we were going to have a day of science), he came with a package, and opened it up. He said, "Now, Jiry, you're going see the world beyond your sight. We're going to look through a microscope." He set it up, and I looked through, and there was this most beautiful, most incredible round object, with prismatic colors going into space and disappearing, with reds, greens, blues, you know. It was the eye of a fly, a common fly. And then he said, "Now what do you say?" It was beautiful, of course, but at a larger dimension it was still a fly.

I have a friend who's an artist and he's taken a view which I don't agree with very well. He'll hold up a flower and say, "Look how beautiful it is!" and I'll agree. And he says, "You see, I as an artist can see how beautiful this is, but you, as a scientist . . . oh, you take this all apart and it becomes a dull thing." And I think that he's kind of nutty!

First of all, the beauty he sees is available to other people—and to me too, I believe. Although I might not be quite as refined aesthetically as he is, I can appreciate the beauty of a flower.

At the same time, I see much more about the flower than he sees. I could imagine the cells in there, the complicated actions inside, which also have a beauty. I mean, it's not just beauty at this dimension of one centimeter; there is also beauty at a smaller dimension—the inner structure. The fact that the colors in the flower are evolved in order to attract insects to pollinate it is interesting—it means that the insects can see the color. It adds a question: does this aesthetic sense also exist in the lower forms? Why is it aesthetic? All kinds of interesting questions which a science knowledge only adds to the excitement and mystery and the awe of a flower. It only adds. I don't understand how it subtracts.

Does it make any less of a beautiful smell of violets to know that it's molecules? To find out, for example, that the smell of violets is very similar to the chemical that's used by a certain butterfly (I don't know whether it's true, like my father's stories!), a butterfly that lets out this chemical to attract all its mates? It turns out that this chemical is exactly the smell of violets with a small change of a few molecules. The different kinds of smells and the different kinds of chemicals, the great variety of chemicals and colors and dyes and so on in the plants and everywhere else, are all very closely related, with very small changes, and the efficiency of life is not always to make a new thing, but to modify only slightly something that's already there, and make its function entirely different, so that the smell of violets is related to the smell of earth. . . . These are all additional facts, additional discoveries. It doesn't

Feynman

take away that it can't answer questions of what, ultimately, does the smell of violets really feel like when you smell it. That's only if you expected science to give the answers to every possible question. But the idea that science takes away is something I don't understand.

It's true that technology can have an effect on art that might be a kind of subtraction. For example, in the early days painting was to make pictures when pictures were unavailable, that was one reason: it was very useful to give people pictures to look at, to help them think about God, or the Annunciation, or whatever. When photography came as a result of technology, which itself was the result of scientific knowledge, then that made pictures very much more available. The care and effort needed to make something by hand which looked exactly like nature and which was once such a delight to see now became mundane in a way (although of course there's a new art—the art of taking good pictures). So yes, technology can have an effect on art, but the idea that it takes away mystery or awe or wonder in nature is wrong. It's quite the opposite. It's much more wonderful to know what something's really like than to sit there and just simply, in ignorance, say, "Oooh, isn't it wonderful!"

Jirayr Zorthian Well, anyway we could never get anywhere with this science-versus-art argument. Years later, and after he was dead, I thought of an example I should have used, and I wish I'd thought of it earlier, because it was funny. What I wanted to say to him was, "Dick—here you are, a virile nineteen-year-old physicist. You love physics, you're curious about all the aspects of science and so forth, and in walks this girl that you're very excited about. She bares her breasts, walks toward you. Are you going to look at these breasts and start analyzing how beautifully they're formed, scientifically? That they form glands to make milk for the baby to suck on? Or are you going to want to just spontaneously go over there and bury your face between them and go "brrrrrrr!" I think that would have been a much better argument than the flower!

Jirayr Zorthian, photographed by Michelle Feynman in the late 1980s.

Every Thursday we would meet for lunch, just for fun, at Gianone's bar. I always wanted to sit right at the front where the girls, you know, wiggled their bottoms, but Richard always said, "No, no. Let's sit at the back." So he'd sit right at the back somewhere, and he worked on his mathematical equations. But he loved the excitement of the place.

His relationship with other people, not just me, but other artists, musicians and so on, were very important to him. I heard Murray Gell-Mann, who I know quite well, complain once:

"Feynman is supposed to be a brilliant physicist, and we need his input at Caltech, we need him to talk to us about physics. But what does he do? He goes off and spends all his time with go-go girls and bongo drummers and artists. He wastes so much time on people, and I don't see what they give him."

Well, I think Feynman got a lot out of people—me, and many others. He was interested in so many other things beside physics, and I think it enriched his life and personality. Other physicists couldn't understand it.

Kathleen McAlpine-Myers I think I was his favorite model. He was my friend, and my confidant. We had a very intimate relationship, but it never went past a point that could make anyone unhappy. It was a total, blown-out love affair—it was! But in the most romantic sense of the word. Richard was a great romantic, and so was I. We meant a great deal to each other, but it was never more than that, as far as being something wrong, or sexual or anything like that. He loved his family and would never do anything to harm them or his relationship with his wife, Gweneth. He may have been a womanizer, and he loved women and liked to see what he could get away with, but there was always a point past which he would not go. He had tremendous integrity, and his word meant everything to him.

He was fascinated with women. He loved women's bodies, and their appearance, and their emotions, and their vulnerability. I don't know if I could really explain, but he always had this very great curiosity in all situations. It didn't matter what it was—any situation to him was vastly curious, and he just had to know what was going to happen.

I never thought of him as a male chauvinist. Well, maybe he was a male chauvinist in a way, because if he went out with a girl, or a group of girls, he would never pay for their entrée or drinks. So you had to really love Richard to go somewhere with him—you always had to pick up the tab! He was great the way he thought highly of himself, and thought he should just be appreciated and cared for.

Once he was commissioned by his friend Gianone to do a nude. We worked on this nude for many, many weeks until finally he finished it, and it was hung over the bar. Richard would love to go there and enjoy the atmosphere of the music and the girls dancing. But his interest was a little bit more extended than what most men's is when they go into a girlie bar. He would sit in the back and draw pictures of the faces of the men watching the girls!

He got very frustrated when he was drawing, ripping the page off to start another one. When he drew he did a funny thing. He stuck his tongue out all the time, like a lizard. His eyes would do something very peculiar, and his face would screw up, and he'd put so much energy and interest into it. He liked the challenge of learning to do something that he hadn't succeeded in doing before, and he was very interested in getting things right.

He liked to tell stories while he drew—it was a way for him to relax. If the telephone rang, and it might be someone calling from a faraway place, he'd say, "I'm sorry, I can't talk to you right now. I'm drawing," and he'd slam the phone down. We'd draw for three hours, one night a week, every week. We had these sessions together for over twenty years, and it was a very special time. He liked to give advice, and he helped me solve many personal problems. I think he understood human nature and life circumstances to a far greater degree than many people who had studied formally for many years. Everything Richard did, he did exceptionally well. He had an innovative way of looking at things that always cut through to the heart of the matter, and that was always one thing I loved about him—the way he could really see what the point was, and do away with all the frills, or the unnecessary. He used to call it "crap." "Get rid of all the crap!" he'd say.

Richard felt about small children, for example, that if they just wanted to ride a bicycle around in a circle for an hour, then that was okay—they should do that. He felt that this idea of structuring and channeling children's interests and time into programs was very destructive to small children. He felt that each child should be allowed to have his own pattern and way of being and self-expression, that everyone was okay just the way they were, and that you should never tamper with that.

He liked children a lot. When he met a small child, if he was visiting a friend maybe, he would capture this child in his Grip of Steel. No child could ever escape the Grip of Steel, no matter how hard they tried. Until, of course, they touched his nose and turned him to jelly! He greeted everyone at their level, and I think that was part of his great intelligence, that he could go anywhere with anyone and fit in. Not everybody can do that.

He liked the innocence of children, he loved animals, and he was very kind-hearted and generous, and he always appreciated laughter.

You make him sound like a combination of Einstein, Francis of Assisi, and Jesus Christ.

I've always thought of him that way! He certainly walked upon this earth, and it seemed like he came from a different time, but he was here with us, and I wish he'd come back.

Richard Davies[8] Feynman and I had a kind of a jovial relationship. We did discuss many serious things, but his approach—and mine—to life was that much of life is a bit absurd, and you kind of make the best of it. You had to recognize that you were absurd and ridiculous at times—otherwise you couldn't stand all the things that go on. He would say, "Oh, the poor human beings. They struggle as best they can, and somehow work it out, bit by bit, don't they?" He was very, very sympathetic to those people of a lower economic and social status than himself. He could be pretty tough, very intimidating, with the guys in his own profession—I mean, he could really cut them up—but when it came to people who were working on their hands and knees, he was very considerate. I liked him for that.

He considered himself a lucky man in so many ways— in his adventures, in the way he picked out the right problems, and all that. He could be humble, too. I remember when he met me in Paris. He had just come back from

CERN and he was talking about how the good news was that quantum electrodynamics had been proven out to eight decimal places. Then he had started to cite a few other ideas he had, and they shot this down, they shot that down. And he said, "I've got to go back to the drawing board. I guess I've got to eat a bit of humble pie."

He was sometimes very intolerant of himself. He didn't strive to be anything perfect, and he had the point of view that maybe people try too hard to be good, or to be do-gooders. He'd say, "That isn't the point. The point is not to do anybody else any harm."

When his friend Gianone was charged with indecency, or whatever the phrase was at the time, there were all kinds of people who said, "Oh, yes! We'll testify that this isn't true." But when it came to it, and the case really came up, they weren't around. Feynman said he would continue to testify. His mother was a bit embarrassed, so he very carefully explained to her, "Look, I haven't got anything to lose, and a man is entitled to a trial." So he went through with it, and that's the way he was. He was willing to do that in other ways. I remember there was a Caltech student who was arrested for being in possession of marijuana, before marijuana became partially legalized in this state. Feynman told me that the students were going to make a protest, and they had asked him if he would show up, and do something. He said he'd kind of like to do it, but he didn't know what kind of statement he could make. So we walked around and we thought about it, and we came up with a statement which he carried on a sign— "Foolishness should not be a felony."

One night in 1973 we were sitting around the fireplace at his house, and his wife, Gweneth, said to me, "Say, Dick, think of some adventurous place for us to go during the spring break in March."

I thought a little bit, and I told them a place I'd like to go to, which was the Copper Canyon down in Mexico, some place southwest of Chihuahua. I'd flown over it. It's bigger than the Grand Canyon, and you can take a one-track railroad from Chihuahua along the north rim. The train journey ends down on the coast at Los Mochis, and

Richard P. Feynman   Andrew P. Telfer
                                      Times photos

SAT NOV 8 1969

Bottomless Helps Nobel Physicist With Figures

Caltech's Feynman Tells Lewd Case Jury He Watched Girls While Doing Equations

BY JACK BIRKINSHAW
Times Staff Writer

PASADENA—A Nobel Prize-winning Caltech physicist testified Friday that he worked at mathematical equations during frequent visits to a Pasadena bottomless restaurant.

"When my calculations didn't work out, I would watch the girls," Richard P. Feynman told a Municipal Court jury hearing charges against the proprietor and seven women dancers.

Angelo Gianone, 43, owner of Gianone's Steak House, 1453 N. Lake Ave., is accused of permitting lewd performances and the women with giving such performances.

Judge John F. Hassler announced at the close of Friday's testimony that court would reconvene Monday at 9 at Gianone's to witness the dancers' performances.

Feynman, who said he visited Gianone's five to six times a week over a long period of time, testified, "I'd like to use the place to work in."

November 1969. Feynman helps out his friend Gianone.

CHIHUAHUA, MEXICO
INCREDIBLE ADVENTURE

The Chihuahua–Los Mochis railroad runs along the rim of the vast Cañon de Cobre complex, home of the Tarahumara (or Raramuri) Indians.

then you can take the boat across the Gulf of California to La Paz.

"Oh, that's great! Let's do that!" they both said. Then, right out of the blue, Richard said, "You know, I've never been anyplace you can't get to by car." So we decided we would try to find some community down there that you had to walk into.

Gweneth was pretty good at setting up the logistics. Richard knew some Spanish, so he said he'd be the interpreter. I said I'd be the beast of burden. Then Richard recruited one of his students, Arturo, in Mexico, and that chap brought us some Mexican maps of the area—very detailed maps, difficult to get hold of. We picked out a place that we'd have to walk to. It was called Cisneguito, which, as I understand it, means "little swan." We would have to get off the railroad and work our way down into the canyon, and make a two-or three-day walk to get there. We got off the train and stayed in some little motel. That night, we could hear tom-toms all over the place, and we wondered what was going on. It was like an old John Wayne movie, or *Drums of the Mohawk* or whatever it was called. We had the idea it had something to do with Easter, or some other great celebration. We never did find out what it was, although later on we saw a boy walking along beating a drum and we asked him, "Why do you beat the drum?" The boy said, "Makes me feel good!"

In the end, we got to Cisneguito. I don't know how. Feynman had a lot of pluck, because shortly before this backpack trip he'd fallen down in Chicago and broken a kneecap. So walking wasn't very easy for him. It was a beautiful little community, elevation about six thousand feet. Gweneth and I imagined it was what Scotland was like back in the early eighteenth century. There was a little house, and Feynman and Arturo talked to the people and they invited us to come and stay on their patio. We spent a fair amount of time there. They had a couple of boys, just as wonderful as could be. They showed us a burial ground—more a burial cave, really, full of skeletons.

I think Feynman liked to go to places where the people had to live close to the soil. He always felt the same way about that—how you can go all over the world, and every-body always wants to take you to the richest place in town, and show you all the big bags. They're essentially the same everywhere. But when people have to live off the soil, they are different. A man who has to live off a bare rock is different to a man who lives near the ocean. That's the sort of thing that interested him a lot, to get close to that. These people in Mexico were living a very marginal exis-tence, and necessarily they all had to cooperate, or they couldn't make it at all. They had a few chickens, and a little bit of grain. There's another thing he found interest-ing and we laughed about it: same as people all over the world, they didn't like the government. We asked them whether they voted and they said it was an awful long way to go. They never spoke of distance, they always talked of time—twelve hours. They meant twelve hours' fast walk to get to the polling place. So it was a little bit difficult to be a voter under those circumstances.

The kids showed us the minuscule schoolhouse, but they said a schoolhouse wasn't any good because they didn't have a professor. Well, Feynman begins to talk to them, and he gets off into the subject of optics. He bor-

Feynman and Gweneth in Mexico, 1973.

Tarahumara in Cisneguito—"a place you can't get to by car."

rowed a little magnifying glass from me to illustrate how the rays go through the lens and how they bend, and so on. He was getting more and more worked up, as he always did in a lecture, whether it was at Caltech or any other place. So he built up a lot of momentum, with his arms going off this way and that, while Gweneth and I were lying back, laughing at the idea that he's forever the Professor, no matter where he is. Suddenly he turns to me and shouts, "Why couldn't you bring a better magnifying glass?"

I don't know if he ever could take a complete holiday from physics. We were stuck in a monsoon one time and we talked about physics through three days of rain. We might flip off into world politics or some other subject, but physics, I think, was always in the back—well, the front of his mind. When we left Cisneguito, there was one hard walk to do. It was getting late, and where were we going to stay? We didn't want to sleep in the middle of a steep trail. Then we spotted a little cabin down near the river. To get there we had to plow through a whole lot of brush, but we did it. Richard threw his gear down, opened his sleeping bag, flopped down, and said, "Why did I ever think the Dirac equation was so important?" He went off, and snored.

I woke him up next morning, and I said, "Hey! How important is the Dirac equation?" He put his head up, and he said, "Damned important!"

In September and October of 1974 we decided to go back. This time we decided we would get a little plane to take us to the bottom of the canyon, and we would climb out of the canyon to see our friends in Cisneguito on the way back. Beforehand, Feynman had decided he would spend a little time on the language of the Raramuri. He went over to UCLA and studied, and he learned a few hundred words. We set off on the trip, and we got into some very remote places. I remember going through a tiny village, so small I don't know why it had a name, but it was called Serro Colorado, and along came one of these Tarahumara, or Raramuri, fellows, carrying some boards across his shoulder. I stopped him because he was such a handsome fellow, and I hoped we could talk to him. Feynman came up, and I said, "Well?"

Feynman says, "What do I say?" I thought about it, and I said, "Why don't you count to ten?" So that's what he did, and this fellow broke out in tremendous laughter as

On the second trip Gweneth took a Polaroid camera.

Feynman was counting to ten in Raramuri. He sat down, and he spent hours trying to talk with us. We found out his name, we made a little fire together, and shared things. So there you are—Richard had a kind of a gift that way, of communicating whatever the circumstances. It was a great experience, and I think it illustrates the way he went about things in this straightforward, somewhat naive way. Actually, less naive than you might think.

Feynman tried to avoid the kind of "make-work," whatever kind of work you want to call it, that goes on in the academic establishment. He shook off committees as often as he could. He called it his Principle of Social Unresponsibility. Well, he happened to be one of the few professors that maybe could get away with that because he was so productive. He once had a bet with Victor Weisskopf about it. Weisskopf said, "In ten years' time you'll be doing administrative work, the definition of 'administrative work' being that you'll be supervising people whose work you don't understand." Well, Feynman collected his bet, ten dollars or whatever it was.

Victor Weisskopf and Freeman Dyson, 1952.

- On this the FIFTEENTH DAY of DECEMBER of the YEAR ONE THOUSAND NINE
  HUNDRED AND SIXTY FIVE, at a Luncheon given at the Laboratories of
  the European Organization for Nuclear Research (CERN), Meyrin, Geneva,
  the following WAGER was made between Professor Viktor F. WEISSKOPF and
  Professor Richard P. FEYNMAN.
  The terms of the said WAGER are as follows:

- Mr. FEYNMAN will pay the sum of TEN DOLLARS to Mr. WEISSKOPF if at any
  time during the next TEN YEARS (i.e. before the THIRTY FIRST DAY of
  DECEMBER of the YEAR ONE THOUSAND NINE HUNDRED AND SEVENTY FIVE), the
  said Mr. FEYNMAN has held a "responsible position".

- Conversely, if on the THIRTY FIRST DAY of DECEMBER of the YEAR ONE
  THOUSAND NINE HUNDRED AND SEVENTY FIVE, the said Mr. FEYNMAN shall
  have held or be holding no such position, Mr. WEISSKOPF will be deemed
  to have forfeited his WAGER and will be in duty bound to pay the sum of
  TEN DOLLARS to Mr. FEYNMAN.

- For the purpose of the aforementioned WAGER, the term "responsible
  position" shall be taken to signify a position which, by reason of its
  nature, compels the holder to issue instructions to other persons to
  carry out certain acts, notwithstanding the fact that the holder has
  no understanding whatsoever of that which he is instructing the afore-
  said persons to accomplish.

- In case of contention or of non-fulfilment of the aforementioned
  conditions, the sole arbiter shall be Mr. Giuseppe COCCONI.

  Signed at Meyrin on this the FIFTEENTH DAY of DECEMBER of the
YEAR ONE THOUSAND NINE HUNDRED AND SIXTY FIVE.

Richard P. Feynman

Richard P. Feynman

Viktor F. Weisskopf

Signed and witnessed:

G. Cocconi

Feynman's 1965 wager with theoretical physicist Victor Weisskopf.

Feynman When I was a young fellow, in the 1940s and '50s, there was a myth around that theoretical physics can only be done by young people. The reason was historical—that relativity and quantum mechanics had recently been developed by young men. If you look at the history of older discoveries, you find it isn't really true, and if you look at mathematics in particular, you would find that there were very many mathematicians who were quite old and still doing fine, original work.

I hadn't read the history then, and I sort of believed the myth. But I kept going, and sometimes I would have these long periods, all my life, when I just couldn't do anything or get anywhere, and every once in a while I would think, "This is the end." If I could somehow get working again, I'd make some new discovery and then I'd say, "Okay, that's it. I'm satisfied. I don't have to do any more because I'm fifty." But I can't stop! Now I'm sixty-three, I keep working, and I think I'm still making contributions.

It is necessary to avoid certain pitfalls—it seemed to me that many of my friends were going into administrative work of one kind or another at the university. That's important, but it really is exhausting, and to do the kind of real good physics work, you do need absolutely solid lengths of time. When you're putting ideas together which are vague and hard to remember, it's like—I get this feeling very much—it's like building those houses of cards, and each of the cards is shaky, and if you forget one of them, the whole thing collapses and you don't know how you got there. You have to build them up again. If you are interrupted, and you forget how the cards go together (the cards being different parts of the idea, or different kinds of idea that have to go together to build up the main idea), it's quite a tower, and it's easy to slip. It needs a lot of concentration—solid time to think. If you've got a job in administering anything, say, then you don't have the solid time. So I have invented another myth for myself—that I am irresponsible. "I am actively irresponsible," I tell everybody. "I don't do anything." If anybody asks me to be on a committee to take care of admissions . . . "No! I'm irresponsible . . . I don't give a damn about the students!" Of course I give a damn about the students, but I know that somebody else'll do it! So I take the view "Let George do it," a view which you're not supposed to take. But I do, because I like to do physics, and I want to see if I can still do it. I'm selfish, okay? I want to do my physics.

I got the idea of "active irresponsibility" in Los Alamos. We often went on walks, and one day I was with the great mathematician von Neumann and a few other people. I think Bethe and von Neumann were discussing some social problem that Bethe was very worried about. Von Neumann said, "I don't feel any responsibility for all these social problems. Why should I? I'm born into the world, I didn't make it." Something like that. Well, I've read von Neumann's autobiography and it seems to me that he felt perpetually responsible, but at that moment this was a new idea to me, and I caught onto it. Around you all the time there are people telling you what your responsibilities are, and I thought it was kind of brave to be actively irresponsible. "Active" because, like democracy, it takes eternal vigilance to maintain it—in a university you have to perpetually watch out, and be careful that you don't do anything to help anybody!

From time to time I do feel responsibilities, and I have gotten involved. I helped the state choose school math textbooks once, and after a while I resigned because I saw it was an ineffective use of my time. Now I'm one hundred percent in physics, and I don't do anything for the university. I don't do a damned thing except think and teach my classes and take care of students.

Marvin Minsky

I must say I have a little of this sense of social irresponsibility, and Feynman was a great inspiration to me—I have done a good deal of it since. There are several reasons for a scientist to be irresponsible, and one of them I take very seriously: people say, "Are you sure you should be working on this? Can't it be used for bad?" Well, I have a strong feeling that good and bad are things to be thought about by people who understand better than I do the interactions among people, and the causes of suffering. The worst thing I can imagine is for somebody to ask me to decide whether a certain innovation is good or bad.

It so happens that in August 1945 I was in the Navy being trained to go to the South Pacific and kill people. Then here was this bomb going off, and I wasn't going to be shipped to the Pacific after all. From a personal, selfish point of view, that was maybe the best thing that ever happened to me—I could very well have been killed that year. So if you had asked me at the time to decide, I suppose I would have said, selfishly, "Oh yes, drop it!"

The idea that a scientist should be responsible for his discoveries is absurd—a scientist is very busy trying to find new ways to think, and he's not in tune with traditional ways to think. There's another view, which is that if I am very good at understanding something and developing a new kind of knowledge for the world, then that's what I should do. There are plenty of other people who are better at ethics. I think Feynman had a deep sense that he wasn't the best person to make such decisions. Not even better than average.

Hans Bethe Feynman somehow was proud of being irresponsible. He concentrated on his science, and on enjoying life. There are some of us—including myself—who felt after the end of the Second World War that we had a great responsibility to explain atomic weapons, and to try and make the government do sensible things about atomic weapons. We didn't succeed very well, but at least we brought to the common knowledge of the public the tremendous destructive power of atomic weapons. No government has used atomic weapons since the end of the Second World War, and I believe that we scientists have deserved some credit for that.

Feynman didn't want to have anything to do with it, and I think quite rightly. I think it would be quite wrong if all scientists worked on discharging their responsibility. You need some number of them, but it should only be a small fraction of the total number of scientists. Among the leading scientists, there should be some who do not feel responsible, and who only do what science is supposed to accomplish.

VIETNAM
AN AMERICAN VIEW

● We, citizens of the United States, who are deeply concerned over the war in Vietnam, wish to put it on record that we do not subscribe to the official view of our country and of yours that Hanoi alone blocks the path to negotiations. On the contrary, there is considerable evidence which has been presented to our Government but which has never been answered by them, to show that escalation of the war by the United States has repeatedly destroyed the possibilities for negotiations.

● We assure you that any expression of your horror of this shameful war — a war which is destroying those very values it claims to uphold — ought not to be regarded as anti-American but, rather, as support for that America we love and of which we are proud.

GAR ALPEROVITZ
JAMES BALDWIN
STRINGFELLOW BARR
S. N. BEHRMAN
HARRY BELAFONTE
BETSY BLAIR
KAY BOYLE
MARLON BRANDO
ROBERT McAFEE BROWN
Professor of Religion, Stanford University
ROBERT BRUSTEIN
Dean of Drama School, Yale University
ALEXANDER CALDER
SERGE CHERMAYEFF
Professor of Architecture, Yale University
NOAM CHOMSKY
Professor of Linguistics, M.I.T.
RICHARD A. FALK
Professor of International Studies, Princeton University
JULES FEIFFER

JEROME FRANK
Professor of Psychiatry, Baltimore
ERICH FROMM
NAUM GABO
MAXWELL GEISMAR
JACK GELBER
ALLEN GINSBERG
DICK GREGORY
PEGGY GUGGENHEIM
ELIZABETH HARDWICK
GEORGIA HARKNESS
Professor of Applied Theology, Pacific School of Religion
KYLE HASELDEN
Editor, Christian Century
JOSEPH HELLER
IRVING HOWE
Professor of English, City University, New York
H. STUART HUGHES
Professor of History, Harvard University
STANLEY KAUFFMANN

R. B. KITAJ
ALEXANDER LAING
Professor of Belles Lettres, Dartmouth College, Hanover
OWEN LATTIMORE
Professor of Chinese Studies, Leeds University
RICHMOND LATTIMORE
Professor of Greek, Bryn Mawr College
TOM LEHRER
VIVECA LINDFORS
ROBERT LOWELL
DWIGHT MACDONALD
MILTON MAYER
THOMAS MERTON
Master of Novices Abbey of Gethsemani
ARTHUR MILLER
JESSICA MITFORD
ASHLEY MONTAGU
PHILIP MORRISON
Professor of Physics, M.I.T.
LEWIS MUMFORD

PAUL NELSON
Director of Franco-American Atelier of Architecture, Paris
MIKE NICHOLS
JAY OREAR
Professor of Physics, Cornell University
J. C. PHILLIPS
Professor of Physics, University of Chicago
ANATOL RAPOPORT
Professor of Mathematical Biology, University of Michigan
PHILIP ROTH
MEYER SCHAPIRO
Professor of Fine Arts, New York University
MARK SCHORER
Professor of English, University of California
PETE SEEGER
ROGER SHINN
Professor of Religion, Columbia University
WILLIAM L. SHIRER
WILLIAM SLOANE COFFIN
Senior Chaplain, Yale University
SUSAN SONTAG

BENJAMIN SPOCK
JOSEPH STRICK
WILLIAM STYRON
ALBERT SZENT-GYORGI
Nobel Laureate for Medicine
GEORGE TABORI
HAROLD TAYLOR
Director, League of Industrial Democracy, American National Theatre and Academic National Repertory Theatre
LOUIS UNTERMEYER
RICHARD W. VAN ALSTYNE
Professor of History, Huntington Library, San Marino
SAM WANAMAKER
VICTOR F. WEISSKOPF
Professor of Physics, M.I.T.
WILLIAM APPLEMAN WILLIAMS
Professor of History, Wisconsin University
MARY C. WRIGHT
Professor of Chinese Studies, Yale University
HOWARD ZINN
Former President, Israeli Science Library College

Names of Institutions are given for purposes of identification only.

This advertisement appeared in the *Times* on June 2, 1967. Weisskopf was among seventy prominent Americans who signed the petition. So was the theoretical physicist Philip Morrison, Feynman's friend and colleague at Los Alamos. Feynman declined to sign.

15 May 1967

Miss Margaret Gardiner
35 Downshire Hill
London N. W. 3, England

Dear Miss Gardner:

I would like to sign your letter for I am completely in sympathy with its spirit and its its last paragraph. However, I am, unfortunately not familiar with the evidence that escalation has destroyed the possibilities for negotiation. Certainly escalation has failed in its attempt to "force" Hanoi to negotiate -- but I have not been following things closely enough to know that there would have been any real possibility of negotiation without escalation. It has seemed to me that Nanoi's policy has never included such an alternative -- but that that is no justification for our being there and destroying what we claim to wish to save.

I feel unhappy that I am not sure enough of my position to be able to sign your letter. As next best alternative I am enclosing a small check to help to make sure your advertisement is published.

Sincerely yours,

Richard P. Feynman

RPF:bb
Enclosure

CHAPTER FIVE

Imagine!

It was my father who got me into this business of having to imagine things all the time. He would start out by supposing we were Martians who came here, didn't know anything, and had to find out all about it. Things like "Why does everyone go to sleep every night?"

I don't know why it is that some people find science dull and difficult, and other people find it fun and easy, but there's one characteristic that I get a big kick from, and that is that it takes so much imagination to try to figure out what the world is really like. I find myself trying to imagine all kinds of things, all the time, and just like a runner gets a kick out of sweating, I get a kick out of thinking about these things.

I don't want you to take this stuff too seriously. I think we should just have fun imagining it, and not worry about it—there's no teacher going to ask you questions at the end!

Feynman

For a very long time I thought everybody in physics understood physics like he did—except me. But Richard sort of internalized it. Just as you and I know there's a chair here, he knew the laws of physics and how things worked,

Joan Feynman

sort of internally and with a total, deep understanding. I suppose other people have it, but I have never met it. I've talked to other people about this. They'll know the equations that describe something, like the equations for electricity and magnetism. But they will need to find solutions to the equations to know how anything acts. Richard had developed this intuition, so that he just knew what the solutions were. Like most people are aware of walls and objects and know their properties because they've touched them, he had the same feeling and knowledge about what physics was. He was always aware of all the physical things that were happening all around. I remember him once talking about electromagnetic waves coming through the room. . . . It had a reality for him that it doesn't have for most people—even physicists.

Here are four examples of the kind of pleasure Feynman took in explaining physical things to a nonscientist. They formed part of a series of short films for BBC TV which we called Fun to Imagine. *He just made it up as he went along, talking about heat, light, electricity, and magnetism in a way I don't remember anyone doing at school. The fourth example is especially interesting—a lucid refusal to explain how magnets work.*

Jiggling Atoms

Nothing is really as it seems. We're used to hot and cold, but all that "hot" and "cold" are is the speed that the atoms are jiggling—they jiggle more and it corresponds to "hotter," and "colder" is jiggling less. So if you have a bunch of atoms—a cup of coffee, maybe, sitting on a table—the atoms are jiggling a great deal, they bounce against the cup, and the cup gets shaking. The atoms of the cup shake, and they bounce against the saucer. . . . The "hot" thing spreads its heat into other things by mere contact—the atoms that are jiggling a lot in the hot thing shake the atoms that are jiggling only a little in the cold things, so that the heat, we say, goes into the cold thing. It's easy to understand, and it brings up another thing that's kind of curious: I say that things jiggle, and if you're used to balls bouncing, then you know that they slow up and stop after a while. But with the atoms we have to imagine a perfect elasticity—they never lose any energy, every time they bounce they keep on bouncing, and they never lose anything. They are perpetually moving. When a ball comes down and bounces, it shakes irregularly some of the atoms in the floor, and when it comes up again it has left some of those floor atoms moving, jiggling. As it bounces, it's passing its extra energies, extra motions to little patches on the floor. It loses a little each time, until it settles down, we say, as if all the motion has stopped. But really what's left is that the floor is shaking more than it was before, and the atoms in the ball are shaking more than before—and the floor is a little bit warmer than it was before! Unbelievable, but anyone who has hammered a great deal on something knows that it's true, that if you pound something you can feel the temperature difference—it heats up simply because you're jiggling it. With the ball, it's not much heat—you'd need sensitive instruments to detect it, but it's there.

So, you can either have the idea that heat is some kind of a fluid which flows from a hot thing, and leaks into the cold thing; or you can have a deeper understanding, which is closer to the way it is—that the atoms are jiggling, and their jiggling passes their motion on to the others.

This picture of atoms is a beautiful one, and you can keep looking at all kinds of things in this way. You see a little drop of water, a tiny drop, and the atoms attract each other—they like to be next to each other, they want as many partners as they can get! Now the guys that are on the surface have partners only on one side, and the air on the other, so they're trying to get in to get closer, and you can imagine these teeming people all moving very fast, all trying to have as many partners as possible—the guys at the edge are very unhappy and nervous, and they keep pounding in, trying to get in, and that makes it a tight round ball instead of a flat thing. When you see a water drop sitting on a table, nice and round, you can imagine that it sits like that because everybody's trying to get in, and at the same time, while all this is happening, there are also atoms that are leaving the surface, and the water drop is slowly disappearing—it's evaporation.

If you cooled off the water so the jiggling is less and less, and it jiggles slower and slower, then the atoms get stuck in place—they like to be with their friends, there's a force of attraction and they get packed together, they're not rolling over each other, they're in a nice pattern, like oranges in a crate, all jiggling in place but not having enough motion to get loose from their own place and break up the structure. What I'm describing is a solid—it's ice. It has a structure. If you held some of the atoms at one end in a certain position, all the rest are lined up, sticking out, and it's solid. Whereas, if you heat that, then the atoms begin to get loose and roll all over each other, and that's the liquid. If you heat that still harder, they bounce more, and simply bounce apart from each other (I say atoms, but it's really little groups of atoms—molecules, which come flying and hit each other). Although they have a tendency to stick, they're moving too fast—their hands don't grab, so to speak, as they pass, and they fly apart again, and this is the gas we call steam.

I've got so many things in mind—friction, what's friction? Why does it make heat? You rub your hands together and they get warm. They get warm because they are made out of atoms, lots of piles of atoms, and when you push them against each other you bump the atoms together and it shakes them, and the remaining shaking motion that's left when you take them apart is the warmth you feel.

Atoms like each other to different degrees. Oxygen in the air, for example, would like to be next to carbon, and if you get them near each other, they snap together. If they're not close enough, though, they repel, and they go apart and they don't know that they could snap together. It's just as if you had a ball that could climb a hill and there was a hole it could go into, like a volcano hole, a deep one. It's rolling along, and it starts to climb the steep hill but it doesn't go in the hole—it rolls away again. But if you could make it go fast enough up the slope it would go over the top and fall into the hole. If you have something like wood and oxygen, then there's carbon in the wood from the trees, and the oxygen comes and hits the carbon, but not quite hard enough. It goes away again, and nothing happens. But if you can get it started, by heating it up somehow, some way, then a few oxygen atoms come in fast—over the top, so to speak. They come close enough to the carbon atoms and snap in, and that gives a lot of jiggly motion which might hit some other atoms, making them go faster so they can "climb up" and bump against other carbon atoms, and they jiggle and make others jiggle, and you get a terrible catastrophe—that catastrophe is a fire.

It's just a way of looking at it. This terrible snapping is producing a lot of jiggling, and with all that activity of the atoms there, if I put a pot of coffee over that mass of wood that's doing all this, then it's going to get a lot of jiggling. So that's what the heat of a fire is.

Then of course, you have to wonder about where the wood came from. Well, it came from a tree, and the substance of a tree is carbon. Where did that come from? It comes from the air, it's carbon dioxide from the air. People look at trees and they think they come out of the ground, but really trees come out of the air. The carbon dioxide in the air goes into the tree, and it changes it: it kicks out the oxygen, pushing the oxygen away from the carbon, and leaving the carbon substance with water. (The water comes out of the ground, but how did it get in there? It came out of the air, down from the sky. So in fact most of a tree is out of the air. There's just a little bit from the ground, some minerals, and so forth.) Now as we know, oxygen and carbon stick very, very tight. How is it that the tree is so smart as to manage to take the carbon dioxide, which is the carbon and oxygen so nicely combined, and undo it that easily? "Ah!" you say, "Life has some mysterious force. . . ." But no—the sun is shining, and it's the sunlight that comes down and knocks this oxygen away from the carbon, and now the oxygen is some terrible by-product which the tree spits back into the air, leaving the carbon and water and stuff to make the substance of the tree.

When we take the substance of the tree and stick it in

the fireplace, all the oxygen made by the trees and all the carbon in the wood would much prefer to be close together again. Once you get the heat to get it started, off it goes and makes an awful lot of activity while they're getting back together again, all this nice light and heat—that's the light and heat of the sun that went in. It's sort of "stored sun" that's coming out when you burn the log.

Next question—how is it that the sun is so jiggly, so hot? I have to stop somewhere, and leave you something to imagine!

An Insect of Sufficient Cleverness

If I'm sitting next to a swimming pool, and somebody dives in, and she's not too pretty, then I can think about something else. I like to think about the waves that are formed in the water, and when lots of people have dived into the pool, there's a very great choppiness of all these waves all over the surface.

Now to think that it's possible, maybe, that in those waves there's a clue as to what's happening in the pool: that an insect of sufficient cleverness could sit in the corner of the pool, and just by being disturbed by the waves and by the nature of the irregularities, the insect could figure out who jumped in where, and when, and what's happening all over the pool. It seems incredible, but that's what we're doing when we look at something.

The light is waves, just like in the swimming pool, except in three dimensions, as they're going in all directions. We have an eighth-of-an-inch black hole into which these things go, which is particularly sensitive to the waves that are coming in a particular direction. It's not so sensitive when they're coming in at the wrong angle, what you would call "the corner of your eye." If you want to get more information from "the corner of your eye," you swivel the eyeball about so that the hole will move from place to place.

It's quite wonderful that we can "see," or figure it out so easily. (Light waves are easier; waves in the water are more complicated, and it would be harder for the bug than for us. But it's the same idea.)

Now, someone who's standing at my left can see somebody who's standing at my right—that is, the light can be going this way across, or that way across, or this way up, or that way down; it's a complete network. It's easy to think of the waves as arrows passing each other, but it's not like that because all this is something shaky—it's called the electric field, but we don't have to bother with what it is, it's like the water height in the pool going up and down. Some quantity is shaking about, in a combination of motions so elaborate and complicated the net result is to produce an influence which makes me see you, completely undisturbed by the fact that at the same time there are influences that represent the guy on this side seeing the guy on the other side. So there's this tremendous mess of waves all over in space, which is the light bouncing around the room we're in, going from one thing to another. Because, of course, most of the room doesn't have eighth-inch black holes to catch the light. I mean, the light's there anyway . . . it bounces off this, and it bounces off that— all this is going on, and yet we can sort it out with this instrument, our eye.

Those waves in the water could be very small and quick, or there could be slower swashes, which are longer and shorter. Maybe our animal that's making this study is using only waves between this length and that length? Well, it turns out that the human eye can only use waves between certain lengths, except that the two lengths are hundred thousandths of an inch. So what about the slowest swashes, the waves that go more slowly but have a longer distance from crest to trough? Those represent "heat." We feel them, but our eye doesn't see them focused very well, in fact not at all. The shorter waves are "blue," the longer waves are "red," and when they get even shorter or even longer we call it "ultraviolet" and "infrared." The pit vipers they've got down there in the desert, they have a little thing that they can see the longer waves and pick out mice, which are radiating their heat, body heat, in the longer waves, the infrared, by looking at them with this kind of "eye" that is the "pit" of the pit viper. We can't do that. And then the waves can be longer and longer, but all going through the same space—all these things are going on at the same time, so that in this space there's not only your vision of me, my vision of you, but also information from Moscow Radio that's being broadcast at the present moment, and the singing from somebody in Peru. The radio waves are just the same kind of waves, only much longer waves. Then there's the radar from the airplane which is looking at the ground to figure out where it is, which is coming through this room too, plus X-rays, cosmic rays, all these other things which are exactly the same kind of waves, just shorter and faster, or longer and slower—it's all the same thing. So this big field, this big area of irregular motions, this electric field, this vibration, contains a tremendous information.

It's all really there—that's what gets you! If you don't believe it, then you pick a piece of wire and connect it to a box, and in the wire the electrons are pushed back and forth by this electric field, swashing just at the right speed from certain of the long waves . . . you turn some knobs on the box to get the swashing just right, and you hear Radio Moscow—so you know that it was there! How else did it get there? It was there all the time, but it's only when you turn on the radio that you notice. Everybody knows all this, but you do have to stop and think about it to really get the pleasure about the complexity, the inconceivable nature of nature!

Bigger Is Electricity!

This business of fantasizing about the world and imagining things (which isn't really fantasy, because you're only trying to imagine the way it really is), it can come in useful sometimes. The other day I was at the dentist, and he's getting ready with his electric drill to make holes. I thought, I'd better think of something fast or else this is going to hurt. So I thought about this little motor going around, and what was it that made it turn? What's going on is there's a dam some distance away from here, and water going over the dam turns a great big wheel, a turbine. This wheel is connected by nothing by long "tubes"— thin pieces of copper which go a long distance, and then

divide into two, and then again into two, until little fila-
ments of this copper are spread all over the city. They're
connected to another little gadget that makes a little wheel
turn. When the big wheel turns, all the little wheels of the
city turn; and if the big wheel stops, all the little wheels
stop. If the big wheel starts again, they all start turning
again, and I think that's kind of a marvelous thing of nature. It's extremely curious, and a phenomenon I like to
think about a lot. All it is, is copper and iron. Sometimes
we think, well, it's a man-made generator, very complicated, and that the phenomenon is the result of some
special something that we have made. But it's nature doing
it, and it's just copper and iron. If you took a big long loop
of copper, and had iron at each end, and moved the piece
of iron at one end, the piece of iron will move at the other
end. If you get right down to it, just moving a piece of iron
in a loop of copper, and seeing another piece of iron move,
then you realize what a fantastic mystery nature is. You
don't even need the iron! You could, if you could get
this "pump" primed—started by jiggling copper strands
around fast enough, knotting them and unknotting them—
you can get other copper strands to move at the other end
of a long connection, a long wire. And what is it? It's only
copper and motion.

We are so used to circumstances in which these electrical phenomena are all canceled out, where everything's
sort of neutral, and that's kind of dull. But nature has these
wonderful things, magnetic and electrical forces—you
comb your hair with your comb and get some strange
condition, because if you put the comb over some paper,
it lifts the paper up, or jiggles it about at a distance, far
away. Strange!

Now in fact it turns out that this is the thing that's
deeper inside of everything than the things we're used to.
We are used to forces that only act directly, right? You
push with one finger against another finger, it only acts
directly. But my fingertips are made out of atoms—there's
one bunch of atoms here, pushing against another bunch
of atoms there. There's space between the atoms, and the
pushing is going through the space between.

The only thing that happens with the comb and the paper is that circumstances have arisen which makes it possible to see that the forces go through a bigger distance than just the short distance between the atoms. We have charges, like electrons, which are both the same, they repel each other with a force which is enormous—it's inversely as the square of the distance, just like gravity is inversely as the square of the distance (but gravity is attractive, and this force is repulsive; for two electrons the gravity is so weak compared to the electrical force . . . electricity is so much more enormous than the gravity that I can't express it because I don't know the name of the number—it's a one with thirty-eight or forty-eight zeroes after the one: bigger is electricity! However, there is also for electrical things another kind of charges, positive charges. Protons are positive, they are inside the nucleus of the atom, and they attract electrons—opposite charges attract, and like charges repel. So you have to try to imagine positive and negative things; the like ones repel each other, and the unlike ones attract each other, with a tremendous amount of force.

What would happen if you had a lot of them? All the likes would collect with unlikes—they'd attract each other and there'd be an intimate mixture of pluses and minuses all on top of each other, and very close together. So you get these little "knots" of pluses and minuses (the reason that the knots don't get smaller and smaller is because they are particles, and there's quantum mechanical effects that we won't discuss here, that makes it so you can't get any smaller than a certain size), and so you get these little "lumps" which are balls—they are the atoms. The atoms are positive and negative charge, and they are neutralized—they cancel out their charges as nearly as they can, so there's always exactly the same number of pluses and minuses in any normal material.

When you comb your hair, it rubs just a little bit extra on, just a few extra minuses here, and a few extra pluses somewhere else. But the forces are so big that just those few extra ones can make a force that we can see, and it seems to be at a long range. That we find mysterious! We need an explanation, and we try to find an explanation in terms of ideas like the forces that are inside rubber bands, or steel bars, or twisted things. We would like to have some "puller" or "pusher" because that's what we're used to in our lives—we don't get any push until we're touching. But the fact is that the reason you don't get any push until you're touching is that it's the same force as you see at a distance, only the distance has got so small because the pluses and minuses have canceled out so well that you don't feel anything until it's very very close.

It's kind of fun to imagine this intermittent mixture of highly attractive opposites which are so strong that they cancel out the effects, and it's only sometimes when you have an excess of one kind or another that you see this mysterious electrical force.

So, in fact it's the electrical forces and the magnetic forces that we have to accept as the base reality with which we're going to explain all the other things. It turns out it's hard to understand, and you have to do a lot of imagining of what the real world has in it.

In the example of the generator, for instance, what happens is that the electrons (which are part of an atom) are pushed by the motion of the copper wire. It's wonderful to think that if you push a few electrons here, then they get too close together so they push the others because they repel at a long distance—it's like a wonderful fluid which can go very quickly through the wire, zinnnnnnnng, all over the city at once. And you can use that stuff to make signals—you can push a few electrons here and there by talking on the telephone, and at the other end of the line, a long line of copper, the electrons respond, and someone can hear what you said.

You can imagine the city electricity as being like a water system, if you like. You can visualize the electrons going in pipes all over the place, with a big pump at one end. In fact, look at any book and they'll tell you that the voltage is the pressure, and the amperage is the amount of the flow. That's a very nice analogy, but why is it that there are always two wires on the plug? Why isn't it all right with just one wire, like it would be for water? That puzzled me a great deal, actually, and I had to think awhile as to why. Because the water analogy is pretty good, and I wondered what went wrong. The answer is it's because the electricity—the electrons—can't go easily through the air; they come to the end of one of the wires and they're stuck, because they can't escape. The analogy with water would be that if we had a pipe and opened it, the water would just run out into the room because the water finds it easy to go through the air. To make the analogy better, we've got to fill the room with some kind of stuff that's impervious to water—some kind of plastic, or something, so the water can't escape from the pipe. You'd pump like mad, and the water wouldn't get anywhere. Well, if you want to get this water to do anything, you'd have to have a pipe to take the water in, and another one to take it out back to the pump, and that's why you have two wires.

The discovery of these long-range forces and these rapid motions, actions and so forth, was a tremendous thing for human beings. I think that the discovery of electricity and magnetism, and the working out of the electromechanical effects in the full equations by Maxwell in 1873, is probably the most remarkable thing, the biggest change in history.

(The dentist's drill, by the way, was run by compressed air, but never mind!)

"Why?" Questions

If you get hold of two magnets and turn them one way you can feel an attraction, and the other way, a pushing between them. Now what is it, the feeling between the two magnets?

What do you mean, what's the feeling between the two magnets?

Well, the sensation is that there's something there when you push the two magnets together.

Listen to my question. What do you mean when you say there's a feeling? Of course you feel it. Now what do you want to know?

I want to know what's going on between the two bits of metal.

The two magnets repel each other.

But what does that mean? Why are they doing it, or how are they doing it? I think that's a perfectly reasonable question.

Of course it's a reasonable question. It's an excellent question. But the problem is . . . when you ask why something happens, how does a person answer? For example, Aunt Minnie is in hospital. Why? Because she slipped on the ice and broke her hip. That satisfies people. But it wouldn't satisfy someone who came from another planet. First, you'd have to understand why when you break your hip you have to go to the hospital. How do you get to the hospital when the hip was broken? Well, because her husband, seeing that her hip was broken, called the hospital up and they sent someone to get her—all this is understood by people. So when you explain a "Why" you have to be in some kind of a framework where you allow something to be true, otherwise you are perpetually asking "Why?" Why did the husband call up the hospital? Because the husband is interested in his wife's welfare. Not always—some husbands aren't interested in their wife's welfare, when they're drunk, or angry. And so you begin to get a very interesting understanding of the world and all its complications. If you try to follow anything up you go deeper and deeper in various directions. For example, why did Aunt Minnie slip on the ice? Well, ice is slippery, everybody knows that. No problem. But then you ask why is ice slippery? That's kind of curious. Ice is extremely slippery. How does it work? Now you're involved with something, because there aren't many things as slippery as ice. It's very hard to get—greasy stuff, but sort of wet and slimy. A solid that's so slippery? Because in the case of ice, they say, when you stand on it the pressure momentarily melts the ice a little bit, so you have a sort of instantaneous water surface on which you are slipping. Why on ice and not on other things? Because water expands when it freezes, so the pressure tries to undo the expansion and melts it. But all other substances contract when they freeze, and when you push on them it's fine to remain a solid. Why does water expand when it freezes and other substances don't?

I'm not answering your question, but I'm telling you how difficult a "why" question is. You have to know what it is you're permitted to allow to be understood and known, and what it is you're not. You'll notice in the example, by the way, that the more I ask why, the more interesting it becomes—that's my idea, that the deeper a thing is, the more interesting it is! We could go even further and ask why did she fall down when she slipped? That has to do with gravity, and involves all the planets and so on. . . . Never mind! It goes on and on.

Now when you ask why two magnets repel, there are many different levels. It depends whether you are a student of physics, or an ordinary person who doesn't know anything. If you are somebody who doesn't know anything at all about it, then all I can say is that there is a magnetic force that makes the magnets repel, and that you are feeling that force. And you say, "That's very strange, because I don't feel a force like that in any other circumstances."

Well, there's a very analogous force—the electrical force, which is the same kind of a question, and you say that's also very weird. But you are not at all disturbed by the fact that when you push your hand on the arm of a chair, the chair pushes you back. Yet we've found out by looking at it that as a matter of fact it's the same force, this electrical force (not magnetic exactly in that case, but it's the same electrical repulsions that are involved in keeping your finger out of the chair, because everything's made out of it!). It turns out that the magnetic force and the electrical force with which I wish to explain these things—this repulsion in the first place—is ultimately the deeper thing that we have to start with in order to explain many other things. You know that you can't put your hand through the chair—that's taken for granted. But that you can't put your hand through the chair, when looked at more closely, why, it turns out to involve those same repulsive forces that appear in magnets. The situation you then have to explain is why in magnets it goes over a bigger distance than it ordinarily does. That has to do with the fact that in iron all the electrons are spinning in the same direction and they all get lined up and they magnify the effect of the force until it's large enough at a distance that you can feel it. But it's a force which is present all the time, and very common.

I could go a little further back if I were to be a little more technical, but at an early level I've just got to tell you that one of the things you're going to have to take as an element in the world is the existence of magnetic—or electrical— repulsion and attraction.

I can't explain that attraction to you in terms of anything else that's familiar to you. For example, if we say that the magnets attract each other "as if they were connected by rubber bands," I would be cheating you because they are not connected by rubber bands, and I would be in trouble because you would soon ask me about the nature of the bands; if you were curious enough you'd ask me why rubber bands tend to pull back together again, and I would end up explaining it in terms of the electrical forces which are the very things that I'm trying to use the rubber bands to explain! I would have cheated very badly, you see.[1]

So I'm not going to be able to give you an answer to why magnets attract and repel each other, except to tell you that they do, and to tell you that that's one of the elements in the world. There are different kinds of forces, electrical forces, magnetic forces, and gravitational forces and others, and those are some of the "parts."

If you were a physics student I could go further. I could tell you that the magnetic forces are related to the electrical forces very intimately, that the relationship between the gravity forces and the electrical forces remains unknown, and so on. But I really can't do a good job—any job—of explaining magnetic forces in terms of something else that you are more familiar with because I don't understand it in terms of anything else you are more familiar with.

Sometimes the explanations of physics can look very easy because you'll ask me a question the explanation of which requires only knowing something that you already know. Then I can explain how it works. Other times you want more details and the explanations involve something that's true but you don't happen to know about.

I must, in order to answer a question satisfactorily, al-

Feynman in the 1970s.

ways bring it to a point that either you understand it, or I have to say that this is an element that you'll have to learn in order to be able to understand. Because, you know, people have been studying this for a long time, asking these kinds of questions—that's what science is. And if you ask that four hundred years of such an activity should come down to things you can understand in a few minutes, you're asking a lot. If it's something easy to understand, it was discovered early; if it's something that was discovered later, then you're going to have to learn some of the concepts that have been found out—about the world being made out of atoms, about electrical forces, and so on. It looks complicated because you're not used to it, but it's the way it is, and I can't help it. Okay?

*   *   *

You ask me if an ordinary person could ever get to be able to imagine these things like I imagine them. Of course! I was an ordinary person who studied hard. There are no miracle people. It just happens they get interested in this thing and they learn all this stuff, but they're just people. There's no talent, no special ability to understand quantum mechanics, or to imagine electromagnetic fields, that comes without practice and reading and learning and study. I was not born understanding quantum mechanics—I still don't understand quantum mechanics! I was born not knowing things were made out of atoms, and not being able to visualize, therefore, when I saw the bottle of milk that I was sucking, that it was a dynamic bunch of balls bouncing around. I had to learn that just like anybody else. So if you take an ordinary person who is willing to devote a great deal of time and work and thinking and mathematics, then he's become a scientist!

4 January 1967

Master Ashok Arora
217 Rajpur Road
Eric Villa
Dehra Dun (U. P.) INDIA

Dear Master Arora:

Your discussion of atomic forces shows that you have read entirely too much beyond your understanding. What we are talking about is real and at hand; Nature. Learn by trying to understand simple things in terms of other ideas -- always honestly and directly. What keeps the clouds up, why can't I see stars in the daytime, why do colors appear on oily water, what makes the lines on the surface of water being poured from a pitcher, why does a hanging lamp swing back and forth -- and all the innumerable little things you see all around you. Then when you have learned to explain simpler things, so you have learned what an explanation really is, you can then go on to more subtle questions.

Do not read so much, look about you and think of what you see there.

I have requested the proper office to send you information about Caltech and the availability of scholarships.

Sincerely yours,

Richard P. Feynman

RPF:bb

"Feynman diagrams" on the blackboard.

CHAPTER SIX

Doing the Physics

In general, we look for a new law by the following process. First, we guess. . . . No! Don't laugh—it's really true. Then we compute the consequences of the guess to see if this law that we guessed is right—what it would imply. Then we compare those computation results to nature—or, we say, to experiment, or experience—we compare it directly with observation to see if it works. If it disagrees with experiment, it's wrong. In that simple statement is the key to science. It doesn't make any difference how beautiful the guess is, it doesn't make any difference how smart you are—who made the guess, or what his name is. If it disagrees with experiment, it's wrong. That's all there is to it.

Feynman[1]

It's an aesthetic appeal. It's the feeling that nature is marvelous, that it's enormously beautiful, and the more you know about it, the more beautiful it gets. There's a poem by Whitman about watching the learned astronomer measuring the stars or something, while he goes out and gazes silently up at the sky. Well, when a poet gazes silently up at the sky he sees these little points of light in the blackness; when a scientist gazes silently up at the sky he sees

Joan Feynman

enormous suns, and galaxies, and magnetic fields, and turbulence, and heat and cold, and molecules in space, and endless distances, and great mysteries. So you have the feeling, if you're a scientist, that you see a lot more than the person who doesn't look into what these things really are. It's a wonderful mystery, and a wonderful game to play to try to find out what's going on.

Feynman One way that's kind of a fun analogy in trying to get some idea of what we're doing in trying to understand nature is to imagine that the gods are playing some great game, like chess, say. You don't know the rules of the game, but you're allowed to look at the board, at least from time to time, at a little corner perhaps. From these observations you try to figure out what the rules are of the game, the rules for how the pieces move.

You might discover after a bit, for example, that when there's only one bishop around on the board that the bishop maintains its color. Later on you might discover the rule for the bishop that it moves on the diagonal, which would explain the one that you understood before that it maintained its color. That would be analogous for how we discover one law and then later we find a deeper understanding of it. But things can happen: you've got all the laws, everything's going good, and then all of a sudden some strange phenomenon occurs in some corner so you begin to investigate it. It's "castling," something you didn't expect. (In the fundamental physics, by the way, we are always trying to investigate those things we don't understand; we are not trying to check our conclusions all the time—after we've checked them enough, we're okay. The thing which *doesn't* fit is the most interesting—the part that doesn't go according to what you expected.)

There can be revolutions in physics: after you've noticed that bishops maintain their color, and they go along the diagonals, and so on, for such a long time that everybody knows that's true, then you suddenly discover one day, in some chess game, that the bishop has changed color! Only later do you discover a new possibility—that a bishop was captured and that a pawn went all the way down to the other end to produce a new bishop. That can happen, but you didn't know it. That's very analogous to the ways our laws are—they look positive, they keep on working, and all of a sudden some little gimmick shows they're wrong, and then we have to investigate, and learn the new rule that explains it more deeply.

In the case of the chess game, however, the rules become more complicated as you go along; in the physics, it can get simpler. When you discover new things, new particles and so on, it appears more complicated; but what's kind of wonderful is that as we expand our experience into wilder and wilder regions, every once in a while we have these integrations, when everything's pulled together into a unification which turns out to be simpler than it looked before.

Why does physics have to be done in mathematics? Why is it that you can't explain it in words?

It's a very interesting, mysterious thing that I really don't understand. For certain aspects of physics you can understand why there has to be mathematics. For instance, one of the laws discovered by Faraday, for electrolysis, is how much current, how much electricity, you need to make a plating of, let's say, so-and-so much gold, and there's a formula that the amount of gold is proportional to the current. What it comes down to is electrons, that electricity comes in little lumps called electrons, and it takes one electron to turn one dissolved gold ion into a gold atom, so all you're doing is counting the atoms, and so although you're not looking at the individual atom, the numbers you are using—like the current, and so on—is really the number of electrons per second, and the number of atoms, so since you are obviously counting things and they're gross, very large numbers, it's perfectly understandable that the relationship you'll discover will be a mathematical one. Because you're trying to count objects in large numbers which will tell how much gold comes for how much electricity, it'll look at first like a mathematical thing: one electron makes one ion turn to an atom. That is qualitatively simple, and it becomes a quantitative formula. But all the laws of physics are not like that, at least as far as we understand them today. The first one was the law of gravitation, which said that the force of attraction is inversely as the square of the distance between two particles, between two objects. But how does it do that? Why does it measure the square of the distance and divide one over . . . you know—if you double the distance, the force is a fourth as much, and there isn't any simple mechanism known for why that mathematical relation comes. So from the earliest discoveries of the character of the laws of physics, we find that these mathematical relationships help us to understand the laws, describe the laws very well, and it's simply gotten more and more that way, as we've pursued it—the equations are more and more mathematical, and we don't really understand why it is that nature happens to come out that way.

Is it because mathematics somehow dictates the way the questions are asked, and that maybe nature isn't like that at all? That what you find out is determined by the language you are using?

Many people have proposed various things like that, but in the end we have to predict what happens, and therefore the thing that we're doing is real in the sense that we are ultimately figuring out patterns by which we can predict what happens. Now the way nature actually works to make these things happen didn't have to be mathematical—why is it that the mathematical reasoning is what makes it work that way? There's another possible explanation, which is that as we found out more about physics, we developed the mathematics as we went along to help us, and that the evolution of mathematics was partially driven by the need to understand the physical world, and that the two things developed together. That's also possible.

But if you are interested in the ultimate character of the physical world, or the real, the complete world, then at the present time our only way to understand that is through a mathematical type of reasoning. I don't think a person can fully appreciate, or in fact appreciate much of these particular aspects of the world, the great depth and character of the universality of the laws, the relationship of things, without an understanding of mathematics. It's just that I don't know any other way to do it; we don't know any other way to describe it accurately, how to see the interrelationships without it. So I don't think a person who hasn't developed some mathematical sense is capable of fully appreciating this aspect of the world. Don't misunderstand me—there are many, many aspects of the world that mathematics is unnecessary for, such as love, which are very delightful and wonderful to appreciate and to feel awed and mysterious about, and I don't mean to say that the only thing in the world is physics, but we're talking about physics, and if that's what you're talking about then to not know mathematics is a severe limitation in understanding the world.

Freeman Dyson

Feynman and I had quite different ideas about mathematics. To me, mathematics was the natural language. I grew up as a mathematician, and moved into physics only afterwards. So to me, it was natural to think in terms of equations; for Feynman, that wasn't true. He was a natural physicist, and he thought in terms of concrete objects. The mathematics was an encumbrance, something you had to stick on afterwards, more or less. So we never came eye to eye on this. It was a matter of taste, and to the end of his life, he never really enjoyed mathematics. For him it was a necessary evil, whereas for me, the beauty is all in the mathematics.

Feynman used to say that if you need any mathematics, you can easily invent it for yourself. So when he needed it, he would invent something which had been discovered by the mathematicians a hundred years earlier. I always had a much more historical view of science. For him history really didn't exist. He came to everything with fresh eyes.

Feynman

When I'm actually doing my own things, and I'm working in the high, or "deep," esoteric stuff, I don't think I can

147

describe very well what it's like. First of all, it's like asking a centipede which leg comes after which—it happens quickly, and I'm not exactly sure what flashes and things go on in the head. I do know it's a crazy mixture of partially solved equations and some kind of visual picture of what the equation is saying is happening, but not as well separated as the words I'm using. It's kind of a nutty thing—very hard to describe, and I don't know if it does any good to describe it. There's something that struck me as very curious: I suspect that what goes on in every man's head may be very, very different—the actual imagery or semi-imagery—so that when we're talking to each other at these high and complicated levels of physics or whatever, we think we're speaking well and that we're communicating, but what we're really doing is having some kind of big "translation" scheme going on, for translating what this or that fellow says into our own images, which might be entirely different. The reason why somebody has great difficulty understanding a point which you see as obvious, and vice versa, may be because it's a little hard to translate what you've just said into his particular framework, and so on—but now I'm talking like a psychologist, and you *know* I know nothing about this!

Sometimes I wonder why it's possible to visualize or imagine reality at all. (That sounds like a very profound philosophical question, like "Why is it possible to think?" But that's not what I really mean.) It's easy to imagine, say, the earth as a ball with people and things all stuck on it, because we've all seen balls and can imagine one going around the sun—it's just a proportional thing, and in the same way I can imagine atoms in a cup of coffee, at least for elementary purposes, as little jiggling balls. But when I am worrying about the specific frequencies of light that are emitted in lasers or some other complicated circumstance, then I have to use a set of pictures which are not really very good at all—they're not good images. But what are "good images"? Probably something you're familiar with. But suppose that little things behave very differently than anything that was big, anything that you're familiar with? Animals evolved brains designed for ordinary cir-

cumstances, but if the gut particles in the deep inner workings of things go by some other rules, and were completely
different from anything on a large scale, there would be
some kind of difficulty, and that difficulty we are in—
the behavior of things on a small scale is so fantastic, so
wonderfully and marvelously different than anything on a
large scale! You can say, "Electrons behave like waves"—
no, they don't, exactly; "they act like particles"—no, they
don't, exactly; "they act like a kind of fog around the
nucleus"—no, they don't, exactly. Well, if you would like
to get a clear, sharp picture of an atom, so that you can
tell correctly how it's going to behave—have a good image
of reality, in other words—I don't know how to do it,
because that image has to be mathematical. Strange! I don't
understand how it is that we can write mathematical expressions and calculate what the thing is going to do without actually being able to picture it. It would be something
like having a computer where you put some numbers in,
and the computer can do the arithmetic to figure out what
time a car will arrive at different destinations but it cannot
picture the car.

For certain approximations, it's okay. With the atom
pictures, for example, the idea of a fog around the nucleus,
which repels you when you squeeze it, is good for understanding the stiffness of materials; the idea of a wave is
good for other phenomena. The picture of atoms, for instance, as little balls is good enough to give a nice picture
of temperature. But if you ask more, and you get down to
questions like "How is it that if you cool helium down,
even to absolute zero where there's not supposed to be
any motion, you find a fluid with no viscosity, no resistance—it flows perfectly, and it isn't frozen solid?" Well,
if you want to get a picture of atoms that has all that in it,
I just can't do it. But I can explain why the helium behaves
as it does by taking the equations and showing the consequences of them is that the helium will behave as it is
observed to behave, so we know we have the theory
right—we just don't have the pictures that will go with
the theory.

I wonder whether you could get to know things better

than we do today, and as the generations develop, will they invent tricky ways of looking at things—be so well trained that they won't have our troubles with the atom-picturing? There is still a school of thought that cannot believe that the atomic behavior is so different than large-scale behavior. I think that's a deep prejudice, a prejudice from being so used to large-scale behavior. They are waiting for the day that we discover, underneath the quantum mechanics, some mundane, ordinary balls hitting each other. I think they're going to be defeated. I think nature's imagination is so much greater than man's that she's never going to be defeated!

David Goodstein   In most cases, when Feynman solved a problem, it was the result of very intense work over a short period of time. The way I work, and the way every scientist I know works, there are very intense periods of time when you forget to eat, you forget to sleep, you forget your wife, and your students, and everything else, and you get consumed by a problem until you solve it—or else decide that you can't solve it, and give up. Most of the rest of the time is quite routine, and your life is like everybody else's. I think Feynman was much the same way.

He had long, long fallow periods. I remember going on a trip with him one time—this is an interesting story. We were at the University of Chicago, where he had been invited to give a talk. I came down to join him for breakfast one morning in the faculty club there, and he was talking to somebody. I didn't know who this person was, and Feynman sort of mumbled the introductions, so I didn't catch the name. I just listened, and ate my eggs, and after a while it dawned on me that this was Jim Watson, of Watson and Crick. Watson had a manuscript with him, which one day would be *The Double Helix*. But this was a year before it was published, and it was still in manuscript form. He asked Feynman to read it—he was hoping to get a testimonial for the dust jacket. Feynman agreed.

That night there was a party for Feynman, and he wasn't there, which was embarrassing. I went looking for him, and I found him in our room reading Watson's book. I made him come to the party for a while, but he left early, and when I arrived back at the room, very late, he said, "You've got to read this book."

I said, "Great! I'll look forward to it."

And he said, "No, I mean now."

So I read that book, from one o'clock to five o'clock in the morning, with Feynman sitting across the room watching me, waiting for me to finish so we could discuss it. At a certain point, I said, "Watson must have been either very lucky or very smart, because he never knew anything that anybody else was doing, and he still made the crucial discovery."

Feynman had been doodling on a pad of paper, and he had written the one word DISREGARD, which he had then illuminated, decorated. He jumped up and said, "That's what I learned from reading it. I used to know it, and I forgot it—I have to disregard everybody else, and then I can do my own work."

As soon as it was a respectable hour in California he called his wife, and he said, "I think I'm going to be able to work again!"

Gweneth Feynman

Richard doesn't really discuss his work with me, but he's superb at explaining a complicated thing simply. I feel I really understand it—though I could never tell a third person what I think I understand.

When Richard works, when he gets a new idea, he's way off. He's just so excited. He paces around, he talks aloud too. He worries day and night, and then suddenly— "Oh, no! It doesn't work!" And if it really and truly doesn't work, that's it. On the rare occasions when something works—it doesn't happen very often—then it's really something!

Feynman

I don't understand my motives. I certainly get pleasure from finding out about nature. It's also possible that there's a tendency to show off—you know other people can't solve this problem, and you can prove that you can. So you're trying to show that you're smarter than the other guy. Maybe that's what's involved, okay? I don't know. I get a big kick out of it.

I know that if you give me puzzles, I love to solve them. They have to be puzzles of a certain kind, in which mathematical or rational analysis is involved. Not puzzles that require knowing the name of who won the cricket match in 1953, or something—they're artificial, and they have no depth because they depend on accidents and circumstances of human life. I mean things like finding a formula for the sum of the third powers of the integers from one to n, or whatever.

In the physics, one of the things I have to do in trying to surmount one of these apparently insurmountable problems that all the other guys are also working on (and to me they all seem smarter than I am—they know the kind of mathematical things that I don't know about, groups and so on), I have to think that I have some sort of inside track, that I'm thinking of a way that they're not thinking of. Because if I'm going to solve it in the same way they think about the problem, I'm not going to solve it because they've thought of that already, and they would have told us what the answer is. So I can't do it by doing it the same way as everybody else. I fool myself perhaps into thinking that I have an inside track, that I have the nerve to do the thing in two dimensions first, or that I have some special mathematical trick that I'm going to use which they don't have, or some kind of a talent, a way that I'm going to do it without group theory or whatever. So I have to motivate myself by inventing this illusion. I appreciate the possibility that it is indeed an illusion, but I don't bother myself about that—I work myself up into thinking I'm on that inside track.

For example, in the case of the quantum electrodynamics where I had the idea that electrons don't act on themselves, and that there's a direct interaction at a distance, ultimately having those ideas made me think I had a chance to solve the problem when I was a young man, when all those big experts had been working so hard. I told myself, "They're on the wrong track; I've got the track!" Now in the end, I had to give up those ideas and go over to their ideas of retarded action and so on—my original idea of electrons not acting on themselves disappeared, but because I had been working so hard I found something. So, as long as I can drive myself one way or the other, it's okay. Even if it's an illusion, it still makes me go, and this is the kind of thing that keeps me going through the depths.

It's like the African savages who are going into battle—first they have to gather around and beat drums and jump up and down to build up their energy to fight. I feel the same way, building up my energy by talking to myself and telling myself, "They are trying to do it this way, I'm going to do it that way" and then I get excited and I can go back to work again.

It's true that you can't talk in great detail about what's going on to nonphysicists, but it's not always lonely. There are sympathetic people who will sit there and nod even though they don't know what you are talking about, but they are good actors and let you keep going. That helps. Of course, in your own field there are all the people who understand the problem you are trying to solve, and if you get anywhere you can discuss your success—I can't resist the moment I get anywhere, running to school and telling colleagues about this thing. They may squelch it, or they may be delighted: "Hey! That looks like you're getting somewhere!" And then they're with me, and I'm not alone.

Richard Sherman

I can recall one episode that I found particularly awesome. Midway through my first year I was doing research on superconductivity, and one afternoon I went into his office to discuss the results of the previous week or two. I started to write these equations on the blackboard, and he began to analyze them very rapidly. We were interrupted by a phone call. I couldn't hear the person on the other end of the line, but Feynman immediately switched from superconductivity into some problem in high-energy-particle physics, into the middle of an incredible complicated calculation that was being performed by somebody else, somewhere else. He talked with that person for maybe five or ten minutes on the phone. When he was through, he hung up and continued the discussion on my particular calculations, at exactly the point he had left off.

The phone rang again. This time it was somebody in theoretical solid-state physics, completely unrelated to anything we had been speaking about. But there he was, telling them, "No, no, that's not the way to do it. . . . You need to do it this way. . . . This is the reason you're stuck right now. . . . If you follow this technique . . . if you this, and then you do that . . ."

This sort of thing went on over about three hours— different sorts of technical telephone calls, each time in a completely different field, and involving different types of calculation.

There are many people who can do calculations in a variety of fields, but normally they stop what they are thinking about, pick up somebody else's calculation, and examine that calculation for thirty minutes or an hour or so. So this absolutely lightning speed made a tremendous impression on me. It was staggering. I have never seen that kind of thing again.

Al Hibbs At a typical Feynman lecture, he would be there before most of the class showed up, and he would be drumming on the lecture table, a long, black counter in the front, smiling, always happy, always charming, delighted with himself, with his class, and with something that clearly he enjoyed—the process of lecturing. He used the blackboard pretty effectively and thoroughly, throwing in little quips every now and then. When he wrote equations, instead of normally, he started at the back end of an expression and wrote it from right to left. That was the way he thought about building up the various terms in the expression which had to be included or to lead to the answer to the problem: you had to take account of this force and that factor . . . each term in the expression had to do with some

Al Hibbs: "His lectures were like a Chinese meal. . . ."

physical parameter, and he stacked them up from the end towards the beginning.

Occasionally when he was writing on the board he would flip up his left hand, glance at it, and then go back at the board. I remember once he turned round and said, "You may notice every now and then I hold up my left hand. The reason is, I keep forgetting which is right and which is left, but I know my left hand has two small brown spots on the back of it."

One on one with me as his student, he was very good. In advanced lecture courses he was inspiring. But there was a saying: that a lecture from Feynman was like a Chinese meal—an hour later you wondered what you had learned. While he was talking—and this was a common experience which I had, and so did many of my fellow students at the time—everything seemed clear. He carried you along with his stream of thought from one idea to the other, to the conclusion. But an hour later, when you tried in your mind to reconstruct this stream of thought, you

couldn't. You had lost some of the key elements which seemed so obvious when he was talking.

Feynman I don't know how to teach. A large class—twenty, thirty students, and everybody comes with different interests. Should we teach science by describing the history of how things are discovered? For some students, that's very interesting, for others not at all—they want to know what the facts are, and never mind how they were discovered. Or should we teach science by letting them do the experiments? Well, they don't get far because the experiments a kid can do in school is only a very tiny fraction of all the facts, and he isn't going to learn much, however delightful the experiments. Another kid is very interested in the applications of science to social problems; he really wants to help people, and the science for him is a means to do that—maybe he'll become an engineer or something. Another one is delighted by the magic and mystery of mathematics, and the methods of analyzing things—he likes the abstract questions, the deeper, more fundamental things, and he's not at all interested in applications to human beings.

My theory is that the best way to teach is to have no philosophy, to be chaotic and confuse it in the sense that you use every possible way of doing it. That's the only way I can see, to catch this guy or that guy on different hooks as you go along, so that during the time when the fellow who's interested in history is being bored by the abstract mathematics, the fellow who likes the abstractions is being bored another time by the history—if you can do it so that you don't bore them all, all the time, perhaps you're better off. I don't know how to answer this question of different kinds of minds with different kinds of interests—what hooks them on? What makes them interested? How you direct them? One way is by a kind of force—"You have to take this course; you have to pass that examination." It's a very effective way, and many people go through schools that way, so it may be good. I'm sorry—after many, many years of trying all different kinds of methods, I really don't know how to do it.

Carl Feynman

My father certainly influenced me tremendously in the direction of science, just because I was raised in a sort of scientific atmosphere. My father would notice things, and say, "Look at that. That's diffraction, and it's caused by this effect and that effect." I never had the feeling that it was a deliberate attempt to influence me in that direction, it was just that it was fascinating and wonderful, he loved talking about it, and it was obviously a great thing.

When I was a kid, he was doing things just because they were sort of interesting little science demonstrations, like you get in school, except less formal. He would say, "Come on, Carl, today we're going to do some chromatography." We'd go into the backyard, pick some grass, boil it in

alcohol, dribble some of it down toilet paper, and watch it separate into different-colored stripes. And that's what I thought parents did.

I think he wanted me to go into science, or something like it. I never felt any pressure, that I would be letting him down if I didn't do that.

He was rather dismayed when I went into philosophy as an undergraduate. But I soon saw the error of my ways, and I ended up in computer science, which is really more engineering. He was happy about that.[2]

Feynman I'm the son of my father, and I got a kick when I was a boy from my father telling me things, so I tried to tell my son things that were interesting about the world. When he was very small, when he went to bed, I used to tell him stories, and I'd make up a story, say, about little people that were so high and lived in the ventilator. They went on picnics and they'd go through these woods which had great big long tall things like trees, but without leaves or branches—only a stalk, and they had to walk between them. And Carl would gradually catch on that this was the nap of the rug, the blue rug. He loved this game, because I would describe all these things from an odd point of view. There were all kinds of wonderful things—they even went into a moist cave, where the wind kept going in and out; it would go in cool and come out warm . . . it was inside the dog's nose that they went. Of course, I could tell him all about physiology in this way, and so on. I enjoyed it because I was telling him stuff that I liked, and he had fun guessing what it was.

Then I have a daughter, and I tried the same thing. Well, my daughter's personality was different—she didn't want to hear these stories; she wanted the story that was in the book repeated again and again. She wanted me to read to her, and not to make up stories. It's a different personality. So if I were to say, "A very good method for teaching children about science is to make up stories about the little people . . ." Well, it doesn't work at all on my daughter; but it happened to work on my son, okay?

Carl Feynman age twelve: "That's what I thought parents did. . . ."

Carl and his father, August 1983.

159

Michelle Feynman

Michelle Feynman in 1992, age twenty-four.

I never really knew when I was a child that some people could leave their jobs at the office, and come home. You could never separate my father from physics—the two were always together. He doodled all the time—on the edges of newspapers, on Kleenex boxes in the car. I didn't realize that he was working on something, and that all the bits of paper could have anything to do with it. If they were so important, why didn't he ever keep them, or catalogue them in some way? It seemed very strange, you know, almost a stream-of-consciousness kind of physics, pouring out of him. He had to write it down, and then he could go on to something else. So yes, every Kleenex box, every spare scrap of paper, had some sort of physics on it.

I don't know anything about physics, and I'm not interested at all in physics. He knew that, and he thought it was fine. He didn't expect me to. Had I expressed a desire to learn a great deal about physics, he would have supported me wholeheartedly, there's no question about it. But I wasn't. I don't think many parents would let it go like that.

I don't think he had any expectations for us at all—he left it completely open. Once I tried to shock him by saying I wanted to be a politician, sort of his most hated kind of person, and he said, "Oh, great! I'm sure you'll do fine!"

"Don't take anything at face value"—I don't know if he ever said exactly those words, but that's what I got from him. He wanted us to be happy, and that sounded like the easiest, but it might be the hardest. "Go to college, be educated, learn all you can," but no "I want you to follow in my footsteps." Nothing like that. I think he realized they were awfully large footsteps.

Marcus Chown[3]

In 1981, the BBC screened a profile of Feynman in its *Horizon* series, and my mother watched from beginning to end. Now, there's nothing extraordinary about that, except that my mother had never shown interest in any science program, or in anything to do with science for that matter. (I have never been able to explain to her satisfaction why people in Australia don't fall off into space.) Later, when

Her father, photographed by Michelle.

I was at Caltech, I had an idea. I would go to Feynman, explain that my mother had watched him on TV, and ask him whether he would help me out by dropping her a note. If he did, I reasoned naively, then perhaps the next time I tried to explain to my mother why the sky is blue, she might be more receptive.

Happy Birthday Mrs Chown!

Tell your son to stop trying to fill your head with science — for to fill your heart with love is enough!

Richard P. Feynman

(the man you watched on BBC "horizon")

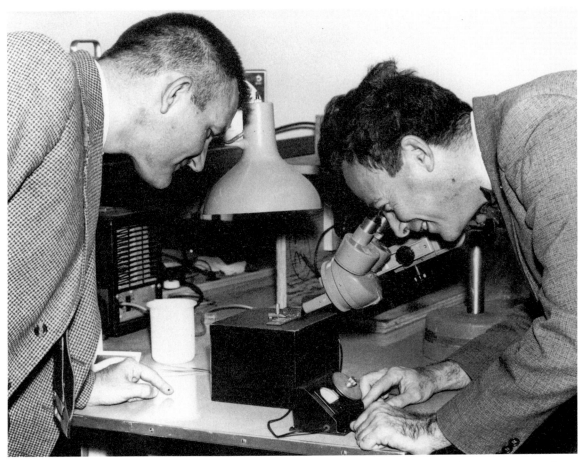

November 1960. Feynman examines McLellan's micromotor—one millionth of a horsepower, six thousandths of an inch in diameter. "Now don't start writing small. . . ."

CHAPTER SEVEN

Crazy Ideas: Tiny Writing and Huge Computers

I'm going to talk about how small can you make machinery, okay? That's the subject. I've heard people around the place muttering, "Tiny machines? What's he talking about—tiny machines!" And I say to them, "You know: *very—small—machines.*"

But first, before I start on machines, I'd like to talk about very small writing. How small can we make writing, or numbers? What's the smallest you can possibly make them? I don't mean if you're very delicate with your fingers how small you can make them; I mean with special machinery, and so on—what is the ultimate limit?

You say, "Any size, any size." But you can't make it smaller than atoms. You can't write on an atom. You can't mark the atom, because marks, you see, are just more atoms spread over other atoms—black atoms on top of white ones, or whatever.

There's a laboratory at Cornell that's doing this particular research—the micro-something-or-other laboratory. Now, I have a friend, Tom Van Sant, who's an artist. He loves art and science, and commerce, and everything else too. He's a real man of the present era, and not one of those artists who sneer at science and don't understand the world they are in!

Feynman[1]

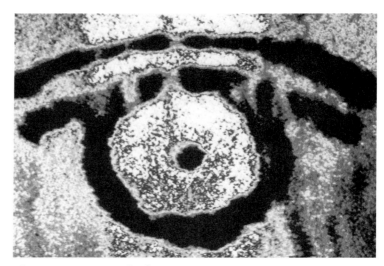

The eye on a grain of salt.

Tom made a drawing which is the smallest drawing ever made by anybody in the world. It's supposed to be an eye, on a salt crystal, and a beam was moved around to make holes—to dig away the salt, so as to make the image. Then the image is looked at through an electron microscope.

Compared to a normal human eye, this drawing is a hundred thousand times reduced! It's very beautiful. There is a slight flaw in the drawing that was caused by a truck that went by, shaking the apparatus and the beam a little—even the tiniest vibration at this scale is a big movement.

To get some idea of the scale, the distance across this picture of the eye is approximately a hundred atoms, which is as small as anything has been made yet. Tom wanted it a hundred thousand times smaller than a human eye, for a reason that I'll explain in a moment. Well, the people at the lab at Cornell were disappointed, because they said they could make the dot about half as big, and the lines about half as thick, so that the whole drawing would be about half the size. But Tom insisted. You see, he had another drawing of an eye, which I would like to show you.

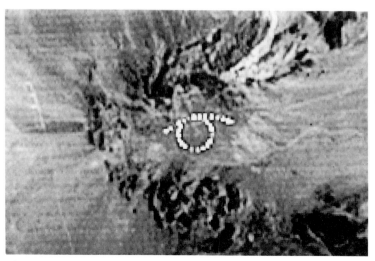

The eye in the desert.

It's the largest picture in the world that has ever been drawn—one hundred thousand times larger than a normal human eye, and it's out there in the desert, northeast of the city of Los Angeles.

Now I'd like to tell you a little bit about how the picture was made. It is, of course, a picture from the Landsat satellite. This drawing's so big you can't just look at it—you've got to go up six hundred miles into the sky and look down with the Landsat satellite to see it!

What happens with the Landsat satellite is this. It has a beam, and it looks down as it sails over the ground. The beam goes back and forth, and it's computed—the light that comes at any moment into the cell, moment after moment, it's all computed. And an image, a spot, a little square, is made, for that area, at that moment. Each little square is called a pixel. They are too small to see in a normal picture, but if you magnify it, they are big enough to see. Each pixel covers about an acre of the earth below.

Now how did Tom Van Sant have the energy to cover all these acres with white, over a distance of two and a half kilometers, which is what this drawing, this picture, corresponds to?

This is the way he did it. He set up twenty-four mirrors

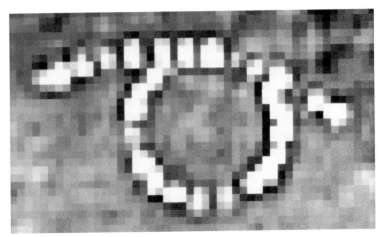

Landsat image with burned-out pixels.

in the desert. The Landsat people gave Tom the timings for the satellite, and he exactly calculated the angle for each mirror, so that at the precise moment that the Landsat beam went to look at his particular acre, the angle was just right such that the sun was reflected straight up into the camera, and saturated it, so that a whole one-acre pixel would come out white.

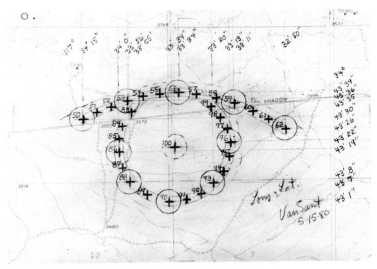

Van Sant's mirror layout.

One pixel didn't come out quite right—there's an error there. After Tom saw the picture, he went back to discover what had happened. Well, a jackrabbit had run over one of the mirrors and changed the angle, so it didn't work!

So, the same artist who made the smallest drawing ever has also made the largest.

The tiny eye is one hundred thousand times smaller than a normal eye; the big eye is one hundred thousand times larger than a normal eye. Let's go up another scale, the same amount again, another hundred thousand, and then try to draw an eye: where would we have to draw it? Well, it turns out that it's there—it's a beautiful eye in the heavens, namely Saturn with her rings!

Feynman was fascinated by scaling things up and down. In December 1959 he gave a visionary talk at the American Physical Society titled "There's Plenty of Room at the Bottom." He speculated on the design and manufacture of very small components and machinery, effectively inventing the field of research into what is now called nanotechnology. (Greek nanos = dwarf; a nanometer is one billionth of a meter.)

Feynman[2]

I would like to describe a field in which little has been done, but in which an enormous amount can be done in principle. This field is not quite the same as the others in that it will not tell us much of fundamental physics (in the sense of "What are the strange particles?"), but it is more like solid-state physics in the sense that it might tell us much of great interest about the strange phenomena that occur in complex situations. Furthermore, a point that is most important is that it would have an enormous number of technical applications.

What I want to talk about is the problem of manipulating and controlling things on a small scale.

As soon as I mention this, people tell me about miniaturization, and how far it has progressed today. They tell me about electric motors that are the size of the nail on your small finger. And there is a device on the market, they tell me, by which you can write the Lord's Prayer on the head of a pin. But that's nothing; that's the most primitive, halting step in the direction I intend to discuss. It is a staggeringly small world that is below. In the year 2000, when they look back at this age, they will wonder why it was not until the year 1960 that anybody began seriously to move in this direction.

Why cannot we write the entire twenty-four volumes of the *Encyclopaedia Britannica* on the head of a pin?

Let's see what would be involved. The head of a pin is a sixteenth of an inch across. If you magnify it by twenty-five thousand diameters, the area of the head of the pin is then equal to the area of all the pages of the *Encyclopaedia Britannica*. Therefore, all that is necessary is to reduce in size all the writing in the encyclopedia by twenty-five thousand times. Is that possible? The resolving power of the eye is about 1/120th of an inch—that is roughly the diameter of one of the little dots on the fine halftone reproductions in the encyclopedia. This, when you demagnify it by twenty-five thousand times, is still eighty angstroms in diameter—thirty-two atoms across, in an ordinary metal. In other words, one of those dots still would contain in its area one thousand atoms. So, each dot can easily be adjusted in size as required by the photoengraving, and there is no question that there is enough room on the head of a pin to put all of the *Encyclopaedia Britannica*.

Furthermore, it can be read if it is so written. Let's imagine that it is written in raised letters of metal; that is, where the black is in the encyclopedia, we have raised letters of metal that are actually one twenty-five-thou-sandth of their ordinary size. How would we read it?

If we had something written in such a way, we could read it using techniques in common use today. (They will undoubtedly find a better way when we do actually have it written, but to make my point conservatively I shall just take techniques we know today.) We would press the metal into a plastic material and make a mold of it, then peel the plastic off very carefully, evaporate silica into the plastic to get a very thin film, then shadow it by evaporating gold at an angle against the silica so that all the little letters will appear clearly, dissolve the plastic away, and then look through it with an electron microscope!

There is no question that if the thing were reduced by twenty-five-thousand times in the form of raised letters on the pin, it would be easy for us to read it today. Furthermore, there is no question that we would find it easy to make copies of the master: we would just need to press the same metal plate again into plastic and we would have another copy.

The next question is: how do we write it? We have no standard technique to do this now. But let me argue that it is not as difficult as it first appears to be. We can reverse the lenses of the electron microscope in order to demagnify as well as to magnify. A source of ions, sent through the microscope lenses in reverse, could be focused to a very small spot. We could write with that spot like we write in a TV cathode ray oscilloscope, by going across in lines, and having an adjustment which determines the amount of material which is going to be deposited as we scan in lines.

A simpler way might be this (though I am not sure it would work). We take light and, through an optical microscope running backwards, we focus it onto a very small photoelectric screen. Then electrons come away from the screen where the light is shining. These electrons are focused down in size by the electron microscope lenses to impinge directly upon the surface of the metal. Will such a beam etch away the metal if it is run long enough? I don't know. If it doesn't work for a metal surface, it must be possible to find some surface with which to coat the original pin so that, where the electrons bombard, a change is made which we could recognize later.

That's the *Encyclopaedia Britannica* on the head of a pin, but let's consider all the books in the world. The Library of Congress has approximately nine million volumes; the British Museum Library has five million volumes; there are also five million volumes in the National Library in France. Undoubtedly there are duplications, so let us say that there are some twenty-four million volumes of interest in the world.

What would happen if I print all this down at the scale we have been discussing? How much space would it take? It would take, of course, the area of about a million pinheads, because, instead of there being just the twenty-four volumes of the encyclopedia, there are twenty-four million volumes. The million pinheads can be put in a square of a thousand pins on a side, or in an area of about three square yards. That is to say, the silica replica with the paper-thin backing of plastic, with which we have made the copies, with all this information, is on an area of approximately the size of thirty-five pages of the encyclopedia. All of the information which mankind has ever recorded in books can be carried around in a pamphlet in your hand—and not written in code, but as a simple reproduction of the original pictures, engravings, and everything else on a small scale without loss of resolution.

What would our librarian at Caltech say, as she runs all over from one building to another, if I tell her that, ten years from now, all of the information that she is struggling to keep track of—120,000 volumes, stacked from the floor to the ceiling, drawers full of cards, storage rooms full of the older books—can be kept on just one library card! When the University of Brazil, for example, finds that their library is burned, we can send them a copy of every book in our library by striking off a copy from the master plate in a few hours and mailing it in an envelope no bigger or heavier than any other ordinary airmail letter.

Now the name of this talk is "There's Plenty of Room at the Bottom"—not just "There's Room at the Bottom." What I have demonstrated is that there is room—that you can decrease the size of things in a practical way. I now want to show that there is *plenty* of room. I will not now discuss how we are going to do it, but only what is possible according to the laws of physics. I am not inventing antigravity, which is possible someday only if the laws are not what we think. I am telling you what could be done if the laws *are* what we think; we are not doing it simply because we haven't yet gotten around to it.

Suppose that, instead of trying to reproduce the pictures and all the information directly in its present form, we write only the information content in a code of dots and dashes, or something like that, to represent the various letters. Each letter represents six or seven "bits" of information; that is, you need only about six or seven dots or dashes for each letter. Now, instead of writing everything, as I did before, on the surface of the head of a pin, I am going to use the interior of the material as well.

Let us represent a dot by a small spot of one metal, the next dash by an adjacent spot of another metal, and so on. Suppose, to be conservative, that a bit of information is going to require a little cube of atoms $5 \times 5 \times 5$—that is 125 atoms. Perhaps we need a hundred and some odd atoms to make sure that the information is not lost through diffusion, or through some other process.

I have estimated how many letters there are in the encyclopedia, and I have assumed that each of my twenty-four million books is as big as an encyclopedia volume, and I have calculated, then, how many bits of information there are (10^{15}). For each bit I allow one hundred atoms. And it turns out that all of the information that man has carefully accumulated in all the books in the world can be written in this form in a cube of material one two-hundredth of an inch wide—which is the barest piece of dust that can be made out by the human eye. So there is plenty of room at the bottom! Don't tell me about microfilm!

There may even be an economic point to this business of making things very small. Let me remind you of some of the problems of computing machines. In computers we have to store an enormous amount of information. The kind of writing that I was mentioning before, in which I had everything down as a distribution of metal, is permanent. Much more interesting to a computer is a way of writing, erasing, and writing something else. (This is usually because we don't want to waste the material on which we have just written. Yet if we could write it in a very small space, it wouldn't make much difference: it could just be thrown away after it was read. It doesn't cost much for the material.)

I don't know how to do this on a small scale in a practical way, but I do know that computing machines are very large; they fill rooms. Why can't we make them very small, make them of little wires, little elements—and by little, I mean little. For instance, the wires should be ten or one hundred atoms in diameter, and the circuits should be a few thousand angstroms across. Everybody who has analyzed the logical theory of computers has come to the conclusion that the possibilities of computers are very interesting—if they could be made to be more complicated by several orders of magnitude. If they had millions of times as many elements, they could make judgments. They would have time to calculate what is the best way to make the calculation that they are about to make. They could select the method of analysis which, from their experience, is better than the one that we would give to them. And, in many other ways, they would have new qualitative features.

If I look at your face I immediately recognize that I have seen it before. (Actually, my friends will say that I have chosen an unfortunate example here for the subject of this illustration.) At least I recognize that it is a man and not an apple. Yet there is no machine which, with that speed, can take a picture of a face and say even that it is a man; and much less that it is the same man that you showed it before—unless it is exactly the same picture. If the face is changed; if I am closer to the face; if I am further from the face; if the light changes—I recognize it anyway. Now, this little computer I carry in my head is easily able to do that. The computers that we build are not able to do that. The number of elements in this bone box of mine are enormously greater than the number of elements in our "wonderful" computers. But our mechanical computers are too big; the elements in *this* box are microscopic. I want to make some that are submicroscopic. . . .

I would like to discuss, just for amusement, that there are other possibilities. Why can't we drill holes, cut things, solder things, stamp things out, mold different shapes, all at an infinitesimal level? What are the limitations as to how small a thing has to be before you can no longer mold it? How many times when you are working on something frustratingly tiny, like your wife's wristwatch, have you said to yourself, "If I could only train an ant to do this!" What I would like to suggest is the possibility of training an ant to train a mite to do this. What are the possibilities of small but movable machines? They may or may not be useful, but they surely would be fun to make.

A friend of mine (Al Hibbs) suggests a very interesting possibility for relatively small machines. He says that, although it is a very wild idea, it would be interesting in surgery if you could swallow the surgeon. You put the mechanical surgeon inside the blood vessel and it goes into the heart and "looks" around. (Of course, the information has to be fed out.) It finds out which valve is the faulty one and takes a little knife and slices it out. Other small machines might be permanently incorporated in the body to assist some inadequately functioning organ.

Now comes the interesting question: how do we make such a tiny mechanism? I leave that to you. However, let me suggest one weird possibility. You know in the atomic energy plants they have materials and machines that they can't handle directly because they have become radioactive? To unscrew nuts and put on bolts and so on, they have a set of master and slave hands, so that by operating a set of levers here, you control the "hands" there, and can turn them this way and that so that you can handle things quite nicely.

Most of these devices are actually made rather simply, in that there is a particular cable, like a marionette string, that goes directly from the controls to the "hands." But, of course, things have also been made using servo motors, so that the connection between the one thing and the other is electrical rather than mechanical. When you turn the lever, they turn a servo motor, and it changes the electrical currents in the wires, which repositions a motor at the other end.

Now, I want to build much the same device—a master-slave system which operates electrically. But I want the slaves to be made especially carefully by modern large-scale machinists so that they are one fourth the scale of the "hands" that you ordinarily maneuver. So you have a scheme by which you can do things at one-quarter scale

173

anyway—the little servo motors with little hands play with little nuts and bolts; they drill little holes; they are four times smaller. Aha! So I manufacture a quarter-size lathe; I manufacture quarter-size tools; and I make, at the one-quarter scale, still another set of hands again relatively one-quarter size! this is a one-sixteenth size, from my point of view. And after I finish doing this I wire directly from my large-scale system, through transformers perhaps, to the one-sixteenth servo motors. Thus I can now manipulate the one-sixteenth-size hands.

Well, you get the principle from there on. It is a rather difficult program, but it is a possibility. . . .

As we go down in size, there are a number of interesting problems that arise. All things do not simply scale down in proportion. There is the problem that materials stick together by the molecular (Van der Waals) attraction. It would be like this. After you have made a part and you unscrew the nut from a bolt, it isn't going to fall down because the gravity isn't appreciable; it would even be hard to get it off the bolt. It would be like those old movies of a man with his hands full of molasses, trying to get rid of a glass of water. There will be several problems of this nature that we will have to be ready for. . . .

Now you might say, "Who should do this and why should they do it?" Well, I pointed out a few of the economic applications, but I know that the reason that you would do it might just be for fun. But *have* some fun! Let's have a competition between laboratories. Let one laboratory make a tiny motor which it sends to another lab which sends it back with a thing which fits inside the shaft of the first motor.

Just for the fun of it, and in order to get kids interested in this field, I would propose that someone who has some contact with the high schools think of making some kind of high school competition. The Los Angeles high school could send a pin to the Venice high school on which it says, "How's this?" They get the pin back, and in the dot of the *i* it says, "Not so hot."

Perhaps this doesn't excite you to do it, and only economics will do so. I want to do something; but I can't do it at the present moment, because I haven't prepared the ground. It is my intention to offer a prize of one thousand dollars to the first guy who can take the information on the page of a book and put it on an area twenty-five thousand times smaller in linear scale in such manner that it can be read by an electron microscope.

And I want to offer another prize—if I can figure out how to phrase it so that I don't get into a mess of arguments about definitions—of another one thousand dollars to the first guy who makes an operating electric motor—a rotating electric motor—which can be controlled from the outside and, not counting the lead-in wires, is only a one-sixty-fourth-inch cube.

I do not expect that such prizes will have to wait long for claimants.

The tiny-motor prize was claimed within a year by a Pasadena electrical engineer named William MacLellan.

World's Smallest Motor

World's smallest motor, shown in contrast with normal sized pinhead, was built by a Pasadena optical company engineer in answer to a challenge.

$1,000 Paid to Inventor

Caltech Prof Writes Check

By MARGARET STOVALL

The world's smallest motor went into operation today with no present logical reason for existence except to provide its inventor with $1000 he didn't have before.

The tiny machine, 1/64-inch cubed which is considerably smaller than the head of a pin, was developed by William McLellan, Electro-Optical Systems engineer, in response to a challenge by Dr. Richard Feynman, professor of physics at the California Institute of Technology.

The challenge was part of a lecture the professor delivered last December in which he outlined the need for microengineering and stated he was willing to pay the thousand dollars to anyone who could construct a working electric motor of the 1/64-inch size.

McLellan started his project in his spare time a little more than two months ago, proving as he did so that it was not necessary to scale down lathes and other instruments to produce the product as Dr. Feynman had believed.

"I worked with a watchmaker's lathe, a microscope and sharp toothpicks," McLellan said. "I had to use the toothpicks because even the tiniest tweezers would have damaged the parts, and I had to use the microscope be-

MOTOR: See Page 6

November 15, 1960

Mr. William H. McLellan
Electro-Optical Systems, Inc.
125 North Vinedo Avenue
Pasadena, California

Dear Mr. McLellan:

I can't get my mind off the fascinating motor you showed me Saturday. How could it b e made so small?

Before you showed it to me I told you I hadn't formally set up that prize I mentioned in my Engineering and Science article. The reason I delayed was to try to formulate it to avoid legal arguments (such as showing a pulsing mercury drop controlled by magnetic fields outside and calling it a motor), to try to find some organization that would act as judges for me, to straighten out any tax questions, etc. But I kept putting it off and never did get around to it.

But what you showed me was exactly what I had had in mind when I wrote the article, and you are the first to show me anything like it. So, I would like to give you the enclosed prize. You certainly deserve it.

I am only slightly disappointed that no major new technique needed to be developed to make the motor. I was sure I had it small enough that you couldn't do it directly, but you did. Congratulations!
Now don't start writing small.
I don't intend to make good on the other one. Since writing the article I've gotten married and bought a house!

Sincerely yours,

Richard P. Feynman

RPF:n

McLELLAN MICROMOTOR

WHAT IT IS

The micromotor is an AC electric motor 1/64 inch on a side. It weighs 250 micrograms. Its output is one millionth of a horsepower. It operates on milliamperes at millivolts. It is a two-phase permanent magnet synchronous motor, if you wish to be exact. The micromotor was made in response to a challenge by Dr. Richard Feynman of Caltech, who offered "$1000 to the first guy who makes an operating electric motor only 1/64 inch cubed". Dr. Feynman's purpose was to encourage the development of new techniques in the field of microminiaturization.

HOW IT WAS DESIGNED

The motor design was based on known coil possibilities -- that .0005 inch diameter copper wire was available and could be wound around a .004 inch diameter mandrel using 3 grams winding tension. An AC design was made because the brushes and the commutator of a DC motor would be difficult to make. In order to get the most torque, a permanent magnet rotor was chosen. A copper or aluminum rotor would make a less efficient eddy current motor out of the same design. Except for the square base and the coils, the parts are disks, rods, or sleeves with no shoulders to permit simple rolling or drawing operations. In general, the raw material is finished to diametral size, then cemented in a close fitting hole in a suitable carrier. The carrier (and captive blank) is then sawed into slices of the desired thickness for that part. The blank is then released from the carrier for use or for further machining such as hole drilling.

HOW IT WAS MADE

The principal tool was a microscope, because every operation required at least one. Sometimes two microscopes at right angles to each other were used when drilling holes, particularly for the locating of imaginary center-lines. A watchmaker's lathe with attachments and a microdrill press were the machines used. Flat pivot drills down to .0016 inch diameter are commercially available. Tweezers were not used at the final stages to avoid damaging the small parts. A fine bristle brush or a sharpened toothpick was used for handling the parts.

THE MOTOR AND ITS FUTURE

The motor was designed by William H. McLellan and built by him and two laboratory technicians, all of Electro-Optical Systems, Inc., in the company's miniaturization laboratory. It required about two months of spare time. There are no commercial plans for the motor at this time. Commercial rights involving the micromotor are assigned to Electro-Optical Systems, Inc., by prior agreement with Mr. McLellan.

How to build a micromotor.

McLELLAN TWO PHASE PERMANENT MAGNET SYNCHRONOUS MICROMOTOR

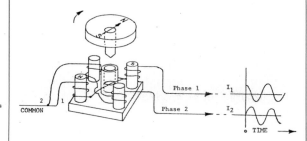

MICROMOTOR -- OBLIQUE VIEW, PARTIALLY EXPLODED

Parts List	(All dimensions in inches)
4 coils -----------	.0005 enameled copper wire, 21 turns
4 poles -----------	iron pins -- .0035 D x .010 L
1 base -----------	steel shim stock -- .003 x .014 Sq.
1 sleeve bearing ----	quartz tubing -- .002 ID x .003 OD x .007 L
1 thrust bearing ----	quartz rod -- .0018 D x .005 L
1 shaft -----------	molybdenum -- .0016 D x .009 L
1 rotor -----------	permanent magnet (Vicalloy) .003 x .014 D

Each coil has two layers, 11 turns and 10 turns, making a total of 21 turns. Coil I.D. is .0042. Coil O.D. is .0065. The resistance of one coil is 1.25 ohms. Phase resistance is 2.5 ohms.

DESCRIPTION OF OPERATION

At time t = 0, the current in Phase 1 is maximum and the stator magnetic field polarity is as labeled on the poles in the above figure. Assume that the magnetized rotor is oriented as shown, but remember that the rotor actually fits down close to the poles and is part of the magnetic path for both phases. The current in Phase 2 is zero at this instant and consequently the magnetic field in Phase 2 is zero. A very short time later, as I_1 decreases and I_2 increases from zero, the pole of Phase 2 clockwise from the temporary N pole of Phase 1 becomes an increasingly stronger N pole. A similar action occurs at the S poles. Eventually Phase 2 is at full strength and the current and magnetic field of Phase 1 are zero. The action repeats and the effect of the two phases alternately increasing and decreasing is a rotating stator field. The magnetized rotor, being free to turn, goes around in step with this field. The synchronous speed of rotation depends on the frequency of the two phase supply. A single phase source may be used if the current in one phase is shifted by the use of a series capacitor. The motor has been run at 1800 rpm, but is usually operated much slower because it is easier to observe rotation at low speed. The rotor revolves one turn for each electrical cycle.

Marvin Minsky   One day I was in Los Angeles for some meeting or other with my friend Ed Fredkin. We rented some Honda trail motorcycles, which I had never ridden before. They are wonderful things—very high torque, so you can go through all sorts of woods as though you were walking (but very destructive, of course).

We rode up towards Mount Wilson because we thought that would be a good place to visit, and then Fredkin said, "Why don't we go and visit Pauling?" Linus Pauling had been one of Ed's teachers when he was at Caltech. So we rang up Pauling, but he wasn't home. Then we thought, why don't we ring up Feynman, whom we had heard of, but never met. He was home. Ed and I were both interested in computers and small machines, so we said we would like to come and talk about that. Feynman said come over, and we did. He had offered a prize for anyone who could build a tiny electric motor—I forget the size, but maybe a cubic millimeter—and some fellow had built one! So we talked all about the future of small components. It was wonderful.

I don't know the structure of his thinking, but Feynman once mentioned to me that he was always more interested in computing than in physics. In his first job at Los Alamos he was in charge of getting people to do calculations. That was in the early 1940s, when of course there weren't any computers—there were desk calculators. So one of his jobs was to get rooms full of people with calculators to do reactor-shielding calculations, or whatever. He became very interested not only in algorithms in general for computing, but also in how do you make parallel algorithms with a lot of processors, because that's what the people in this room were doing. I think this is why eventually he became so interested in the Thinking Machines company and the "Connection Machine."

Carl Feynman   When I went to MIT, my father introduced me to Marvin Minsky, and Marvin introduced me to Danny Hillis. Danny was living in Marvin Minsky's basement at the time. I was a freshman, and Danny was a graduate student.

He had this crazy project to build a giant computer. Well, what did I know? I was seventeen years old, and I thought it would work—nobody else did.

I started working for Danny, and gradually it turned into an actual project. I introduced Danny to my father; they really hit it off.

Danny Hillis

I got to know Feynman through his son, Carl. Once when I was going out to Los Angeles, Carl said, "You should go and visit my father." I was very surprised that Feynman came out to the airport to pick me up—it's a two-hour drive from their house, and here was Richard Feynman wanting to know about this crazy project his son was involved with. So we began talking about the basic ideas of the computer, which at that time was really only on the drawing board. His first response was, "That's a kooky idea." That meant he was interested in it.

A lot of times, I guess, Richard wasn't so much worried about whether something was a real idea or not, but was it a way of generating new ideas? I guess he had an interest in things that were on the edge of the conventional, and it led him to deal in a lot of cases with pretty flaky people. But I think he found flaky people stimulating, because the people who are doing the ideas that really change the world are—or appear—flaky. "Flaky" means it doesn't fit in with the conventions; you are not recognized as an acceptable part of how "we" think, an acceptable part of the structure of things. Well, anything that's going to change anything is not going to be recognized as part of the structure of things. My friend Stewart Brand has a nice way of saying it—"You look at the edges to see where the center is going to go."

I think Richard did that a lot. He talked to physicists with crazy ideas that bucked standard ideas about gravitation, say, or perpetual motion. Or to mathematicians who had kooky ideas. Computer scientists, even! Of course, you have to go through a lot of chaff to get a little bit of wheat that way, but I think he enjoyed that too. Even ideas that were wrong. He found it stimulating to try and figure it out—"Is this person a fake? In which case let's figure out their trick. How are they trying to fool us?" In either case you learn something by dealing with them. So Richard liked learning by engaging in things that were out of the ordinary. He would never write off something just because on the surface it sounded absurd.

I think this was maybe one of the things that made him unusual for a scientist. Scientists in general have a pretty narrow range of things that come up on their radar. They tend to reject an awful lot if it doesn't fit into their pattern of things. I think he was just the opposite: he was always looking for things that didn't fit into his pattern of things. He was always deliberately turning any piece of conventional wisdom on its head and questioning it. The thing that he loved the best was if he could find some absolute gospel truth that somebody believed, and then ask some very simple question that caused it to fall apart. He loved that!

Richard did have stupid ideas sometimes, and it was pretty hard to derail him once he got started even if it *was* stupid. In particular, he would often dive into a field without paying much attention to the work that had been done there before, sort of starting from scratch. Sometimes that would let him get at the essentials, but sometimes it also let him miss the essentials.

I remember a crazy thing he was trying to work on. He had a little box that he wanted to talk to by sending in symbols, and getting it to repeat things. So he would say "Blue" and show it a blue thing. Then next time he showed it a blue thing, he wanted it to say "Blue." I guess his idea would be that it was kind of like a baby and he would teach it, which I think is a great idea—that's in some sense what I work on. But his idea of how it ought to work inside was pretty naive. He kind of stuck with it for a while—who knows what would have happened if he had stuck with it for a few years more?

A lot of times he'd get crazy ideas of how physical things worked. He was always putting his theories to the test, and that was a great thing about Richard—whenever you asked a question and couldn't think of the answer, Richard would say, "Well, what experiment can we do to figure it out?"

Once we were making spaghetti, which was our favorite thing to eat together. Nobody else seemed to like it. Anyway, if you get a spaghetti stick and you break it, it turns out that instead of breaking in half, it will almost always break into three pieces. Why is this true—why does it break into three pieces? We spent the next two hours coming up with crazy theories. We thought up experiments, like breaking it underwater because we thought that might dampen the sound, the vibrations. Well, we ended up at the end of a couple of hours with broken spaghetti all over the kitchen and no real good theory about why spaghetti breaks in three. A lot of fun, but I could have blackmailed him with some of his spaghetti theories, which turned out to be dead wrong!

I think when he first started looking at the Connection Machine, it was just another sort of perpetual motion machine, another crazy gadget. So he was pretty surprised when he started taking it apart and it began looking like a real idea. I don't think he ever thought in the beginning that we were actually going to build it. When I told him I was going to leave MIT and start a company, he said, "That's a really wacky idea!" He started telling me about how it could never possibly work, how starting a company would bring all these terrible distractions, and so on. But at the end of the conversation, he said, "By the way, do you want anybody for a summer job?" And that's when he said he'd come to the company and work on the machine.

The idea of the Connection Machine is that instead of making one big fast computer, you use a lot of simple little cheap computers together to work on a single problem. It's a bit like breaking up a problem by having a team of people work on it at the same time, and in this case it's a team of sixty-four thousand. It turns out that on the computer, it's actually possible to coordinate the action of sixty-four thousand processors on the solving of a single problem. So that's what's inside the black box—sixty-four thousand little bitty simple processors, sixteen of them on each chip.

181

If you have a lot of people working in a team, they have to talk to each other. So built into the chips is a sort of telephone system that allows them to communicate with one another: this chip can call up that chip, this chip can call up that other chip, and so on. You can have sixty-four thousand "conversations" going on at once. The details of that communication system, between the chips, is what Feynman worked on.

Carl Feynman In a big engineering project like the Connection Machine, there are people who worry about the whole thing, and there's also many little bits that have to be gotten right. My father and I were both inclined to work on the little bits, things that could be reduced almost to puzzles. Some of the stuff I worked on with him was the design of the "router" network, that connects the processors together. People at the company had been trying to prove that it would work, and not get itself hopelessly jammed, and never unjam—which was a possibility. We didn't really understand whether that would happen or not.

My father proved that, given certain features of the design, this was impossible. He did it through methods entirely unlike anything else that anyone at the company was thinking about, methods derived from thermodynamics, and statistical mechanics—entirely unlike what computer scientists usually think about.

The stuff he did at Thinking Machines tended to be a problem which was large enough to have a real impact on the effectiveness of the machine, and yet sufficiently straightforward to be amenable to a really crisp and exact solution. There are things—puzzles—that are no more intellectually stimulating than crossword puzzles, or jigsaw puzzles, but which have to be done; that's not the kind of puzzle I mean. I mean a puzzle that has a very simple statement, and then you do a lot of thinking, and you come to a very simple answer. That's a really good puzzle, and that's the kind of thing you want to work on.

Picking a problem is almost the hardest part of doing good work. There are plenty of problems that are hard beyond human comprehension, and there are plenty of problems that can be solved merely by working through all the possibilities in a tedious fashion. A good problem is neither of those. Out of the whole world, you want to pick a problem that is of the right kind, and he had a tremendous sense for picking those kinds of problems, much better than most people I know. He wouldn't find himself going down blind alleys very often.

People use the machine for simulating reality. For example, you're designing an airplane and you'd like to know if it's going to fly before you build it. One way is to build a little model inside a wind tunnel. But another way to do it is to build a model inside the computer—you tell the computer the shape of the airplane, and the computer tells you how it's going to fly. You can also simulate reality for things that are much too big to model, like what happens if two galaxies collide; or things that are much too small to see, like what happens if two quarks bump into each other in a certain kind of situation. In fact, using it to model quarks is something Feynman was interested in. At Caltech, they were building a special machine for modeling the interactions of quarks, and Feynman said, "Well, Danny, let's see if your machine here is any good. Let's see if it can do this thing they're trying to do at Caltech."

I really didn't think the Connection Machine could do something like that, but Feynman worked out a way to use it to model quantum chromodynamics—one of Murray Gell-Mann's theories.[3] It turned out the machine was really good at it—Richard came to me one day and says, "Hey, Danny! You're not going to believe it, but this crazy box of yours can actually do something useful."

Something "useful" to Richard was physics, of course, as opposed to this artificial intelligence stuff which I was interested in!

A computer is a high-class, super-speed, nice, streamlined Filing Clerk. . . .

Danny Hillis

Feynman[4]

I would like to say some words about what the computers can do and can't do, and you'll see they can do only what you would expect to be able to do with a filing system, and a reasonable File Clerk.

What we need to do, of course, is to convert what we want the Clerk to do into an absolutely definite procedure, where every step is precisely defined in a stupid way, but exactly. If you can do that, then you can get the system to work.

Now, will computers think? Nobody knows how to define a series of steps which correspond to something abstract like "thinking." Nevertheless, we can make machines which play chess, which was supposed to be something that takes thinking. What exactly do they do? What definite procedure can you make with a big file system, a very fast operating gadget, by which the thing could be used to play chess?

Well, there's a given position on the board, which is a whole lot of information of where everything is, and we want to know which way to move. You look at the rules for how to move—the knight goes this way, the queen goes that way, and so on. You just list all the different ways the things could move, and the way the other guy could move. You see all the new possible positions. Getting pretty big, isn't it? But they're big machines, and they've got lots of storage space, memory. So what's the next move? If he does that, what can I do? You just check every one of the positions there for, let's say, four or five or six half moves. These are called half moves—one side moves, and the other side moves. See which of the final positions you're better off in. "Better off" might be some little rule like "I haven't been in check," or "I've got more pieces than the other guy." So you look down, six steps down, say, to see which move is the best to make, where you've got the best possible outcome, and you make that move. Then your opponent makes a move. You start again, this time going down six again. Of course, you're going deeper now because the game has proceeded a little bit further. And that's all there is to it.

What the machines do is just a tremendous amount of

trying different positions. A human being doesn't; a human being tries about thirty-five positions, as far as we can tell, before he makes a decision. A machine checks something like thirty-five million positions. But that doesn't make the machine better than the other guy. A human says, "His knight can fork my king and queen if it goes there, so I'll have to watch out about that square." Human players see patterns, or at least they describe it that way. And we really don't know how it works. The human player says, "I saw that it was a good idea to try this, and I tried it." We don't know how he does that. So we can't make a machine play like a human plays, but we can make it play better than almost all humans.

You've probably heard that machines have been used to be like doctors—expert systems which can diagnose disease. Now how can a damn File Clerk be a doctor? Well, it's easy, isn't it? How would you diagnose a disease? You write down all the symptoms, and then you'd like to have a book that you could look up that says, in a complicated case, "It's either common morbis of the borbis or it's bactracaemia." However, you can tell the difference by looking with ultraviolet light up the nostril. All right! But usually you don't bother to look with ultraviolet light up the nostril, so you don't know what to look for. So the book (or the machine) says, "Look with ultraviolet in the nostril and tell me whether it gets through or not." You try it, and you say, "Yes." Okay. The machine says, "It's bactracaemia." This filing system contains all this stuff, plus the incomplete decisions that require more information, and it's been arranged so that when it comes to a place where it's incomplete, it simply sends back and says, "Make the following test and tell me the result." The thing doesn't work as well as a real doctor, of course. But anyway, you can get some idea of how machines can be doctors, how machines can be chess players, and how machines can be designers of equipment, how they could route trucks in the most economic way, and so on.

That's all there is to it. It's a filing system. I'm done, but I'll answer questions. . . .

Oh, there's something I left out, which is: what kind of a File Clerk can't be imitated by the machine? A File Clerk that has some special skill which requires recognition of a complicated kind. For instance, a File Clerk in the fingerprint department, which looks at the fingerprints and then makes a careful comparison to see if these fingerprints match—it's hard to do, and as yet it's almost impossible to do by computer. You'd say there's nothing to it: "I'll look at the fingerprints, and see if all the black dots are the same." But of course it's not the case—the finger was dirty, or the print was made at a different angle, or the pressure was different, and the ridges are not exactly in the same place. If you were trying to match exactly the same picture, it would be easy, but where the center of the print depends on which way the finger is turned, whether it's been squashed a little more or a little bit less, whether there's some dirt on the finger, whether in the meantime he got a wart on his thumb, and so forth . . . these are all complications which make the comparison so much more difficult for the machine. A human can go across all that somehow, just like they do in the chess game—they seem to be able to catch on to patterns rapidly, and we don't how to do that, automatically, mechanically, yet. Okay? Are there any questions? Yes sir!

I think a question that everybody asks themselves is whether the supercomputers, real fancy computers, will be more useful or more destructive, ultimately, to the world.

Well, I haven't any idea, of course. I have no idea about that. Whether anything is more useful or destructive to the world, whether yoga is more useful or more destructive to the world! All these things give us the power to do something, to do many things, and the power to do something may or may not be destructive. We don't know how to guarantee to produce only creative things—with the exception of the telephone, as far as I can tell. I mention that because it's rather interesting: if you think about inventions, almost all the inventions have a destructive element in war. The telephone has an effect in war, it helps communications, and maybe in that sense it's destructive because it helps the army to destroy you. But other than that, it's a relatively peaceful device; it doesn't kill, not at least directly. That's rather interesting because it's hard to find a device that isn't directly available for killing. A knife—when the knife was invented, and a guy was explaining what a knife is: "It's a sharpened piece of stuff—metal, or maybe stone, a very sharp piece of stone, and you can use it to cut things, so it's easier to get the vegetables off the plants," and some other guy was sitting there saying, "On the other hand, it's very destructive, because you can cut my head off with it." That problem's been with us forever, and there's nothing special about computers. Absolutely anything that can do anything has this problem, but it's not a problem for computers particularly, I think. That's my view, but I don't know.

There's the Big Brother element with computers that you didn't have with stones and knives.

I know, but which is better? Big Brother, or the cutting the head off, huh? In fact, that's what makes Big Brother possible—he has the knives. It's not so easy. It's true that we could worry about the fact that they'll be able to store information better, and have more information about people, and will that produce Big Brother? Rather interestingly, the country which is more democratic, and which is less interested in all the information about what everybody is doing to make sure they're not doing something wrong, is where the computers have developed the most. And the places where you'd think the government would find computers of greatest use, because it can file all the information about everybody, those countries don't develop the computer very much, and they don't know how to use it. It's only a curiosity—it's one of life's contradictions.

Will they be able to do everything humans can do?

They can do lots of things, like play chess quite well. There have been computers which can do things like theorem-proving in geometry, say, in which they've converted the problem of finding a proof of a theorem into a definite procedure. It's an elaborate and dumb way to do proofs, but the computers can do it. At the present time, a computer can't do all the different things that a person can do, of course. But it's very difficult to find some way of defining rather precisely something we can do that we can say a computer will never be able to do.

There are some things that people ask while the computer's doing something: "Does it feel good?" Or, "While it's doing it, will it understand what it's doing?" Or some other abstraction like that. I rather feel that these are things like "While it's doing it, will it be able to scratch the lice out of its hair?" No, it hasn't got any hair, or the lice to scratch from it. So you've got to be careful when you say "Will they be able to do what the humans do?"

Human beings have a tendency to want to be sure that they can always do something that no machine can do. Somehow it doesn't bother them anymore (although it must have bothered them in earlier times) that machines are stronger, physically, than they are—the machines can lift huge weights, they can move things faster, they can run faster than people, they can fly, and so forth. We don't sit around worrying about that. I think it will be the same with the computing machines.

---

4 Part II/Wednesday, July 30, 1986

Los Angeles Times
A Times Mirror Newspaper

Small Wonder

In the Middle Ages scholars wondered how many angels would fit on the head of a pin. This puzzle was never satisfactorily answered. But as the result of a recent technological advance at Stanford University we now know that the entire Encyclopaedia Britannica would comfortably fit there.

In 1960 Richard Feynman, the Caltech physicist, offered a $1,000 prize to anyone who could make a printed page 25,000 times smaller while still allowing it to be read. A Stanford graduate student, Tom Newman, has now done it, and Feynman has paid him the grand.

Newman's technique is based on the same technology that is used to imprint electronic circuits on those tiny computer chips that are everywhere. Newman uses several electron beams to trace letters made up of dots that are 60 atoms wide. The resulting text can be read with an electron microscope.

Some technological advances bring instant rewards to humanity, while some have no practical use—at least for the moment. They are just amazing. In the latter category, chalk one up for Tom Newman, with an assist from Richard Feynman.

Crazy Ideas: Tiny Writing and Huge Computers

While Feynman worked on the Connection Machine in Boston and talked about computers and tiny machines at Esalen, a Stanford graduate named Thomas Newman was working at making very small writing. In 1986, Newman claimed his thousand dollars. Using the microscopic etching techniques Feynman had suggested almost twenty-five years earlier, Newman had reduced by twenty-five thousand times the first page of Dickens's A Tale of Two Cities. Feynman paid up.

CHAPTER EIGHT

Challenger

At 11.38 a.m. EST on Tuesday January 28, 1986, the *space shuttle* Challenger *lifted off from Cape Kennedy. Seventy-three seconds later, it disintegrated with the loss of all seven crew members.*

That night on television President Reagan postponed his planned State of the Union address (which was to have included a live conversation with Challenger astronaut-teacher Christa McAuliffe) and instead paid an eloquent tribute to NASA and the dead astronauts:

The future doesn't belong to the faint-hearted—it belongs to the brave. The *Challenger* crew was pulling us into the future, and we will continue to follow them. I have always had great faith in and respect for our space program, and what happened today does nothing to diminish it. We don't hide our space program, we don't keep secrets and cover things up. We do it all up front, and in public—that's the way freedom is, and we wouldn't change it for a minute. . . . Nothing ends here. Our hopes and our journeys continue. I want to add that I wish I could talk to every man and woman who works for NASA, or who worked on this mission, and tell them, "Your dedication and profession-alism have moved and impressed us for decades, and we know of your anguish—we share it. . . . The crew of the space shuttle *Challenger* honored us by the manner in which they lived their lives. We will never forget them, nor the last time we saw them, this morning, as they prepared for their journey and waved goodbye, and slipped the surly bonds of Earth to touch the face of God.

A week later, Feynman was asked to join the presidential commission of inquiry into the accident. His health was not good—he had survived two major operations for abdominal cancer, and now he had a rare type of blood cancer, and heart problems too.

Al Hibbs   I think it was quite a decision for him. He called me up about it before he had made up his mind. He told me he'd been asked to do this, and what was my advice? I asked him, did he think it was important, and he said he thought it was. So then I asked him did he think he could make a difference? And he said, "Well, probably I could." I didn't say anything more. After a while, he said, "To hell with you, Hibbs," and hung up the phone.

Feynman   I have a policy, practically, of never going near Washington. I called up various friends of mine who are connected to the space program in one way or another, and tried to ask them whether I should go, or if somebody else could do it just as well. They both told me, "No, you ought to do it."

I'm still trying to get out of it, and I'm talking to my wife, and I asked her. I have to be immodest here to explain the effect. Gweneth said, "If you're not on the commission, there'll be twelve members in a little knot which will go from one place to another, figure it all out, and write a report. If you are on this thing, there'll be eleven guys in a knot, going around, writing a report, and one guy like a mosquito running all over the place. You probably won't find anything, but if there is something interesting, if there's something strange, then you'll find it and it wouldn't have been found otherwise."

Well, I had to believe her, because I know how I act. I'm

To Richard Feynman
Thanks for a job well done,

Ronald Reagan

an explorer, okay? I get curious about everything, and I want to investigate all kinds of stuff. So I knew she was right, and I had no further excuse. I could make a contribution that not everybody could make. Could be true, or be untrue. Anyway, she used my lack of modesty to convince me to do it. And I did it.

Well, knowing about his "Principle of Social Unresponsibility," I called him up to say, "Why, you big old faker! What's this about you being on the *Challenger* commission?" He says, "Gweneth asked me to do it." Well, I'm not going to argue with a man's wife, so I shut up.

Richard listened to Gweneth, and if she wanted him to

Dick Davies

do something, he might say no once or twice, but he usually did it. He respected her opinion, and realized she had insights into various issues that he didn't. So if he was worried about something, such as his testimony for Gianone, why, he would ask Gweneth.

I went over to his house and we discussed what the problems were. I suggested who he might talk to get some background. But I had nothing to do with encouraging him into that adventure.

Most commissions of this kind are damage control as much as anything else, but I think he did something that nobody else could do, which was to take away that impression. I think he made some of the people in NASA gasp a little bit.

Carl Feynman I think in the *Challenger* investigation he was doing lots of stuff he had never done before, and that was something he always loved to do—get into a field, start from scratch, bumble around, learn things, and eventually get good at it. So I think he had a lot of fun being an "Inspector-general," which he'd never been before. It was like his drawing, you know, and decoding Mayan hieroglyphics, which he'd never done before. Same sort of thing.

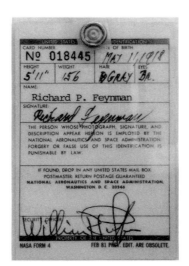 

NASA ID: "Don't tell me any secrets. . . ."

General Donald J. Kutyna: "Copilot to pilot. Comb your hair."

Donald Kutyna[1]

I had been warned that Feynman absolutely hated the military. His dad was, I guess, a uniform salesman back in New York, and had dealt with a bunch of stuffy old admirals and generals who always gave him a hard time. So his son was brought up listening to his dad complaining about those military guys. Then, as you recall, he went to Los Alamos, to help develop the nuclear bombs. Well, his hobby there was safecracking, which isn't the sort of hobby which goes down too well with military types!

The very first day I sat next to him in my uniform, wondering what this guy was going to think of me. I didn't know how to say hello to him, or what to do. I looked at him—it was the middle of February, and his hair was all mussed up by the cold winds of Washington. I tried to think of the lowest position I could think of, and in my experience, a copilot is probably the lowest thing in the world—he carries the flight launchers, the parachutes, the water bottles. I turned to Feynman, and I said, "Copilot to pilot. Comb your hair." He looked at me, and I thought, "Well, I'm really in for it." But he says, "You got a comb?" I gave him my comb, he combed his hair, and that kind of broke the ice.

He kind of latched on to me. That evening we walked out down the steps of the State Department and Secretary of State Rogers, of course, had a large black limousine come and pick him up. Neil Armstrong had a big limo pick him up. Even Sally Ride had a limousine pick her up.

Feynman looked at me, with my two stars on my arm, and said, "Where's your limo?"

I told him, "Two stars don't get a limo in Washington. I ride the subway." He put his arm around me, and he said, "Kutyna, any general that rides the subway can't be all bad!" And that started a great relationship between the two of us.

Feynman had three things going for him. Number one, tremendous intellect, and that was known around the world. Second, integrity, and this really came out in the commission. Third, he brought this driving desire to get to the bottom of any mystery. No matter where it took him, he was going to get there, and he was not deterred by any roadblocks in the way. He was a courageous guy, and he wasn't afraid to say what he meant.

Many of the commissioners had certain ties to NASA— I certainly did. I was the shuttle program manager for the Department of Defense at the time, so I would have been too close to the problem to be totally objective at times. The same goes for some of the gentlemen who were contracted, who'd been working with NASA. The NASA astronauts also would have a closeness that maybe was not as objective, just by their position, as a fellow like Feynman could be.

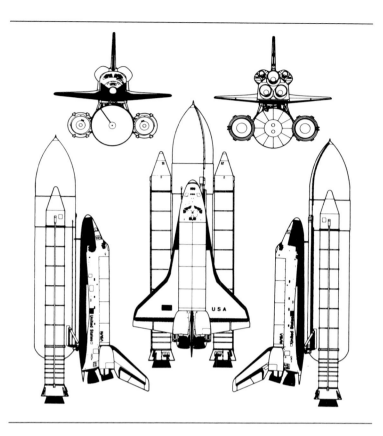

The shuttle stacked for launch: orbiter, external tank, and the two solid rocket boosters.

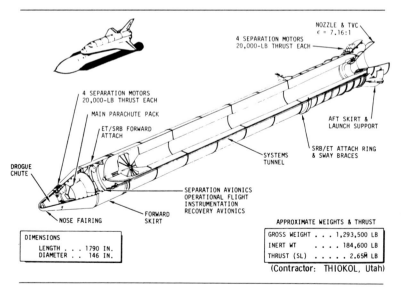

NOZZLE & TVC
ϵ = 7.16:1

4 SEPARATION MOTORS
20,000-LB THRUST EACH

4 SEPARATION MOTORS
20,000-LB THRUST EACH

MAIN PARACHUTE PACK

ET/SRB FORWARD
ATTACH

AFT SKIRT &
LAUNCH SUPPORT

DROGUE
CHUTE

SYSTEMS
TUNNEL

SRB/ET ATTACH RING
& SWAY BRACES

SEPARATION AVIONICS
OPERATIONAL FLIGHT
INSTRUMENTATION
RECOVERY AVIONICS

FORWARD
SKIRT

NOSE FAIRING

DIMENSIONS
LENGTH . . . 1790 IN.
DIAMETER . . 146 IN.

APPROXIMATE WEIGHTS & THRUST
GROSS WEIGHT . . . 1,293,500 LB
INERT WT . . . . 184,600 LB
THRUST (SL) . . . . . 2.65M LB
(Contractor: THIOKOL, Utah)

The solid rocket boosters are made in sections and assembled at the launch site. Between each section is a "field joint" to prevent high-pressure, high-temperature gases from leaking out when the boosters are "lit off."

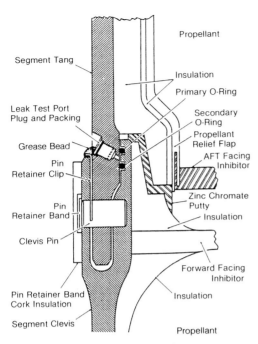

Propellant

Segment Tang

Insulation

Primary O-Ring

Leak Test Port
Plug and Packing

Secondary
O-Ring

Propellant
Relief Flap

Grease Bead

AFT Facing
Inhibitor

Pin
Retainer Clip

Zinc Chromate
Putty

Pin
Retainer Band

Insulation

Clevis Pin

Forward Facing
Inhibitor

Pin Retainer Band
Cork Insulation

Insulation

Segment Clevis

Propellant

SRB field joint showing the dangerous secondary O-ring seal.

Feynman had no ties with NASA, and he had no ties with the DOD. He didn't even know what a space shuttle was, really, except from what he read in the papers.

How important was the shuttle? The shuttle was going to be our only access to space at that time. Every single payload going into space would go on the space shuttle. So—extremely important.

The United States has almost 150 satellites in space. Of those, maybe one hundred are military. In the civil sector, fifty or sixty satellites are providers of communication for television and telecommunications that you're familiar with.

In the military, we use them for weather, we use them for navigation, and we use them for surveillance. They are extremely useful to our military forces. The war in Iraq,

Mission 51-L: countdown to disaster

Seconds

-6.6 — Challenger's liquid fuelled main engines ignited and run up to full thrust while the entire shuttle structure was bolted to the launch pad.

0 — Liftoff

+0.678 — A strong puff of gray smoke spurts from the aft field joint on the right Solid Rocket Booster.

+0.836 to +2.5 — Eight more distinctive puffs of increasingly black smoke.

+4.5 — Three bright flashes appear downstream of the Challenger's right wing, each flash lasting less than a thirtieth of a second.

+58.788 — A small flame appears on the right Solid Rocket Booster in the area of the aft field joint.

+59.262 — The flame becomes a continuous plume, increases in size, and is deflected by aerodynamic slipstream onto the surface of the External Tank.

+64.660 — The flame breaches the External Tank.

+72 — Structural breakup of Challenger begins.

+73.138 — Challenger is totally enveloped in a massive fireball while travelling at Mach 1.92 at an altitude of 46,000 feet.

+73.618 — Last telemetry data received from Challenger.

for example, was the first war where satellites had a major role in helping our forces on the ground. Those forces would not have been able to navigate in the desert without GPS,[2] for example.

It's not a matter of space being just a nice thing to have; it's absolutely imperative to be there, because you can't do it the old way anymore.

The shuttle schedules were very tight. It took a long time to process the flights, and there were only certain windows open in space—you could only launch at certain times, be it a certain time of the year or a certain time of day. If one shuttle launch was delayed for, say, mechanical reasons, it would delay all the shuttles in line following it.

One of the important flights down the pike was a flight called *Galileo*, a satellite that was going out to Jupiter. As the *Challenger* continued to slip, we had less and less time to launch *Galileo*. That window only came around once every few years—it was not something you could launch at just any time you wanted to. If they missed that window it would cost a considerable amount of money waiting for the next window. So there was certainly some pressure to get the *Challenger* off.

The other pressure on NASA to launch was the pressure from the press. The press had full coverage of the launches, and every time anyone dropped a screwdriver it would appear in the press: "Gee, we've goofed up, and we can't fly."

Next, Congress gives you money according to how successful you are. They look at every mission you fly, and if they find something that is unsuccessful, that doesn't test very well, then it affects your budget in the future. I think there was probably pressure to make sure that NASA could prove that this was a very reliable vehicle, and that it could fly the number of missions that had been promised, because that might determine the budget next year. Those kind of pressures exist in every field, in the military, and in civilian life also.

There's also a certain allure attached to man (or woman) in space—if you've got an astronaut on the vehicle it catches the public eye a lot more than just a piece of cold hardware like you have with expendable launch vehicles, and I think that was probably used by folks to sell the shuttle as a prime vehicle.

So there were expectations, and maybe they were too hopeful in the beginning. For example, it was said that it would fly sixty times a year. The cost—this was back in 1972 dollars—the cost was to be $12.5 million a flight. The reliability of the shuttle was almost immortal—one chance in one hundred thousand of failure. That certainly wasn't achieved in any respect.

Well, I thought Feynman needed the full background, so I took him into the Pentagon, and I said, "Let me give you a briefing to give you the whole picture of space, as I know it, so you can look at this thing from the broadest perspective." He agreed to that. Then I offered to get him cleared in at the classified level, since he'd worked with the government before. But he said something like "Absolutely not. I don't want to clog my mind with secrets that I can't talk about. I want to be able to talk about anything that you tell me. So don't give me anything classified."

In the world of space, as in any other world, there are a lot of political pressures, a lot of undercurrents as these agencies (or individuals) battle for position. There was no difference in this particular program, and it happens in every walk of life. As I gave him this briefing, I certainly gave him the technical aspects, but I also gave him a piece of the politics. And there were some strong politics in the shuttle program. Well, he was madder than a dickens. He said, "Kutyna, you've ruined my whole experience here. I thought this was going to be a technical discussion, and you've clouded my mind with all these extraneous, political considerations, and all the things that are going on in Washington. I wish I'd never come and listened to your briefing."

In the end he came to understand that politics was a fairly important factor in what happened to the *Challenger*. He certainly was naive about the politics. I guess that's where we had a great relationship—he was very good on the technical and the scientific aspects, and I think I helped guide him through the pitfalls in the Washington environment. It's a tricky place to work, but he learned very quickly.

A Letter Home

Washington Weds Feb 12th, 2 P.M.

(If you can't read this, get Helen to read it to you. She can read my handwriting)[3]

Dearest Gweneth and Michelle,

This is the first time I have time to write to you. I miss you, and may figure out later how I can get a day off and visit. When a very boring meeting is scheduled? This is an adventure as good as any of the others in my book. You, Gweneth were quite right. I have a unique qualification. I am completely free, and there are no levers that can be used to influence me, and I am reasonably straight-forward and honest. There are exceedingly powerful political forces and consequences involved here, but although people have explained them to me from different points of view, I disregard them all and proceed with apparent naive and single-minded purpose to one end: first why, physically the shuttle failed, leaving to later the question of why humans made apparently bad decisions when they did. As you know, Monday at home at 4 pm they told me I was on the committee and I should fly in Tuesday night for a Wednesday meeting. All day Tuesday, I educated myself with the help of Al Hibbs and technical guys he brought around to help me (I knew nothing about the shuttle, considering before that it was some sort of boondoggle) I was preparing myself technically for the job, and the preparation was excellent. I learned fast. We had an "informal get-together" on Wednesday when we were advised by the Chairman on how important press relations were, and how delicate. We had a public meeting Thursday February 5th which used up the whole day, the entire committee being briefed on facts about the Challenger and its flight. I spent the night making a plan of how I (and we) should proceed, facts to get, a long list of possible causes, make some calculations of loads and so on and so on, ready to roll.

Excuse the paper, I can't find hotel stationery.

Wed. Wed Feb 12
2 P.M.

Dearest Gweneth & Michelle,

[IF YOU CAN'T READ THIS, GET
HELEN TO READ IT TO YOU

(SHE CAN READ
MY HANDWRITING)

This is the first time I have had time to
write to you. I miss you and may figure out later
how I can get a day off and visit (where a very
boring meeting is scheduled?). This is an adventure
as good as some of the others in my book. You,
Gweneth, were quite right - I have a unique qualification,
- I am completely free and there are no levers that
can be used to influence me - and I am reasonably
straightforward and honest. There are exceedingly
powerful forces and political forces and consequences
involved here. But altho people have explained
them to me from different points of view I disregard
them all, - and proceed with apparently naive
and single minded purpose to the one end first
why, physically, the shuttle died, and leaving
were the to later the question of why humans
made bad decisions when they did.

As you know, Monday at home at 4 P.M.
they told me I was on the committee and I showed
flyers (Tues night) for a Wednesday meeting.
All day Tuesday I educated myself with the
help of Al Hibbs and technical guys he brought
around to help me (I knew nothing about the
shuttle considering, before, that it was some sort
of boondoggle). I was preparing myself technically for
the job and the preparation was excellent - I learned
fast.

We had an "informal get together" on Wed. where
we were administrated by title of opinions.

Challenger

Friday February 6th, a General Kutyna on the Commission tells us how such accident investigations have been made in the past using a Titan failure for an example. Very good. I was pleased to see that much of my plans of February 5th are very similar, but not as methodical and as complete. I would be happy to work with him, and a few others want to do that too. Others suggested they could make better contribution by looking into management questions, or by keeping records and writing the report, and so on. It looks good. Here we go.

But the Chairman (Rogers, not a technical man) says that the General's report cannot serve for us because he had so much more detailed data than we will have (quite patently false. Because of human safety questions very much more was monitored on our flight!) Further [said Rogers] it is very likely that we will be unable to figure out just what what happened (!?) and the co-chairman says that the Commission can't really be expected to do any detailed work like that, we shall have to get our technical advice from mutter, mutter. I am trying to get a word in edgewise to object and disagree, but I am always interrupted by a number of accidents—someone just comes in to be introduced around, and the Chairman returns to a new direction, and so on. What is decided is that we, as an entire committee, will go down next Thursday to Kennedy to be briefed there by people there on Thursday and Friday. During the discussion earlier, there are various pious remarks about how we as individuals, (or better small groups called sub-committees) can go anywhere we want, to get info. I tried to propose I do that (and several physicists tell me they would be happy to go with me, among which was Sally Ride) and I have set my affairs so that I can work intensively full-time for a while. I can't seem to get an assignment, and the meeting breaks up practically while I am talking, with the vice-chairman [Neil] Armstrong's remark about our not doing detailed work. So I am leaving, I say to the Chairman that I should go to Boston for a consulting job there for the next five days, Saturday, Sunday, Monday, Tuesday, Wednesday? "Yes, go ahead," he says. (I don't have to explain to you why that drives me up the wall.) I leave very dejected. I then get the idea to call Dr. Graham, Head of NASA, who had been my student and who had asked me to serve. He is horrified, makes a few calls, and suggests possible trips to Houston—Johnson Air Force Base, where the telemeter [sic] data comes in—or Huntsville, Alabama—where they make the engines (I turned down Kennedy because we shall go there later and it is too direct a rebellion from the Chairman). To get the Chairman to OK this, he calls Commissioner Acheson, a lawyer, son of Dean Acheson, good friend of Chairman Rogers. Acheson says he will try, as he thinks it's a good idea. Calls back surprised—he can't get an OK, the Chairman doesn't want me to go: "We must do things in an orderly manner." Graham suggests a compromise: I will stay in Washington, and even though it is Saturday, he will get his men (high-level heads of propulsion, engines, orbiter, and so on) to talk to me. That seems to be OK, although I get a call from Rogers trying to bring me to heel, explaining how hard his job is organizing this, how it must be done in an orderly manner, and so on on. "Do I really want to go to NASA." "Yes," I say. I point out so far two meetings and still no talk on how we should proceed, who can best do what, and so on. (Most of the talk at the meetings was by Rogers, on how he knows Washington, that there are serious questions of orderly press relations, [how we should] tell any reporter he should go to him, Rogers, for answers, and so on.) He asked me if he should bother all the Commissioners, and ask them to come to a meeting Monday which he will convene? "Yes," I say. He drops that subject, OK's that I stay in Washington, and suggests: "I hear that you are unhappy with your hotel. Let me put you into a good hotel." "I don't want any favors. Tell them no, everything is OK, that my personal comfort is less important to me than action," and so forth. He tries again. I refuse again (reminded of "Serve him tea!" at London Airport).[4]

So, Saturday I get briefed at NASA. In the afternoon we talk in fine detail about joints and O-rings, which are critical, have failed partially before, and may be the cause of the Challenger failure. Sunday I go with Graham and his family to see the Air and Space Museum which Carl liked so much. We are in an hour before the official opening, and there are no crowds. Influence! After all, the acting head of NASA.

All this time, evenings, I eat with or go over to the house of Frances and Chuck.[5] It is a very welcome unwinding, but I don't tell stories because they are with the press, and I don't want to spread, or be suspected of spreading leaks. I report to Rogers that I have these close relatives with press connections, and is it OK to visit with them? He is very nice, and says "Of course!" He himself had had some AP connections, he remembers Frances, and so on. I was pleased by his reaction, but now as I write this I have second thoughts. It was too easy, after he explicitly talked about the importance of no leaks and so on at earlier meetings. Am I being set up? (SEE DARLING, WASHINGTON PARANOIA IS SETTING IN.) If when he wants to stop or discredit me, he could charge me with leaking something important. I think it is possible that there are things in this that somebody might be trying to try to keep me from finding out, and might try to discredit me if I get too close. I thought I was invulnerable. Others like Kutyna, Ride, and so on, have some apparent weakness and perhaps may not say what they wish. Kutyna has Air Force interests to worry about, Ride her job at Johnson Air Force Center, and so on and so on. But as I learned, I must keep watching in all directions. Nobody is invulnerable. They will sneak up behind you. This I learned from Kutyna. He said "Check six."[6]

So, reluctantly, I will have to not visit Frances and Chuck any more. Well, I'll ask Fran first if that is too paranoid. Rogers seemed so agreeable and reassuring. It was so easy, yet I am probably a thorn in his side.

Anyway, Monday and Tuesday we have a special closed and open meeting respectively because some internal report saying that the joint seals are, or might be dangerous appeared in the New York Times. Big deal! I knew all the facts in question. I got them at JPL before I started. Very important emergency concerning press relations! At this rate we will never get down close enough to business to find out what happened. Not really, for now tomorrow at 6:15 we go by special airplane (two planes) to Kennedy Space Center to be "briefed." No doubt we shall wander about, being shown everything—gee whiz!—with no time to get into the technical detail with anybody. Well, it won't work. If I am not satisfied by Friday, I will stay over Saturday and Sunday, or if they don't work then, Monday and Tuesday. I am determined to do the job of finding out what happened. Let the chips fall. I feel like a bull in a china shop. The best thing is to put the bull out to work on the plough. (A better metaphor would be "an ox in a china shop," because the china is the "bull" of course). My guess is that I will be allowed to do this, overwhelmed with data and details, with the hope that buried with all the attention on technical details, I can be occupied so they will have time to soften up dangerous witnesses, and so on. But it won't work, because (1) I do technical information exchange and understanding much faster than they imagine, and (2) I already smell certain rats which I will not forget, because I just love the smell of rats, for it is the spoor of exciting adventure.

So, much as I would rather be home and doing something else, I am having a wonderful time. . . .

. . . TUVA OR BUST![7]

Love, Richard

PS This letter need not be splashed around too much. If you do, leave out the personal. . . . Forget it, everything's OK. Uncensored report from the front!

Donald Kutyna The accident was so terrible that the shuttle folks were very cautious about releasing data—they wanted to make sure it was correct. There was an occasion where I had a friend, a classmate of mine and a test pilot at school, who was now a NASA astronaut, and he brought me a piece of paper. The piece of paper showed how the shuttle segments that failed had been put together wrongly. They had violated some procedures in putting those pieces together. We were in the astronaut quarters down at the Cape. He wanted me to know that it was available, but that we would have to find it ourselves—he wasn't allowed to give it to us. He made the mistake of doing this in front of another person, and within a day or two, he was taken off the investigative team, and he came back and told me they'd fired him.

So I was very careful about how I passed on information that had anything to do with the accident that came to us in a different manner. As you recall, we hadn't got any information on the O-rings yet—on cold being a factor. Another astronaut came to me, and again gave me some information that said that the contractor had been testing these O-rings for about six months prior to the accident, testing them in relation to how they reacted under various conditions of cold, and that this data was available. We kind of wondered why we had not been given the data at that time. Again, it was being withheld, for whatever reason. My connection with this second astronaut was as close as it was with the first, and I was afraid he might get fired if I pursued this data. So it was kind of a quandary. I needed to release this data, but if I did, we're in trouble. I had to find some way to get it to someone else so that the astronaut connection wouldn't be there.

Just coincidentally, I had invited Professor Feynman to my home for dinner one night. After dinner, I took Feynman out into the garage and we walked around this old Buick Riviera of mine. I take great pride in these old junk cars that I have. One of my favorites is an Opel GT, 1974. On the workbench there were a couple of Opel carburetors. Feynman asked me about them, and just then the thought hit me.

I said, "You know, Professor Feynman, these damn things leak when it gets cold. Do you suppose cold has any effect on the rubber O-rings in the carburetor?"

He said, "I don't know. I'll chase that down. Maybe that's what happened to the *Challenger*."

And that's what started him down the path that eventually led to the resolution of the O-ring problem. He took off with it, did his experiment, and we were able to surface the information without the astronaut getting fired.

Feynman's experiment focused the commission's inter-

what he has to say and then we, if you would like, after that some time this afternoon, to make further comments about that letter and anything he may say.

We want to give him the opportunity to appear and for the Commission to consider his thoughts, particularly because of the visibility that resulted from the New York Times story, and to have you and anybody else that you want comment upon the contents of

679

that letter.

Is that okay with you?

MR. MULLOY: Yes, sir.

CHAIRMAN ROGERS: Then why don't we have a ten minute recess and reconvene after the recess.

(Recess.)

CHAIRMAN ROGERS: Could we ask the Commission to reconvene, please.

Before we start with Mr. Cook, Dr. Feynman has one or two comments he would like to make. Dr. Feynman.

DR. FEYNMAN: This is a comment for Mr. Mulloy. I took this stuff that I got out of your seal and I put it in ice water, and I discovered that when you put some pressure on it for a while and then undo it it doesn't stretch back. It stays the same dimension. In other words, for a few seconds at least and more seconds than that, there is no resilience in this particular material when it is at a temperature of 32 degrees.

I believe that has some significance for our problem.

CHAIRMAN ROGERS: That is a matter we will consider, of course, at length in the session that we will hold on the weather, and I think it is an important

680

point, which I'm sure Mr. Mulloy acknowledges and will comment on in a further session.

Now, if I may and if there are no further comments, I would like to ask Mr. Cook to come forward.

(Witness sworn.)

The ice-water experiment. Extract from the commission hearing transcript for Tuesday, February 11, 1986.

est, the press's interest, and the public's interest in the relationship of cold and O-rings. Would it have been discovered eventually? Yes, because it was there. But his experiment speeded the process up. We were able to go into this, and get down to the bottom of what really happened.

Donald Kutyna It was a surprise to me that he did it. We were sitting in tiers, with the high rollers, the distinguished members, down on the front row with Neil Armstrong and the Secretary of State. Feynman and I were kind of in the peanut gallery. The television cameras hadn't started rolling yet, and he said, "General, I need a glass of ice water." By this time, I knew him pretty well, so I was able to say, "Why do you need ice water? You haven't said anything yet!" He said, "Don't give me a hard time, just give me some ice water."

There was a lady attendant there, and I asked her, could we please have a glass of ice water for Professor Feynman. She went off somewhere, and the hearing started. The water wasn't coming, the water wasn't coming, and Feynman was fidgeting, "Where's the ice water?"

Next thing we knew, the lady came out and started pouring ice water for the entire commission. Finally she got up to us. At that point in the hearing they had a section, a cross section of this shuttle joint. They had cut it so that you could see the area that had the O-ring in it, and they passed it around to the commissioners. (We'd all seen it the day before, and this time was so the public could see it.) Each commissioner looked at it, like he was interested, and passed it on. It finally got to me, and I passed it on. Feynman didn't. He laid it in front of him, reached in his pocket, and got out a pair of pliers, a screwdriver, and a clamp. I thought, "Oh my God, what's he going to do?"

He proceeded to take this thing apart. He was going to take a piece of this O-ring rubber, put his clamp on it to compress it, like it got compressed in the shuttle joint, then put it in the ice water to cool it down to the temperature on the day of the launch, and show that the O-ring did not bounce back to its original form. He was very anxious to do this. The way you got to talk during that hearing was to press a little red button on your microphone. That would get all the television cameras pointing towards you, and the lights on you, and your microphone would become activated—"hot"—so you could talk.

Feynman started reaching for this button, but it was absolutely the wrong time to press it. The cameras were on some kind of a political discussion going down on the floor, but he was oblivious to that—he wanted to get on with this thing. I remember saying, "No, not now!" He turned around and he said, "Okay. When?"

Well, when the right point came around, he pressed his button, and he did his experiment, to the dismay, I think, of some folks on the commission. It also caught the press by surprise, because during the break the press came up but asked very few pertinent questions. Feynman told me, "You should've let me push it when I wanted to. You ruined my whole experiment." And he stalked out of there, just as sore as could be.

That night, on all the major TV networks, and next day in the *New York Times*, and the *Washington Post*, Feynman's experiment came out. I remember he put his arm round my shoulder and again he said, "Hey, Kutyna! You're not all bad!"

I don't think any of us could have done the experiment. It just would not have been fitting for a two-star general, or a former Secretary of State, or the first man on the moon, to pull out his beaker of water and do that kind of a thing. But Feynman was able to do that. I guess if he had a weakness, it was for showmanship. He was a superb showman.[8]

Al Hibbs I suspect it would have come out as "one of many possibilities we're examining" but never fingered as "that's the problem" so early in the investigation. It would have been immersed in a whole pile of other problems, and I think it would have led to a mushy report.

By forcing this into the open, and doing it right there on television for the world to see, the rest of the commission could not avoid it any longer, and they had to say, "Yeah, that's it. Now, why did it happen?" They might have spent all their time looking at what happened, considering all the technical possibilities, and never getting around to "why?"

I think that he prevented the complete bureaucratic whitewash that it might have turned out to be, saying, "Nobody's really to blame, it was an unfortunate accident," and so on. Feynman said, "No, that's not true. Lots of people were to blame. The system was to blame. And you've got to say that. You've got to say it openly."

I don't believe anybody else on that committee—maybe

NASA Admits Cold Affects Shuttle Seal

Continued From Page A1

rockets at the Marshall Space Flight Center in Huntsville, Ala., acknowledged that low temperatures could slow the rate at which the O rings move to form a tight seal after being hit by hot gases. He said that this, in turn, would increase the erosion of the O rings under the pressure of the gases rushing by.

When asked by Dr. Feynman if there was some temperature below which the O rings should not be used, Mr. Mulloy said that the procurement specifications indicated that they could be safely operated at temperatures down to 30 degrees below zero, Fahrenheit. But he said that tests had indicated that the rings lost resiliency as temperature declined toward 50 degrees Fahrenheit, and he added that Morton Thiokol Inc., which builds the booster rockets, presented data to NASA the day before the launching indicating a further loss of resiliency at 20 or 25 degrees Fahrenheit.

He said that the Thiokol data suggested that the shuttle should not be launched at temperatures below those of previous flights. Nevertheless, he added, NASA experts judged that the O rings would perform properly under the conditions at the time of launch.

NASA officials said that the outside air was about 38 degrees Fahrenheit at the time of launching, but did not say how this temperature compared with previous launchings. No previous launching is known to have raised so many questions about the effects of cold weather. Temperatures plunged to the mid-20's the night before.

William P. Rogers, the former Secretary of State who heads the commission, cut off further questioning about weather and suggested that the topic should be taken up more fully at commission meetings Thursday and Friday at the Kennedy Space Center.

Although the O ring seals were the main focus of today's hearing, NASA officials cautioned that possible failure of the O rings was not necessarily the cause of the accident.

Several Theories Offered

Many theories have been proposed as to the cause of the accident. Photographs released by NASA seem to show a plume of flame emerging from the right-hand booster, raising the possibility that the flame somehow triggered a huge explosion of the shuttle's external fuel tank. The flame seems to emerge from the rocket near a seam, or joint, between two steel segments that are fastened together with steel pins and sealed with the O rings and other barriers to prevent gas from escaping through the seams.

Some analysts have speculated that the seals might have given way under

The New York Times/Marilynn K. Yee

EXPERIMENT: Richard P. Feynman at hearing demonstrating informal resiliency test on material used to make sealing rings. He said he first tried the experiment on lunch break.

tle, or that undetected cracks might have formed in the reusable booster segments on previous flights.

The magazine Aviation Week recently reported that NASA investigators believed that once the gases started escaping out the side of the booster, they severed a connection holding the booster in place, causing it to rotate and crash into the fuel tank.

Another possible explanation, proposed publicly for the first time at today's hearing, was that holes used for testing the O ring seals might have sprung a leak. The holes lead into a section between two seals, the primary seal that is intended to stop the gases, and a backup seal.

Technicians open the test hole, pressurize the gap and determine if both seals are holding properly. Then they are supposed to close the hole with a screw-like plug. Their work is supposed to be checked by a contractor and by Air Force personnel, but if there is undetected human error and the plug is left out, "that would be a leak source," Mr. Mulloy tesitifed. Other analysts have suggested that a manufacturing defect might also cause the test por' to fail.

neers had been concerned last year about erosion observed on the O rings in some previous flights.

The hearing particularly focused on memorandums written by Richard C. Cook, a budget analyst in the NASA comptroller's office, who had warned in a July 23, 1985, memo that flight safety was "being compromised by potential erosion of the seals" and that "failure during launch would certainly be catastrophic."

A parade of agency witnesses testified that Mr. Cook's concerns were overstated, that the issue of seal erosion had been dealt with carefully by top NASA engineering experts and managers, and that seal problems had diminished in 1985. The NASA officials did not specifically dispute the budget analyst's contention that seals had eroded but argued that more competent professionals than he had judged them adequately safe.

Mr. Cook works in the resources analysis branch, which consults with the agency's engineers to determine the budgetary impact of hardware problems. The branch head, Michael B. Mann, told the panel that the possible budget implications of seal erosion was the first assignment he gave to Mr. Cook, who was then a new employee. After Mr. Cook reported back that engineers considered the problem very serious, Mr. Mann said he checked with the engineers and concluded that "maybe the memo overstated their concerns."

Concerns Sent to Others

Mr. Mann said he forwarded the memorandum to superiors and to the office of space flight, and said he thought the issues raised were being handled "in the proper technical channels." Jesse W. Moore, the head of the space flight office, said he had not seen Mr. Cook's memorandum until Sunday.

Mr. Mulloy, the agency's chief witness on the erosion problems, said that some 228 joints had been examined after previous flights. He said there had never been a case of both seals failing, but that 22 of the joints exhibited some erosion of the primary O ring and 10 actually had soot behind it. On only one occasion, he said, was the secondary O ring also eroded, but it sealed effectively anyway.

Mr. Mulloy testified that the erosion "wasn't disturbing from the standpoint of safety" because tests and analyses suggested that the seals could suffer three times the observed erosion and still block gases at far higher pressure than exists in the rocket.

Mr. Cook testified that he had interviewed NASA engineers in July 1985 and found them concerned about erosion of the seals. He suggested that declining budgets for the solid fue'

New York Times, Wednesday, February 12, 1986.

the general, but nobody else with the force of Feynman—
could insist that they not brush it under the rug.

Saturday, May 24, 1986

Dear Mr. Rogers,

I am very sorry I had to leave at noon Saturday, before
we had time to discuss fully the problem that our report
might seem overly critical of the NASA shuttle program.
I would like to explain my views in more detail.

It is our responsibility to find the direct and proximate
causes of the accident, and to make recommendations on
how to avoid such accidents in the future.

Unfortunately we have found, as the proximate cause,
very serious and extensive "flaws" in management. Not
just a crack but a general disintegration. Our report lists
them with our evidence for our view.

This raises serious problems for our nation as to how to
continue on with the space program. There are very large
questions of budget, what other projects to follow to sup-
plement the shuttle (i.e. Expendables?) to maintain scientific and more importantly, military strength, commercial
space applications, etc. Our entire position and program
in space must be reconsidered by people, Congress and
the President. We did not discuss these matters—and
properly so. The President was surely not asking us to
make recommendations in this larger theater. We were
asked, as I see it, to supply information needed to make
such decisions wisely.

It is our duty to supply such information as completely,

R. P. FEYNMAN
UNITED
NATIONS
PLAZA
HOTEL RM 3422

MR. ROGERS, CHAIRMAN
PRES. COMM. ON THE SPACE SHUTTLE CHALLENGER ACCIDENT
CAPITOL GALLERY, EAST WING
SUITE 760
600 MARYLAND AVE. SW
WASHINGTON, D.C. 20024

One United Nations Plaza   New York, New York 10017

doing a wonderful job would weaken our careful report - and might even make us look foolish, ~~worse~~ if it is contrasted with the mass of evidence we ourselves present in a careful documented way.

Well, I'll be back Monday and we can discuss it with other commissioners more fully next week. Maybe they may explain to me where my point of view is off base and I will change my mind — now I doubt it, of course. I feel _very_ _strongly_ about this now.

I am satisfied that my "Reliability" contribution need not go in the main report but will go into the appendix more or less intact rather than being lost in the archives. It is a good compromise we have come to.

See you soon,

Commissioner Feynman, Nobel Prize, Einstein Award, Oersted Medal and utter ignorance about politics.

Feynman signed off with his full credentials.

accurately, and impartially as possible. We have laid out the facts and done it well. The large number of negative observations are a result of the appalling condition [the] NASA shuttle program has gotten into. It is unfortunate, but true, and we would do a disservice if we tried to be less than frank about it. The president needs to know it if he is to make wise decisions.

If it appears we have presented it in an unbalanced way, we should give evidence on the other side. Let us include somewhere a series of specific findings that this or that is very good, or recommendations that they keep up the good work in this and that project specifically. One example is the software verification system, I think, altho I seem to be poly [?] and a little dumb—I thought (apparently incorrectly?) that NASA was very helpful and courteous in giving us all the information (and doing tests) we asked for, especially for our accident panel.

A general statement, without presenting the particular evidence in the report, that NASA is after all actually doing a wonderful job would weaken our careful report, and might even make us look foolish, if it is contrasted with the mass of evidence we ourselves present in a careful documented way.

Well, I'll be back Monday and we can discuss it with other commissioners more fully next week. Maybe they may explain to me where my point of view is off base and I will change my mind—now I doubt it, of course. I feel *very strongly* about this now.

I am satisfied that my "Reliability" contribution need not go in the main report but will go into the appendix more or less intact rather than being lost in the archives. It is a good compromise we have come to.

See you soon,
Commissioner Feynman, Nobel Prize, Einstein Award,
Oersted Medal and utter ignoramus about politics.

The MacNeil/Lehrer Newshour, June 9, 1986

With us now for a "Newsmaker" interview is a key member of the presidential commission. He is Richard Feynman, the Nobel Prize–winning physicist from the California Institute of Technology.

Welcome, sir. Was this an accident that did not have to happen?

Feynman: Yes. Yes, it was. They had many, many warnings that there was something wrong, and that it might sooner or later go off, and the warnings were disregarded.

Disregarded out of incompetence, out of a faulty system, out of bad judgment? For what reason?

I had some difficulty with that. I kind of imagined something like a child that runs in the road, and the parent is very upset and says, "It's very dangerous!" The child comes back and says, "But nothing happened," and he runs out in the road again, several times, and the parent keeps saying, "It's dangerous!" Nothing happens. If the child's view that nothing happened is a clue that nothing is going to happen, then there's going to be an accident. You could hear brakes squealing a couple of times—that's leakage, and the gas going through the seals, and so forth.

Again and again, in looking through this, I saw statements like "This new flight is within our data base," which just means "Nothing happened before, it's about the same as we did before, so it can't be unsafe because it was okay last time." And that's a kind of childish attitude, with the mother corresponding to the engineers here, and the management corresponding to the children. That's the way I look at it, and I don't know what you would say. Sooner or later the child gets run over. Is it an accident? No, it's not an accident.

And yet your commission, and we just heard Chairman Rogers, say, "We're not here to blame anybody." Why not? Why is somebody not blamed?

I don't know how to assign blame, and whether it does any good. The question is, how do we educate the child? You could say you blame the child for being a little foolish, but it's very difficult. I tried to figure out why they had this attitude, and why they weren't paying attention. I've tried various theories, and I really don't know the ultimate cause.

What's your theory?

People say to me there's an idea that in management, incompetence reaches its own level, or whatever. But I had another idea—I don't know whether it's right. That is, that in the beginning all kinds of exaggerations were made about what this thing can do: it can fly sixty flights, it'll only cost so much, it'll be recoverable . . . there'll be no real problems. But the engineers at the bottom are probably screaming (this is my imagination), they're screaming up, "No, no! It can't be this way, it can't be that way. . . . We can only go ten flights. . . . We haven't got enough equipment to train that many crews a year," and so forth, and the people at the top who are talking to Congress don't want to hear this, so they discouraged information from moving up.

You see, it was just after they were so successful with Apollo, and in that case they were doing a project that was just a little bit harder than they could do, just a little bit harder, so they could do it. This is my imagination, right? I wasn't there. Somebody would say, "How are we going to make a space suit?" and finally they get a solution to that. They get excited and tell the others. A fellow who's working on some other problem gets a solution to his problem, and there's a lot of intercommunication, because there's excitement and motivation . . .

Which is not necessarily always a bad thing?

No, not at all! It's what makes it go, and that's why it worked okay with Apollo. But then when they had this other project, which is so to speak impossible from an engineering point of view, it's unrealistic, then they don't want to hear what happens. It just goes up, and each level in a bureaucracy kind of understands what it's supposed to do—keep it from the other guys, so they don't have to hear it. They don't want to hear it, because it would be uncomfortable to be saying "We're going to do sixty flights a year" when just that morning they were told that it's impossible.

That's the theory. Now as you know, I am a professor of physics and not of management and human relations, and it's very likely not right. But you asked me for my theory.

Donald Kutyna Feynman, by nature, always wanted to get to the very basic roots of any mystery, and this was a tremendous mystery. He had found the symptoms that caused the *Challenger* to crash—the technical reasons. But it was obvious to him that there was something that drove the people in the system to make these mistakes. So he went one level beyond, and he found the reasons. He wanted them to come out, because he was so interested in truth and in accuracy, and it would have been only half the story had his work not been published.

His views were not popular, because they attacked the basic structure of an organization. There were folks who didn't necessarily want that to be brought out in public.

Joan Feynman

It became uncomfortable when he was being pressured to sign a report he didn't like. I told him that they were not going to put the report out unless he had signed it; that the appendix he had written should come out at the same time as the main report, otherwise no one would take any notice; that they couldn't reject the appendix because he wouldn't sign otherwise; and that they had to get a report out.

At one point he was sort of giving up, and saying, "Oh well, they probably won't publish the appendix," and so on. I said, "Richard, if you don't push the appendix through, what will be the result of your work on the committee?"

And he stopped for a moment, and he thought, and he said, "Nothing."

From that moment it was clear the appendix was going to get published, with what he believed in it.

Feynman's "Personal Observations on the Reliability of the Shuttle" were finally published as Appendix F in Volume 2 of the Report of the Presidential Commission on the Space Shuttle Challenger *Accident. This is how he ends:*

If a reasonable launch schedule is to be maintained, engineering cannot be done fast enough to keep up with the expectations of originally conservative certification criteria designed to guarantee a very safe vehicle. In these situations, subtly, and often with apparently logical arguments, the criteria are altered so that the flights may still be certified in time. They therefore fly in a relatively unsafe condition, with a chance of failure of the order of a percent (it is difficult to be more accurate).

Official management, on the other hand, claims to believe the probability of failure is a thousand times less. One reason for this may be an attempt to assure the government of NASA perfection and success in order to ensure the supply of funds. The other may be that they sincerely believe it to be true, demonstrating an almost incredible lack of communication between themselves and their working engineers.

In any event this has had very unfortunate consequences, the most serious of which is to encourage ordinary citizens to fly in such a dangerous machine, as if it had attained the safety of an ordinary airliner. The astronauts, like test pilots, should know their risks, and we honor them for their courage. Who can doubt that McAuliffe was equally a person of great courage, who was closer to an awareness of the true risk than NASA management would have us believe?

Let us make recommendations to ensure that NASA officials deal in a world of reality in understanding technological weaknesses and imperfections well enough to be actively trying to eliminate them. They must live in a world of reality in comparing the costs and utility of the shuttle to other methods of entering space. And they must be realistic in making contracts, in estimating costs, and the difficulty of the projects. Only realistic flight schedules should be proposed, schedules that have a reasonable chance of being met. If in this way the government would not support them, then so be it. NASA owes it to the citizens from whom it asks support to be frank, honest, and informative, so that these citizens can make the wisest decisions for the use of their limited resources.

For a successful technology, reality must take precedence over public relations, for nature cannot be fooled.[9]

Donald Kutyna   If anyone knew how to manipulate the system, and work the system to his advantage, Feynman did it beautifully. He illustrated that with getting his report out, which many people tried to stifle.

I did feel slightly guilty that I didn't tell him at the

The White House Rose Garden, June 1986. Feynman far right, Kutyna far left. Kutyna autographed the back of Feynman's copy of the official photograph.

time that I had gotten that information from an astronaut, because Feynman had told me, "Whatever you do, don't ever tell me anything that you want kept secret. I will not keep a secret."

Feynman gave me a lot of credit later on for coming up with this wonderful idea about the O-rings and the problems you might have with the compression and the cold. Of course I couldn't take that credit. So before he died I explained the story to him, and I told him why I had to do it that way. He just got very angry with me. I don't blame him. I'd be angry. I think he probably understood in the end, although he gave me a hard time for quite a while because of it!

Feynman

I found out later that when I thought I was doing something independently, I was being worked—operated by somebody else who wanted to get something done without involving himself. Those guys are clever, you know—I think I'm running around on my own hook, getting a clue here and a clue there, but those clues were just little taps to make me run in the right direction.

So I was being had to a certain extent. On the other hand, I enjoyed it. It was fun to see what that crazy place was like!

CHAPTER NINE

The Quest for Tannu Tuva

One evening in 1986, Feynman told me about somewhere strange called Tannu Tuva which he said was a country in the geographical dead center of Asia. He seemed surprised that I had never seen Tuvan postage stamps—triangular, and depicting archers, wrestlers, and strange animals. He claimed that it was the country "where the reindeer meets the camel," that the Tuvan landscape was dotted with stone statues of men with big mustaches, and that there were Tuvan shepherds who could sing as if they had two separate voices, one voice sounding like an accompanying musical instrument—"throat-singing," it was called.

I told Feynman I thought he was making fun of me, so he picked up the phone and called his friend Ralph Leighton. He told Ralph to come over quick, and to "bring the Tuvan stuff" with him. Ralph brought a large cardboard box. There were the beautiful postage stamps, maps, a tape recording of the indescribably weird throat-singing, and a videocassette of a magnificent Kurosawa film called Dersu Uzala starring a Tuvan actor named Maxim Munzuk. . . . It was all true, and Feynman and Ralph had been trying to get to Tannu Tuva for years.

In early 1988, my wife, Lotte, and I went to Los Angeles

to discuss the idea of making a film with Feynman and Ralph about their efforts to reach Tuva. Feynman was now very frail but said he loved talking about Tuva—it would take his mind off his illness. We decided to record the story on a home video camera, on the veranda at the back of the house. Feynman's face lit up when he talked, but he tired rapidly. He would say, "I'll just go and lie down for five minutes. The doctor says I mustn't go to sleep during the day. I'll be right back." So he would lie down on a sofa, with a blanket and two dogs on top of him, and fall into a deep sleep.

He was clearly dying, but that didn't stop him from going to Chinatown for a Sunday dim sum lunch, or from playing the drums for the camera.

The videotapes became the BBC Horizon documentary The Quest for Tannu Tuva, *from which this chapter is drawn.*

Feynman Ralph's a very good friend of mine, and I like to tease him a little. He was teaching arithmetic and algebra in high school, and then they gave him a geography class. I knew he'd do a fairly good job in geography because he listens to the shortwave, and therefore he gets a very good feel where everything is.

Nevertheless I wanted to tease him, so one evening I said, "You know all about geography, huh?" And he said, "Yeah." I said, "Okay. Whatever happened to Tannu Tuva?" I knew that there was this country when I was a kid, that my father explained was an independent country, and it had these interesting stamps. I think he had shown me on the map where it was, and it was a purple area in the middle of Asia somewhere. As time went on, I never heard of it again. It was supposed to be an independent country, so it must have disappeared somehow. So in the back of my mind always was this question, "Whatever happened to Tannu Tuva?"

I knew damn well Ralph had never heard of it, and that he'd think I was kidding him that there was such a thing, because I like to tease by that kind of method, you see— making up a country that doesn't exist. Sure enough he said, "You're making up a country that doesn't exist!"

"The capital was K-Y-Z-Y-L. That's what did it!"

"Oh yeah?" I said. I got the encyclopedia out and we looked it up on a map, and sure enough there was a Tannu Tuva. I was as surprised as he was, really. It was just outside of Outer Mongolia, in the middle of central Asia, in the depths of Russia, far away from anything, and it was no longer an independent country. It was a part of Russia, and we saw that the capital—this is what did it— the capital was K-Y-Z-Y-L. My wife and I and Ralph at the same time sort of looked, grinned at each other, because any place that's got a capital named K-Y-Z-Y-L has just got to be interesting!

Feynman

We couldn't get any information at all. At first we started out in San Francisco, where we had a job playing drums for a ballet. We would use the spare time to go to the library, but we didn't know where to begin. We went to "Travels in Central Siberia," which is right where Tuva is. We'd find all these books of people traveling in central Siberia and nobody went through Tuva. They went down around below it, or they went around above it, but wherever they went in central Siberia they missed it, because it was a kind of a bowl, and if you went down in you'd have to climb back out. There was no particular reason to go through it—it was just in the way. So everybody seemed to dodge it, and in spite of all these books about "Travels in Central Siberia," we found nothing.

223

One day, Ralph came across a rare book published in Berlin in 1931 and written by the German historian and explorer Otto Maenchen-Helfen. Ralph's brother Alan, a French-horn player in Bochum, Germany, translated it into English. It was a treasure chest of information and pictures from Tuva. It included, for example, a remarkable (if fanciful) account of a visit to the cinema:

I was the first non-Russian to set foot in the Republic of Tuva. It took a lot of trouble to obtain permission to go. I went as an ethnologist, pointing out that ethnologists are as harmless as mushroom connoisseurs or stamp collectors. . . .

I did not bring with me especially high expectations of Kyzyl, though what I encountered was nonetheless astonishing. . . . The Kyzyl electric plant works only when the movie theater is running. I saw the beautiful Pudovkin film *Mother* there. Tuvans rode from far and wide to look at this wonder. The film broke at least twenty times that night, but that only made the audience happy! So much the better! Now the fairy tale could last that much longer. They couldn't understand anything, not the slightest bit. The subtitles were in Russian. They couldn't read them, but their pleasure was nevertheless unending. When horses appeared the whole place went crazy. They screamed and jumped up, they had a magnificent time. They didn't worry at all about who was a gendarme and who was a revolutionary, because they didn't understand what the fight was about. Whoever just fired . . . that was their man! Only once were they incensed and raving. I didn't understand the reason. The film didn't show anything outlandish: running feet, a raised arm, a face. But that was precisely why. What they were shouting was translated for me: "We paid full price! Why do you show us just a foot? Where is the head? We want to see a whole person! Why do you make the screen so small? We demand a screen on which a whole person has room! We want a big screen, a big screen, a *big* screen!"

Feynman It has everything! As far as I know, it still has everything. We had discovered a Shangri-la, you see. A place in the world where nobody visited in a long time. So we all— Gweneth, Ralph, and I—right then and there said, "We've got to go there, of course."

My wife and I often went to places. We had done this before. We've discovered that this trick of picking a place that looks obscure to visit leads to the most interesting trips. It's a place that nobody goes, and it hasn't got all the hotels and hocus pocus. Not like the Holiday Inn in Miami—we know what that looks like. And so it was when we went to the Cañon de Cobre.[1] To get there, we had to go through the strange forests and peculiar towns. In Cisneguito, the kids walked around in bare feet, all over the rocks and so on. They took us into a cave in which there were skeletons, and there was some kind of a story about how the soldiers had pushed the Indians into the cave, or vice versa—I don't remember now. But to find a cave of skeletons! The moral, if there is any, is that you find the unexpected and it's always delightful.

Now there are people who would be afraid to go to such places; they're not sure the accommodations will be good enough, they're not sure of this, they're not sure of that, they wouldn't do it. Well, they're missing the delight of surprise. So yes, the moral is: be brave, forget it, nothing bad will happen! If you get rained on, someone will pick you up. I can't explain it, but it always works well. Sometimes we go on a trip across the country slowly, camping out at night, and to find a site we turn off the highway, and at every turn we take the worst road! We do that in the daytime, too, just to explore. Anyway, Ralph was delighted with this crazy idea. That's how it started.

Part of the difficulty of getting to Tuva was created by Feynman's insistence that no special status or privileges were to be invoked—clearly a reflection of his antipathy to the Nobel Prize and other honors.

Feynman

It's very simple: I propose to give some lectures in Russia. They would be delighted (I think). I arrive there and I say that one of the conditions is that I travel to Tuva. And they say, "Indeed, it's fine!"

And then (having learned a bit, you see) I say, "But I

ИНТУРИСТ
Intourist

USSR COMPANY FOR FOREIGN TRAVEL
SOCIETE ANONYME DE L'URSS POUR LE TOURISME ETRANGER
ВСЕСОЮЗНОЕ АКЦИОНЕРНОЕ ОБЩЕСТВО ПО ИНОСТРАННОМУ ТУРИЗМУ В СССР

МОСКВА, К-9
ПРОСПЕКТ МАРКСА, 16
ТЕЛЕФОН 292-22-60

16 AVENUE MARX,
MOSCOU, URSS
TEL. 292-22-60

CABLE: INTOURIST, MOSCOW
TELEX: 7211, 7212, 7213, 7214, 7215,
7216, 7631, 7632, 7914
ТЕЛЕГРАФНЫЙ АДРЕС: МОСКВА 9 — ИНТУРИСТ

№ 05-I-76/17

«7» January 1981 г.

Mr. Ralph Leighton
2484 N. Page Dr.
Altadena, Ca. 9I00I
USA

Dear Mr. Leighton:

We have received your letter of Nov.29,1980 requesting us
to arrange visit to Tuvinskaya ASSR. We regret to inform
you that the subject area is beyond Intourist travel routes,
therefore we cannot arrange such visit.

Thank you for a pleasant and very interesting letter. Please
accept our best wishes for a happy healthy and prosperous
New Year.

Sincerely,

INTOURIST

USSR Company for
Foreign Travel

give the lectures in Moscow *after* I visit Tuva." And they'll have to say yes to that, and I could go.

Well, I don't want to do it that way. The whole idea is to have adventure. The way to have adventure is to do things at a lower level, not to ride on the freeway and to stop at the Holiday Inn!

We found somehow this Mongolian-Tuvan-Russian phrasebook, which was just wonderful. Now that we had the phrasebook we would write in Tuvan; that would probably wake somebody up, you see. So we struggled, and this is the kind of thing I love—try to put something together, taking all the phrases and trying to make the minimum changes on any of the phrases so that we would be able to put together the phrases in order to say to someone, "Greetings to your country from ours! We have a great interest in Tuva, and we hope someday to come to visit and we would look forward to see you, and if there's any way that you can send us tapes of your language we would appreciate it. . . . All good wishes," all this kind of stuff. It sounds a little odd that you could make all that out of a phrasebook, but actually it was rather a good one, and it had a lot of stuff in it—"phono-recordings," and things like that. So we wrote this letter into the vacuum as usual, and nothing happened.

Then one day Ralph comes running over here waving a letter in the air! He was so excited he didn't open it yet. A letter had come from Tuva. With the stamps—well, Russian stamps, but it had come from Kyzyl. So we opened it. And then of course we couldn't read it because it was in Tuvan!

We worked very patiently back and forth, because we had to go through the phrasebook into Russian, and then from Russian into English. His name was Ondar Daryma. "Greetings from Tuva! Kyzyl is a nice city! You will find we have a statue of the center of Asia. . . ."

It was very much fun, of course, to do that: to discover the different way that they speak, and how their language works, and so on. And that was our first piece of anything

Feynman

248 N. PABE DR.
ALTADENA, CALIFORNIA
С.Ш.А. USA. 91001.

г. Кызыл;
ул. Кочетова, Ч.
ТНИИЯЛИ
ДАРЫМА ОНДАР —
КИШ-ЧАЛАЕВИЧ

Экии, Ралф Лейтон! Чаа чыл-биле!
Мени Дарыма Ондар дээр, 45 харлыг мен.
Силерниң бижээн чагааңарны номчуп танышкан мен. Тывалап бижээниңерге өөрүп четтирдим. Бистиң тыва дыл тюрк дылга хамааржыр.
Силерге чагаа четкен бе? Кымнардан чагаа ап тур силер? Бистиң институттан чагаа алдыңар бе? Кызыл хоорайда ном магазиннери бар. Орус-тыва болгаш тыва-орус словарлар ному бар. Тываның төву Кызыл хоорай. Азияның төп точказы бистиң чараш хоорайывыста. Дыштаныр хүннерде ооң чанындан кижилер үзүлбес. Бисте тыва= англи словарь ному чок. Пластинкада бижээн ыр, хөөмей бар.
Чүну сонуургап турар силер? Биске чагаадан бижиңер.
Мен бо институтта тыва улустуң аас чогаалын чыып бижип турар мен, 15 чыл ажылдап турар мен. Дарый чагаа бижииринерни манап тур мен. Менди-чаагай болурунарны күзедим.
Улуу-биле четтирдим.

The first letter from Tannu Tuva. It began, in the Feynman/Leighton Tuvan-Russian-English translation: "Hello! Happy New Year! Me Daryma Ondar called, forty-five snowy I. Your written-having letter-your reading acquainted I. Tuvan-in written-having-your gladness full-am-I. Our Tuvan language Turk language-to related-is. . . ."

that came out of Tuva. That was the beginning of hope. It took us a number of years till we got to that stage.

It's the kind of a puzzle I love. It's like deciphering hieroglyphics, which I enjoy. There's a Mayan codex, called the Dresden Codex, which is one of three books left

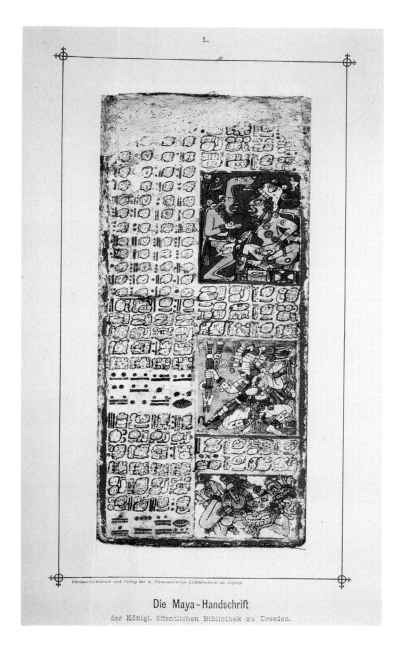

A leaf from "Die Maya Handschrift" (the Dresden Codex) in the British Library.

from the hundreds of thousands of books that were extant at the time when the Spanish conquered Mexico. This is the only good one, the Dresden Codex. I knew that it had been translated in 1850 or something by somebody, but I love puzzles, and I thought to myself, "Suppose I was the one who got hold of this thing for the first time. What would I do? What did he do?" So I made believe I was in the same position.

It wasn't very difficult, because there are bars and dots, and pretty soon you guess they're numbers, and then you find out that five dots is equivalent to a bar, and so on. After that, you notice periodicities and funny symbols which are presumably names of days that go like our week does, etc. Okay? You can work all that out. Then there'd be some very puzzling numbers, a whole lot of calculations involving multiples of 584, and you can't figure out what the heck that is.

Then you get the idea that maybe it's an astronomic thing they're observing. So I went to the library at Caltech and looked up astronomical numbers, for the planets from the point of view of the earth, and Venus appears in the same position in the sky again after 584 days! Well, after 583.92 days. You have to kind of understand the orbits, but you can see that there would be a period when Venus would be a morning star—about 230 days—and a period when it's an evening star—another period of about the same amount. But the transition from the morning to the evening star is very quick. At one part of the orbit, when it's on our side of the sun, you pass it quickly, and when it's on the far side its relative angle of motion is very slow, so it would look like a longer period where you can't see it because it's too close to the sun.

You see all this fit, and you know all of a sudden that you've been reading about Venus and that they have made all these observations. You get one hell of an excitement, just like a physics discovery or something. Although it's all been discovered before, I didn't know it, and that's all—I was doing it for the fun of it, to see what I could discover. I finally figured out eclipse numbers, eclipse prediction tables in this thing. It was very exciting. You know there's sense behind the damn thing. The problem is to extract it with whatever clues and tools you've got, and that's lots of fun.

Feynman

Ralph has this car which has license plates saying TUVA on it.[2] For the fun of it we had the car outside on the street in front here, and we got some friends of ours to take our picture trying to push this automobile up the hill, as if it's kind of run out of gas or something. We're faking, of course, that we're pushing so hard. We sent it to Ondar Daryma and said, "See how hard we're working to get to Tuva. It's Tuva or bust," or something like that, as a joke. He was delighted and took it to their local newspaper, the

ТУВИНСКАЯ ПРАВДА

НАИЛУЧШИЕ ПОЖЕЛАНИЯ!

Мы, жители штата Калифорния Ральф Лейгтон, доктор Ричард Фейнман и Глен Коуэн, хотели бы передать через вашу газету сердечный привет народу Тувинской АССР!

Нас поражают удивительная красота, богатая и разнообразная природа вашей республики, находящейся в самом центре Азии. Мы особенно интересуемся тувинской этнографией и музыкой и слушаем с огромным интересом запись тувинских народных музыкальных стилей — сыгыт, каргы-

раа и хоомей, которую нам подарил доктор С. И. Вайнштейн из Института этнографии им. Н. Н. Миклухо-Маклая в Москве.

Мы считаем, сегодня, когда наша планета переживает такое трудное, напряженное время, очень важно выразить наше пожелание хороших отношений, мира и дружбы между нашими народами. Желаем вам счастья, здоровья, новых успехов.

С калифорнийским приветом и искренним уважением —

Ральф ЛЕЙГТОН,
Ричард П. ФЕЙНМАН,
Глен КОУЭН.
г. Пасадена, США.

На снимке: (слева направо) Глен Коуэн, аспирант Калифорнийского университета в Беркли, доктор Ричард П. Фейнман, физик Калифорнийского технологического института, и Ральф Лейгтон, учитель средней школы им. Маршалла в Пасадене, около автомобиля Ральфа, который достал специальный номерной знак, чтобы рекламировать наш интерес к Туве.

From the *Tuvinskaya Pravda*, January 1983.

231

Kyzyl newspaper, and they printed the picture with a caption that I think we had written, actually.

Somewhere along the line we found out that a group of botanists had been able to go to Tuva. It looked to us that they were counting the leaf buds, or whatever you do when you're a botanist, and we were kind of disappointed that these guys had gotten there ahead of us, and also that they maybe hadn't fully appreciated the wonderful place we imagined they were going to! But we got from them the idea that the reason it was easier to go was that they had something to do, some reason to be there. So we had to find some kind of a thing that would officially make sense that we had to go to Tuva.

Then Ralph found out that there was going to be a great throat-singing contest for a week somewhere way out on the west edge of Mongolia. It was a part of Mongolia you don't ordinarily go to, and it was right near Tuva. Of course, there were various fantasies, dreams of donning old robes, old rags and so on, because we'd meet these guys, we'd meet the Tuvans in Mongolia, and then they'd carry us back in their wagons and we'd see a part of Tuva, maybe. Okay? We were all excited. Even if we didn't get to Tuva, that would be interesting too. You see, you have to understand that every plot, even though there was a high chance of failure as far as the ultimate aim was concerned, it would always turn out well. It would be a big adventure after all and it ain't everybody that goes across the world to visit a throat-singing conference in the western part of Mongolia. We tried to sign up with this and get everything ready, and then there was a change of government in Mongolia. The Minister of Culture decided they weren't going to have a throat-singing conference in Mongolia after all. So that fell through.

Next Ralph discovered that there was a Russian museum exhibit about the Silk Road which had a lot of Tuvan artifacts and things in it. It was at present in Sweden. Ralph's idea was that he would go to Sweden acting as if he could get that exhibit transferred to the United States. We would be the exhibit representatives in the United States and would need to go to look at sites where the things came from, to take pictures that would appear in the exhibit. In other words, we would become "museum people" that had to go to Tuva in order to make the exhibit work. Good, huh?

Ralph went to several museums with details of the Silk Road exhibit. Finally, he and Feynman met with the curator of the Los Angeles County Museum of Natural History.

Ralph was explaining all these costs and things, and the curator finally said, "I think maybe we'll do this, but what is your finder's fee?"

Feynman

Ralph said, "There is no finder's fee."

And the curator says, "Well, that's kind of incredible. Why are you doing this?"

Ralph told him, "Because we want to arrange some way that we can get to Tuva, and that's our finder's fee."

And that was the way that we first got a real chance to go to Tuva—by moving the earth, you know!

"We became museum people. . . ." Feynman and Ralph Leighton at the Los Angeles County Museum of Natural History, 1987.

Feynman   Well, the Russians laughed because two thirds of their protocol were various gimmicks for getting Russians to come here! There were all kinds of people, seventeen different people, coming from Russia for this exhibit. So they understood this trick, see? They would get to see the mysterious Disneyland. The first ones to come were high in the system, the Russian curator and Professor Andrej Kapitsa. We took them around and introduced them to some of our friends, hippie-like friends who have parrots and make music, enjoy life, and have a funny view of things.

Kapitsa was utterly delighted with all this and he said, "You should come to Tuva, and I'm going to guarantee it."

I think that he understands what I understand, that what he likes and what I like are the same—you don't want to be treated as anybody special. I'm just a regular guy, and he's just a Russian that's visiting. It's not the "Vice-President-Deputy-in-Charge of the Academy of Sciences," etc., etc. No, none of that! And he was happy. So I hope that the trip he's arranging for us will turn out that way—if it will turn out at all!

Feynman never did reach Tuva. A couple of weeks after his death in February 1988, Gweneth Feynman received a letter from Moscow.

Some weeks later I went back to Pasadena to see Ralph Leighton and to finish the filming for our Tuva Horizon. One afternoon in his apartment, after we had filmed a short interview and some close-ups of Tuvan postage stamps and so on, Ralph took me over to a closet, opened the door, and reached inside.

Ralph Leighton   Let me show you something here. I'm not usually good at keeping secrets, but this one I kept. I was going to break these out at the monument, when we finally reached our goal. Things like this: a T-shirt with a Tuva map. Another one . . . you know how you have "I love New York" or "I love California"? This one says, in Tuvan, "Kyzyl love I."

АКАДЕМИЯ НАУК

СОЮЗА СОВЕТСКИХ СОЦИАЛИСТИЧЕСКИХ РЕСПУБЛИК

117901, ГСП-I, Москва, В-71, Ленинский просп., 14.   Тел. 237-98-49.

I9.02.88 № _Cons.ekcib_

На № _____

Professor Richard Phillips Feynman,
Los Angeles
California
USA

Dear Professor R.P.Feynman,

I have the great pleasure to invite you, your wife and
four of your collegues to visit the Soviet Union as the guests
of the USSR Academy of Sciences.

I was informed by the corresponding member of the USSR Academy
of Sciences, Prof.A.P.Kapitsa that you would like to visit Tuva
ASSR and get acquainted of its sightseeings. We consider the most
favourable time for such a trip to be the period of May and June
of the next year /1988/. Your trip will take 3-4 weeks.

I hope that during your tour you will have time to meet Soviet
collegues in Novosibirsk and Moscow who knew your activities and
works and , undoubtly, will be very pleased to meet you.

Kindly note that the USSR Academy of Sciences will cover expences
on your and your collegues'staying in the USSR.

Yours sincerely,

Vice President
of the USSR Academy of Sciences
Academician
E.P.Velikhov

And we were going to have these souvenir hats. But the Chief never knew about it, and now I regret I didn't tell him.

I don't know what my feelings are going to be in a few months from now. It's been a consuming kind of a thing, but on the other hand certain factors are working their way into this now, things like tax time is coming up, and my wife and I have got to think, "Can we afford a trip like this?" I never thought of things like that before. Financial considerations never worked into the equation, but now I'm starting to think of things like that. I think that must indicate that I'm not as set on it, because I realize it was the adventure with my friend that this was all about.

Ralph had tears in his eyes, and when I came to edit the film, it seemed unbearably sad. So we ended it with a last word from Feynman on the "meaning" of the quest for Tannu Tuva. . . .

Feynman We're getting a little philosophical and serious, okay? Let's go back to what we're doing. One day we look at a map and its capital is K-Y-Z-Y-L. We decided it would be fun to go there because it's so obscure and peculiar. It's a game. It's not serious. It doesn't involve some deep philosophical point of view about authority or anything. It's just the fun of having an adventure to try to go to a land that we'd never heard of, that we knew was an independent country once, that's no longer an independent country, to find out what it's like and discover as we went along that nobody went there for a long time and it's isolated, and so on. It made it more interesting. Many explorers like to go to places that are unusual, and it's only for the fun of it, and I don't go for any philosophical interpretation of "our deeper understanding of what we're doing." We haven't any deep understanding of what we're doing! If we tried to understand what we're doing, we'd go nutty!

The Quest for Tannu Tuva

Ralph Leighton reached Kyzyl in July 1988. He tells the story of what he found there in his book Tuva or Bust! Ralph has founded an informal organization called Friends of Tuva and organized a Feynman memorial plaque on the Center of Asia monument in Kyzyl. In early 1993, Ralph brought three Tuvan horsemen—throat singers to the United States. They rode in the Pasadena Rose Parade and gave a series of wildly successful concerts. They have also been recording with the legendary Frank Zappa.

Feynman's blackboard at Caltech as he left it for the last time in January 1988.

CHAPTER TEN

Dying

You see, I can live with doubt, and uncertainty, and not knowing. I think it's much more interesting to live not knowing than to have answers which might be wrong. I have approximate answers, and possible beliefs, and different degrees of certainty about different things, but I'm not absolutely sure of anything. There are many things I don't know anything about, such as whether it means anything to ask "Why are we here?" I might think about it a little bit, and if I can't figure it out then I'll go on to something else. But I don't have to know an answer. I don't feel frightened by not knowing things, by being lost in a mysterious universe without having any purpose—which is the way it is, so far as I can tell. Possibly. It doesn't frighten me.

Feynman

One morning in January 1988 I asked Feynman if he would like to talk about death and dying on our home video camera or a tape recorder. I thought that if I didn't ask, I might well regret it when it was too late.

He was still in bed when we turned up at the house to record some more about Tuva, but he said to come upstairs anyway. When I put my question, he said no, he certainly didn't mind my asking, but he'd have to talk

Feynman near his beach house at La Misíon, Baja California, in January 1981. His cancer had first been diagnosed in 1978; now he was heading for a second major operation.

about it for a while to see how it would make him feel. So I sat on the side of the bed while he talked for an hour or so. He told me about the terrible experience of his father's funeral, when he realized that he would not be able to repeat words in Hebrew spoken by the rabbi, in which he, Richard, did not believe. He could not do it, and so the feelings of family and friends had to be badly hurt.

He also told me about his first wife, Arline, and about

her illness and death, how they had agreed that they both knew from childhood that everyone had to die someday, and what difference did it really make as to whether that day was close or far off? It was a quantitative, not a qualitative thing—what mattered was what you did with life, and so their right course of action was to marry even though Arline was going to die very soon. This made him weep.

In the end, he smiled and said that we'd found out something—he didn't want to talk about dying, because it made him feel too depressed.

One day Feynman's secretary Helen Tuck called me up to tell me quietly that Dick had cancer and that he would be going into the hospital for an operation the following Friday. (This would be the first of four operations for the cancer that would ultimately take his life.) It was to be a dangerous operation, and it was not assured that he would survive it. I promised not to tell anyone, and he didn't know that I knew.

This particular Friday, a week before the operation, was Commencement Day at Caltech, where we put on our academic robes and parade for the graduates and their parents. Most people found it remarkable that Feynman would put on those silly robes and hat and march in the parade. But there he was.

I told him that somebody had found an apparent error in a calculation that we had done and published together, and I didn't know what the error was. Would he be willing to spend some time with me to look for it? And he said, "Sure."

On Monday morning we met in my office and he sat down and started working—he had to do the work because my command of this particular problem was not good enough to be much help, except to kibitz a little bit. Most of the time I just sat there looking at him, and thinking to myself, "Look at this man. He faces the abyss. He doesn't know whether he's going to live through this week, and here is this really unimportant problem in two-dimen-

David Goodstein

Commencement Day at Caltech.

sional elastic theory." But he was consumed by it, and he worked on it all day long.

Finally, at six o'clock in the evening, we decided that the problem was intractable, it couldn't be solved. So we gave up and went home.

Two hours later, he called me at home to say that he had solved the problem. He hadn't been able to stop working on it, and finally he had found the solution to this utterly obscure problem. He dictated the solution to me over the phone, and he was exhilarated, absolutely walking on air.

This was four days before the operation. I think that tells you a little bit about what drove the man to do what he did.

Joan Feynman   Like anything else, he found it a very interesting problem—how it worked. He always used his brain to protect himself as well as he could, so he read everything he could on cancer. He wanted to know exactly what was happening to him, and to understand as much as possible. The doctor, Dr. Morton, cooperated with him in this. So Richard found out that the cancer he had was rare, and that sometimes the operations worked. It was a peculiar cancer in that it didn't metastasize. It just grew from the region where it started and went in tendrils all over the place, but it didn't spread from the kidneys, where it started, to some other unconnected place. He also knew that the chances were not great that he would live.

(I think my father also stood back and watched his dying. He had high blood pressure, and I can remember him sitting at the table saying, "Have you seen my bloodshot eye? Now, that's an interesting thing, because the pressure . . ." and so on, and so forth. He said, "One day that's going to happen in my brain.")

Eventually, Richard had a heart condition, two cancers, and a blood condition. Half of his diaphragm was missing, one kidney wasn't operating too well, and a few other items were missing. But it never stopped him for one minute, not even up to the end.

Dick Davies

I don't have many cases to compare with him. He was very brave about it. Obviously it worried him. He thought about it, and probably knew more about the type of sarcoma he had than the physicians who were attending him. He was asking them questions all the time. He wasn't anxious to just cave in and die—he wanted to keep going. But he was very accepting. He would say, "Well, I've been luckier than most people. I've had opportunities for an exciting life and I've taken advantage of all of them."

He approached it in a very positive way, and I think he affected all of us in that sense—that he could be upbeat

Episodes of dizzyness. Momentary syncope on two occasions 1/85
More frequent day after exertion like running.
Longstanding with varying degrees. (Eg similar to 1/79)
    PVC's   present medications diazide, aspirin (5gr/day)
Card. History: Atrial fibrillation on two occasions. (once
                rythum restored in hospital, other spontaneous (?)
            Hypertension now only diazide - previously
                    reserpine, then aldomet, etc then.
            Thrombocytopenia (while taking quinidine)
    4/75 Some dizzyness reported
    4/77 Syncope while jogging. ~~congryogenically slower~~ stress test rate
related left bundle branch block. → angiogram.
        (a stress test some years later - no CHGB)

    10/79 Vertigo. PVC's. Holter monitor test
    (Slightly prolonged PR interval and left axis deviation
        are longstanding > 5 yrs.)
1. echo   Unexplained rise in SGOT 56(Iw 300), 10/82 to 12/82
2. monitor   nearly normal ~50 in 2/83, rose again ~50 in 4/83)
3. Neurologist ← Baylor   Since 1978 (at least) Grade 1 Systolic Murmur in Aortic Region.
4. 80 mg.f

other
Medical History. Retroperitoneal Cancer. two operations - last 1981.
        Thrombocytopenia 12/82
        Subdural Hematoma. Burr holes operation.

Feynman's notes on his condition and treatment.

about it despite the fact that he was in a lot of discomfort from time to time. All four of the operations were massive.

He realized that there were other people in this world besides himself and the physicians, and that his illness was disturbing them. So he went to a great deal of trouble to try to make the rest of us feel pretty good about it, because we cared for him and he cared for us, and he realized his disappearance wasn't going to make life any easier for us. Before his second operation we had a dinner party in the house here with a few close friends. Ralph Leighton came over with a pair of bongo drums and we just pounded away at those drums all evening, and then he went into hospital the next day. He had this adventure on the operating table which was out of this world—some fourteen hours.[1]

I remember once he came over to tell us that his cancer had returned. First there was some good news, but I can't remember now what the good news was. Then he said, "Well, unhappily my cancer's come back. That's not so bad for me, but I know it's hard on my friends." So we came out here in the yard, and we sat down, and tried to think about something else.

I had been playing with a little problem in fluid dynamics and I mentioned that there was an invariant. Feynman said, "What's this invariant? Show me the stuff." I gave him my notebook, and he said, "Now what was it you said?" He wrote it down. "Well, this and this and this and this . . ." He went through it in thirteen steps, and then he said, "Yes. Yes, that's right. Very good. You've got me thinking about physics again. Now I can go home!"

Freeman Dyson

The last time I saw him was at a meeting on Long Island called Shelter Island Two. It was a reunion of the people who had been at a famous meeting, thirty years earlier, or whatever it was, and it was a very emotional occasion. Feynman was by then known to be a dying man, but he never let it show. We all had a good time, and talked about the old days.

That was the last time, but much more memorable was

the time before that, at a little meeting in Texas organized by John Wheeler, who was Feynman's original teacher. Wheeler had arranged this little meeting, a gathering of physicists and astronomers, at a place called the World of Tennis, in the neighborhood of Austin, Texas. It was a hideout for oil millionaires, a terrible place, most garish, the ugliest place you can imagine, and correspondingly expensive. I think the rooms were three hundred dollars a night or so, which some oil millionaire was paying for— we didn't have to pay. But anyway, we arrived in the middle of the night, and we looked at our rooms, which were enormous and hideous, and we all groaned, and said what an awful place this was. But Dick Feynman, who was then well over sixty and recovering from a cancer operation, simply said: "I'm not going to sleep in this place. Goodbye!" And he walked off into the woods by himself, and spent the night under the stars. That was Feynman.

Danny Hillis   **O**ne thing Richard did, which was probably the hardest, was to be always scrupulously honest with himself. When Richard was bad at something he would say, "I'm bad at that." Or when he wasn't making progress on a problem he'd say, "I'm not making progress." When he came up with a stupid solution to something he'd say, "You know, that's a pretty stupid solution I've come up with." So he wouldn't fool himself into thinking a situation was better than it was, or worse than it was. He would just say, "Okay, these are the facts. It's going to be like this." He wasn't afraid of the facts, and he loved reality, I guess. I think an awful lot of people put too much emotional content into the facts of a situation, and end up denying it and being dishonest with themselves.

Richard's cancer is a perfect example of how he accepted the facts of a situation. Instead of denying that he had cancer, he got very interested in it, and he was always very happy to talk about his cancer. I remember once we were walking in the hills behind his house. I hadn't seen him for a while, and he'd just been through another cancer operation. He went through a whole series of them before he died. He started telling these stories about his cancer operation, and the stories were funny stories. They were about how he would secretly read his chart, for example, so that when the doctors came by he would say, "I feel like my blood pressure is up three points today." They would say, "That's amazing, Dr. Feynman! How did you know that?" He would do all these silly things just to fool his doctors—read the textbooks and get doctors to cross-check each other, and so on.

But I began to realize how serious it was this time, that they hadn't got all the cancer out, and he was probably going to die. We were walking along and I'm sure I was pretty quiet and sad, and Richard said, "What's the matter?"

I think that with any other person I would have made up something about what was the matter, but with Richard it seemed natural just to say, "I'm sad because I'm realizing that you're about to die."

Richard said, "Yeah, that bugs me too, sometimes."

But then he said something which I wish I could remember exactly. It was to the effect of, "Yeah, it bugs me, but it doesn't bug me as much as you think it would, because I feel like I've told enough stories to other people, and enough of me is inside their minds. I've kind of spread me around all over the place. So I'm probably not going to go away completely when I'm dead!"

That's the closest to any sort of philosphy or religion I ever got out of Richard, any kind of afterlife sort of concept. But he seemed comfortable with the idea. It was just another piece of reality that he had to deal with. I'm sure he loved life as much as anyone, and I'm sure he hated the idea of dying. But he was also able to talk about it, accept it, and take it as real. That's very typical. He never shied away from what was real. He offended people because of that. He would say to people what he would have liked people to say to him—"Oh, you're sick? You're about to die?"

Of course, that would really throw people off, but when they realized it was just honesty, it had a kind of endearing quality to it.

Tom Van Sant I learned a tremendous amount from Richard's experience with the operations, each of which was life-threatening. The first time, I think I asked him how he felt about it, and he said something to the effect of: "Well, I think I was about seven when I knew I was going to die one day, so it isn't as though it's some big surprise. We'll see what happens."

The last operation was the most dangerous, and in a sense he didn't survive it. I told him we were really going to miss him if he didn't make it this time. He told me he'd already talked to Gweneth about it, and they'd made their arrangements for if he didn't regain consciousness. He didn't want machines keeping him alive and all that stuff—he thought that was sort of dumb. That was the word he used: "dumb."

I guess I showed that I was going to miss him, you know, and he said, "Look, going through all this stuff and, you know, maybe dying—it isn't all that easy. I got enough trouble just taking care of myself. You don't want me to have to take care of you too, do you?" It was like a sort of joke.

My last meeting with Feynman was two or three days before his death. The indirect effects of the cancer were attacking his liver, and his ability to process poisons. He didn't want to go onto dialysis equipment. He couldn't see a future in it, and so he elected checkout time. It was anticipated to be three days, and that's exactly what it was. I was gratified. I saw it as a model for all of us.

Joan Feynman When he was dying in the hospital, we talked at least once a week from about seven p.m. till midnight, about things like consciousness and the universe. Every week. I miss it terribly. About a week before he died, I said to him:

"I figure that whether or not there's a God, or anything like that, is a question of physics, really. Now I've often been wrong, very, very wrong, about physics"—this is me talking—"and so I don't know if there's a God. But you have a problem: you haven't been wrong as much as I have."

He said: "Well, I know there isn't."

When he was a small child, our parents sent him to Sunday school, and in Sunday school he thought he was going to school, and that everything they told him was what was known. So he thought all this business about God and the Creation was literal fact—truth. One day the Sunday school teacher told him something about "Sarah" and how "Sarah thought such-and-such." He went up afterwards and asked about how they knew what Sarah thought. Did she write it down? Did she tell somebody? How do they know? And the teacher said, "Oh, no, we don't actually know what Sarah thought. It's just the way we talk. . . ." Richard began to wonder, and he realized that all the things he had been learning as if they were literal truth were merely opinion. It was devasting for him. And I think it was the reason why, for the rest of his life, he was so intense about not believing any of these things.

You know, it is a question of physics, really, how the universe is put together, and he certainly didn't change his mind about that at any time. He just did not believe the universe was put together by any supernatural being, governing anything. So his belief was that there wasn't anything else.

My family was Jewish, and my father was an atheist. My mother—they—sent me to the temple on Saturdays, and to Jewish Sunday school to learn a little Hebrew and so on, but I gave it up about the age of thirteen. I became an atheist because I didn't believe it.

I could say that my religious position might have nothing to do with my scientific knowledge—I have not, by learning about the physical world, directly discovered that some religious view is wrong. But I do think there is a relationship, and the relationship looks to me something like this:

The religions that I was related to, like Jewish or Christian religions, have a direct personal connection with the Creator of the universe, and in the Christian religion there is even a messenger that comes to earth because they are

Feynman

particularly interested in the problems of human beings. But as you learn about the universe, that it's so vast, and that there was such a long time in which there were no people, that there's such a big region in which there are other than humans, and so many stars, such an intricacy of nature, and so on—well, it looks like human beings are just part of the grand nature. The stage is so huge, and the drama so effective, that I can't believe that God spends His time attending to this little corner.

I see humans as animals that have evolved to this particular point. There are very remarkable mysteries about the fact that we're able to do so many more things than animals can apparently do, and other questions like that, but these are mysteries I want to investigate without knowing the answers to them. So I can't believe those special stories that have been made up about our relationship to the universe at large, because they seem to be too simple, too local, too provincial: "He came to the earth"—one of the aspects of God came to *the earth*, mind you, and look at what's out there! It isn't in proportion. Anyway, it's no use arguing. I'm just trying to tell you why the scientific views that I have do have some effect on my beliefs.

Another thing has to do with the question of how you find out if something is true. If there are all these different theories, different religions about the thing, then you begin to wonder. You ask me, "Is science true?" I say, "No, we don't know what's true; we're trying to find out, and everything is possibly wrong." Start out understanding religion by saying, "Everything is possibly wrong—let's see." As soon as you do that, you start sliding down an edge which is hard to recover from. So with the scientific view (or my father's view), which is that we should look to see what's true and what may not be true . . . well, once you start doubting, which I think is a very fundamental part of my soul, it gets a little harder to believe.

Marvin Minsky Feynman and I agreed that we shouldn't worship mysteries. Mysteries are wonderful because maybe you can solve them. For example, one great mystery is, how does the mind work? The view that Feynman and I shared closely was that someday we would understand this. The mind is what the brain does. The brain is hundreds of computers that have evolved for five hundred million years. It's a wonderful natural phenomenon, and we have to understand how this thing works. We must sweep aside the idea that the mind is animated by a soul or a spirit or anything like that. In fact, my view is that there is something insulting and degrading about the idea of a soul, and the idea of a spirit. Look at what the animals did—four hundred million years ago there were fish. Billions of fish had to live and die by Darwinian evolution. Then there were the amphibia, and the reptiles, and then mammals. It's a tremendous struggle, like nothing in human history—a struggle of trillions and trillions and trillions of these animals living and dying to develop the little changes in the circuits. Now here you are, a person, and thirty thousand genes or more are working to make the brain, the most complicated organ. If you were to say it's just a spirit, just a soul, just a little hard diamondlike point with no structure, a gift from some creator, it's so degrading! It means all the sacrifice by all of our animal ancestors is ignored. It seems to me that the religious view is the opposite of self-respect and understanding. It's taking this brain, with a hundred billion neurons, and not using it. What a paradoxical thing to be taught to do!

Did Feynman agree with all this?

Feynman liked those views, yes.

Feynman

If you expect science to give you all the answers to the wonderful questions about what we are, where we are going, and what the meaning of the universe is, then I think you could easily become disillusioned and look for a mystic answer to these problems. How a scientist can want a mystic answer, I don't know. I don't understand that.

The way I think of what we're doing is, we're exploring—we're trying to find out as much as we can about the world. People say to me, "Are you looking for the ultimate laws of physics?'' No, I'm not. I'm just looking to find out more about the world. If it turns out there is a simple, ultimate law which explains everything, so be it; that would be very nice to discover. If it turns out it's like an onion, with millions of layers, and we're sick and tired of looking at the layers, then that's the way it is. But whatever way it comes out, it's nature, and she's going to come out the way she is! Therefore when we go to investigate it we shouldn't predecide what it is we're going to find, except to try to find out more.

If you think that you are going to get an answer to some deep philosophical question, you may be wrong—it may be that you can't get an answer to that particular problem by finding out more about the character of nature. But I don't look at it like that; my interest in science is to simply find out more about the world, and the more I find out, the better it is. I like to find out.

Jirayr Zorthian

The last time I saw him was in the hospital, and I knew he was going. I spent three hours with him, and it was the first time I saw him cry. (Actually, no. It was the second time. The first time I saw him cry was when my daughter died. Although he was an atheist, he was the one who gave the eulogies at my daughter's death. He loved her very much.) Anyway, he was crying in the hospital when he started talking about his first wife, who died of tuberculosis, was it? I don't remember.

I knew he was going, and he knew he was going. He said, "You know, Jiry, I can live longer, I'm sure I can. But I don't think it's important anymore. It would be a way of life I don't want, in a wheelchair and so on."

So he said he was ready to go, and that he had no qualms about it. We talked about people, ourselves, friends. Finally he started getting tired, and then he said, "Well, I think we'd better stop now."

My wife, Dabney, was with me, of course, and as we walked out of the room into the corridor, he called out, "Jiry, don't worry about anything. Go out and have a good time!"

Dying

One day I got Gweneth on the phone and asked her, you know, what's happening? And she told me: "Richard says he wants to die, and that it's your decision." My decision? That was sort of unexpected.

I think he must have figured out ahead of time, "How do you tell when it's time to quit? When you're feeling sick and you're feeling terrible you might say it's time to quit. But if you have courage, you wouldn't." So I think what he must have done is decide that when he felt it was time to die, and if Gweneth and I agreed, then it was time to go.

We all knew his cancer was now inoperable, and to be taken a few months later by a painful cancer—there wasn't any sense to it. So by the time I got to the hospital I had decided. Gweneth and I met in the hospital chapel (because it was quiet, not because we were asking advice from the supernatural). Gweneth said, "Have we decided?" I said, "Apparently we have." When I came in he was lying there and he said: "Decision?" Because he couldn't talk very well. I said: "Yes, you're going to die." And his whole body just relaxed. That was the beginning. He had pain-relieving drugs, but he didn't seem to need many. He'd fought so long and so hard. He apologized to Dr. Morton, the cancer specialist. He apologized for dying.

There were some things that happened that I think he would want people to know. You can decide what you think about it, okay? You know how Richard was always watching everything, and telling people about nature? Well, as I told you, he had decided—the three of us had decided—it was time for him to die. He soon went into a coma, but occasionally he came out of it. Once he said, "The Mecca Café dancing girls!"

In the coma, his hand was moving, and Gweneth said that the doctors had told her that the motion is automatic, and it doesn't mean anything. So this man who'd been in a coma for a day and a half or something, and hadn't moved, picks up his hands, and goes like this, like a magician, as if to say "Nothing up my sleeve," and then he put his hands behind his head. It was to tell us that when you're in a coma you can hear, and you can think.

Joan Feynman

The other message which I think he wanted out was a little later. He pulled himself up out of the coma and opened his eyes briefly and said, "This dying is boring," and then went back into the coma. This sense of humor is a bit macabre, but that's what he said. That's the last thing he said.

So until the very end he was giving us signals that he knew we were there. Here was this guy who was dying

Student banner at Caltech the morning after Feynman's death.

and yet what he was thinking of was giving the living some more information about life and nature and what dying was. He was still watching nature, as he was leaving.

Feynman died, age sixty-nine, at the UCLA Medical Center on Monday, February 15, 1988, at 10:34 p.m.

Danny Hillis

I miss Richard every time I have something beautiful that I want to explain, because he was always so wonderful to explain something to. A while ago, I was working on this equation, looking for a solution to it. It was a big messy equation. At its worst it covered a page with figures and things. But the solution to it turned out to be $1/e^2$.

It was just beautiful that this big mess could have this very simple little answer. It was something I really wished I could have shown to Richard, because it was exactly his kind of thing.

Well, that night I actually dreamed that I met Richard and explained the equation to him. He looked at it, and he liked it. But the whole time I was saying to myself, "Gee, I wonder if he knows he's dead? I wonder if I should mention it?" I thought, "Well, Richard can handle this sort of thing." So I said, "Hey, Richard! How come you're talking to me? You're dead!"

And he said, "Oh well. At least we won't get interrupted this way!"

Mountain View Cemetery, Fair Oaks Avenue, Altadena.

Notes

1. These remarks appear as a footnote in Vol. I of *The Feynman Lectures on Physics*, tape-recorded at Caltech in 1961–62 and published in three volumes in 1963.

2. Srinivasa Ramanujan, the self-taught Indian mathematical genius, was brought from Madras to Trinity College, Cambridge, in 1914 by G. H. Hardy, to whom Ramanujan had written asking for advice. Hardy later described their relationship as "the one romantic episode of my life." They did magnificent work together, but Ramanujan soon fell ill, probably with tuberculosis exacerbated by vitamin deficiency—his strict adherence to Hindu belief made a proper diet difficult to sustain in wartime England. One day, Hardy visited his dying friend at a nursing home in London and happened to mention that the cab which brought him had "rather a dull number—1729." "Oh no, Hardy!" cried Ramanujan. "It is a most interesting number. It is the smallest number expressible as the sum of two cubes in two different ways." (The two ways are $12^3 + 1^3$, and $10^3 + 9^3$.) Ramanujan died in India in 1920, age thirty-two.

3. Freeman Dyson was born in England in 1923. During the second World War he worked in operations research for RAF Bomber Command. In 1947 he came to Cornell University, where he met Feynman. He decided to settle in America, and he has been professor of physics at the Institute for Advanced Study in Princeton since 1953.

1. The Pleasure of Finding Things Out

4. Hans A. Bethe was born in Strasbourg in 1906. He left Hitler's Germany in 1933 for England, and then America and Cornell University. He was one of the leading members of Oppenheimer's bomb-building team at Los Alamos, where he and Feynman first met. After the war, Bethe went back to Cornell, and he has been a professor there ever since. He was awarded the Nobel Prize in 1967 for discovering the inner workings of the sun and stars.

5. Marvin Minsky is Donner Professor of Science at MIT, where he cofounded the pioneering Artificial Intelligence Laboratory in 1958. Minsky is famous for illuminating and memorable remarks such as "The brain happens to be a meat machine."

2. Love and the Bomb

1. John Archibald Wheeler studied with Niels Bohr in Copenhagen before going to Princeton in 1938, the year before Feynman arrived. He had an intimidating habit of laying his watch on the table when a student came to see him; for his second visit, Feynman bought a cheap watch and laid it alongside the professor's. They became friends as well as scientific collaborators. It was Wheeler who invented the astronomical term "black hole."

2. This was the theory proposed by Dirac, Pauli, Heisenberg, and others, which Feynman was to develop after the war and for which he would share a Nobel Prize. Feynman and others tell the story in Chapter 3.

3. This letter was brought to light and first published by James Gleick in his 1992 Feynman biography, *Genius*.

3. How to Win a Nobel Prize

1. This account was given to a film crew from Swedish TV (SVT) in 1965.

2. These remarks are from the introduction to Feynman's book *QED: The Strange Theory of Light and Matter*.

3. Why getting infinity from a calculation is so annoying:

   "Thinking I understand geometry and wanting to cut a piece of wood to fit the diagonal of a five foot square, I try to figure out how long it must be. Not being very expert, I get infinity—useless—nor does it help to say it may be zero because they are both circles. It is not philosophy we are after, but the behavior of real things. So in despair, I measure it directly—lo, it is near to seven feet—neither infinity nor zero. So, we have measured these things for which our theory gives such absurd answers. We seek a better theory or understanding that will give us numbers close to what we measure. We are seeking the formula that gives the square root of fifty."

> —Letter from Feynman to Miss Barbara Kyle, Dorking, England, October 20, 1965

4. In other versions of this story, the Cornell medallion is red.

5. Gweneth Howarth was born in Yorkshire, England, and met Feynman in 1958 on a Lake Geneva beach. He was forty, she was twenty-four. He persuaded her to come to Los Angeles to be his housekeeper, but soon asked her to marry him. This and the other contributions from Gweneth Feynman are taken from "The Life of a Nobel Wife" in the Caltech magazine *Engineering and Science* for March/April 1977.

6. Albert R. Hibbs was Feynman's Ph.D. student and close friend. He was an early enthusiast for space travel, and worked for most of his career at the Jet Propulsion Laboratory in Pasadena. In the late 1940s, Hibbs and his friend Roy Walford pulled off a spectacular gambling coup in Reno and Las Vegas, based on identifying the bias in casino roulette wheels.

7. Edward Fredkin is a physicist and inventor. Feynman was best man at his wedding.

8. W. Daniel Hillis is Chief Scientist at the Thinking Machines company in Cambridge, Massachusetts. For his Ph.D. thesis at MIT, Hillis designed the world's first "massively parallel" supercomputer—the "Connection Machine." He explains Feynman's part in helping build the machine in Chapter 7.

4. Topless Bars and Other Ways to Have Fun

1. These remarks appear in *Physics Today*, February 1989, in an article titled "Dick Feynman—the Guy in the Office down the Hall."

Gell-Mann—Nobel laureate, polymath, and Caltech physics legend—invented the term "quark" and developed the theory of quantum chromodynamics, which explains how three different types of quark of different "color" relate to each other in different ways to make up atomic nuclei, and so all of matter. In the 1960s, Feynman and Gell-Mann collaborated to create an important theory of the so-called weak interaction that explains why nuclear particles sometimes decay by emitting electrons (or positrons) and neutrinos. There is a story that during an argument, Feynman threatened to start spelling Gell-Mann's name without the hyphen; Gell-Mann countered with the threat of inserting one: Feyn-man.

2. David L. Goodstein is professor of physics and vice provost at Caltech.

3. Richard Sherman was Feynman's Ph.D. student. He is now a free-lance theoretical physicist and Italian-car enthusiast: "There are Ph.D.s, and then there are Feynman Ph.D.s. With the second kind, you get to buy a Ferrari!"

4. Faustin Bray and her partner, Brian Wallace, are musicians and self-confessed "compulsive documentarists." They organized and videotaped a number of Feynman "workshops" at the Esalen Institute in the 1980s.

5. From the question-and-answer session at the Esalen "Tiny Machines" workshop, 1984.

6. Tom Van Sant is the founder of the Santa Monica GeoSphere Project, which is exploring the use of advanced computer-aided graphic techniques to generate revolutionary maps of the earth's surface and resources. Van Sant has also made the world's smallest and largest artworks, which Feynman describes in Chapter 7.

7. Jirayr Zorthian was born in Turkish Armenia in 1911. He wrestled for Yale, served in the U.S. Army Intelligence Corps during World War II, and is the perennial winner of the *Pasadena Star*'s "Most Eccentric Person" award.

8. Richard Davies, physicist, worked at the Jet Propulsion Laboratory in Pasadena. He was one of Feynman's closest friends.

5. Imagine!

1. Feynman was once invited to explain quantum electrodynamics in a one-hour television program. He told the producer that he had recently tried this in a series of lectures in Australia, and had found that it took him about six hours. The producer took the lecture text away for a week, edited it into a one-hour version, and brought it back. Feynman was impressed, but pointed out that a problem remained—the producer had "left out the difficult bits."

6. Doing the Physics

1. From the Messenger Lectures given by Feynman at Cornell in 1964.

2. Feynman liked to say, "Scientists are explorers, philosophers are tourists."

3. Marcus Chown was a physics graduate student at Caltech and is now news editor of *New Scientist*.

7. Crazy Ideas: Tiny Writing and Huge Computers

1. From Feynman's Esalen "Tiny Machines" workshop, 1984.
2. This is an abridged version of Feynman's talk as published in *Engineering & Science*, February 1960.
3. Quantum chromodynamics is concerned with how quarks behave. See the footnote on Murray Gell-Mann in Chapter 4.
4. From Feynman's Esalen workshop on "Computers from the Inside Out," 1984.

8. Challenger

1. General Donald J. Kutyna was commander in chief of NORAD and the United States Space Command until 1992, when he retired from the U.S. Air Force. As a pilot, he flew 120 combat missions over Vietnam.
2. By 1993 there will be a total of twenty-four Global Positioning System (GPS) satellites in earth orbit. They send radio signals to small portable receivers to give longitude, latitude, and altitude to an accuracy of about twenty-five meters anywhere on the earth's surface.
3. Helen Tuck was Feynman's secretary at Caltech. He shared her with Murray Gell-Mann.
4. Feynman explained this reference to Ralph Leighton: "Once Gweneth and I went to London, to Heathrow airport. It was one of my first times in England, maybe even the first. We go to get the baggage, and there isn't any baggage, and we wait and we wait. You look around, and there aren't any people there, no officials. Nothing's coming out, and I swear it was nearly two hours before, finally, somebody with a uniform comes. So I go up to this person, somewhat upset, and I say, 'Why is there a delay on the baggage?' She says this and that, but doesn't give me any kind of an answer. I'm saying, 'What's the problem?' when someone comes up behind her, also in a uniform, but obviously of higher rank, and says, 'Serve him tea.' Obviously this is the solution to all problems in England. So my thought was this is just like 'Serve him tea'—get him a better hotel room."
5. Frances Lewine is Feynman's cousin and a well-known Washington political journalist.
6. Kutyna had told Feynman that when flying a combat aircraft,

it's important to remember to check behind you—six o'clock—whenever you think you are safe. This applied to Washington.

7. The *Challenger* investigation overlapped with Feynman and Ralph Leighton's attempts to reach the mysterious central Asian country of Tuva. While Feynman wrote this letter home, Ralph was pursuing the Silk Road exhibit in Uppsala, Sweden. See Chapter 9, "The Quest for Tannu Tuva."

8. On February 11, the day of the ice-water experiment, Chairman Rogers was overheard telling Neil Armstrong in the men's room that "Feynman is becoming a real pain in the ass."

9. The commission's report is published in five volumes, and they are difficult to come by. The more widely available summarized version does not contain Feynman's Appendix F.

9. The Quest for Tannu Tuva

1. See Dick Davies's account of the trip to Copper Canyon in Mexico in Chapter 4.

2. Ralph Leighton also arranged to be given the telephone number 246-8882—AIM TUVA.

10. Dying

1. During surgery in fall 1981, Feynman's aorta split. He needed transfusions of some seventy pints of blood, much of it donated by Caltech students.

A Feynman Bibliography

By Richard Feynman

Feynman, Richard. *The Character of Physical Law*. British Broadcasting System, 1965; Cambridge, MA: MIT Press, 1967.

———. *QED: The Strange Theory of Light and Matter*. Princeton, NJ: Princeton University Press, 1985.

Feynman, Richard P., with Ralph Leighton. *Surely You're Joking, Mr. Feynman!* New York: W. W. Norton, 1985.

———. *What Do You Care What Other People Think?* New York: W. W. Norton, 1988.

Feynman, Richard, Robert Leighton, and Matthew Sands. *The Feynman Lectures on Physics*. Reading, MA: Addison-Wesley, 1963.

By Others

Bethe, Hans A. *The Road from Los Alamos*. New York: Simon & Schuster/Touchstone, 1991.

Dyson, Freeman. *Disturbing the Universe*. New York: Basic Books, 1979.

———. *Infinite in All Directions*. New York: Harper & Row, 1988.

Gleick, James. *Genus: The Life and Science of Richard Feynman*. New York: Pantheon, 1992.

Gonick, Larry, and Art Huffman. *The Cartoon Guide to Physics*. New York: Harper Perennial, 1991.

Goodchild, Peter. *J. Robert Oppenheimer*. New York: Fromm, 1985.

Hardy, G. H. *A Mathematician's Apology.* Cambridge, MA: Cambridge University Press, 1940; reprint with foreword by C. P. Snow, 1967.

Kac, Mark. *Enigmas of Chance: An Autobiography.* New York: Harper & Row, 1985.

Kanigel, Robert. *The Man Who Knew Infinity: A Life of the Genius Ramanujan.* New York: Charles Scribner's Sons, 1991.

Leighton, Ralph. *Tuva or Bust!* New York: W. W. Norton, 1991.

Rhodes, Richard. *The Making of the Atomic Bomb.* New York: Simon & Schuster, 1987.

Videotapes (VHS/NTSC) of Feynman's Esalen workshops on "Tiny Machines" and "Computers from the Inside Out" can be obtained from Sound Photosynthesis, P. O. Box 2111, Mill Valley, CA 94942-2111.

The BBC TV programs about Feynman are not available on home video.

Illustration Credits

AIP Emilio Segré Visual Archives, pages 52, 73, 80 and 118.

AIP Niels Bohr Library, page 31.

Physical Review, Vol. 76, No. 6 (1949), page 79.

Courtesy Faustin Bray, pages 96 and 97.

By permission of the British Library, page 229.

Courtesy the Archives, California Institute of Technology, pages 33, 45, 47, 82, 84, 88, 90, 91, 119, 140, 141, 155, 156, 162, 176, 236, and 239.

Courtesy Patricia Chown, page 161.

Clemens of Copenhagen, page 87.

Courtesy of Carl and Michelle Feynman, pages 20, 21, 24, 26, 29, 37, 38, 39, 42, 43, 48, 54, 55, 62, 64, 66, 68, 80, 81, 85, 93, 94, 115, 116, 117, 142, 158, 159, 194, 202, 212, 214, 219 (right), 241, 242, and 252.

Michelle Feynman, pages 109 and 161; drawings on pages 105 and 106 are included with permission of Michelle Feynman and by courtesy of Gordon and Breach/Craftsman House Publishers, from the book *The Art of Richard Feynman* (in press).

Courtesy Joan Feynman, pages 22, 25, 35, and 92.

Courtesy Margaret Gardiner, page 123.

Courtesy Ralph Leighton, pages 220, 223, 226, 228, 231, and 235.

Index

Page numbers in *italics* refer to illustrations.